THE KEY

STUDENT STUDY GUIDE

THE KEY student study guide is designed to help students achieve success in school. The content in each study guide is 100% curriculum aligned and serves as an excellent source of material for review and practice. To create this book, teachers, curriculum specialists, and assessment experts have worked closely to develop the instructional pieces that explain each of the key concepts for the course. The practice questions and sample tests have detailed solutions that show problem-solving methods, highlight concepts that are likely to be tested, and point out potential sources of errors. **THE KEY** is a complete guide to be used by students throughout the school year for reviewing and understanding course content, and to prepare for assessments.

Rao, Gautam, 1961 –

THE KEY – Biology 30 Alberta

1. Science – Juvenile Literature. I. Title

Published by
Castle Rock Research Corp.
2340 Manulife Place
10180 – 101 Street
Edmonton, AB T5J 3S4

15 16 17 FP 13 12 11

Publisher
Gautam Rao

Contributors
Susan Ferbey
Ruby Grewal
Crystal Homeniuk
Selma Losic

Reviewers
Alison Donner
Randy Dzenkiw

Dedicated to the memory of Dr. V. S. Rao

THE KEY—Biology 30

THE KEY consists of the following sections:

KEY Tips for Being Successful at School gives examples of study and review strategies. It includes information about learning styles, study schedules, and note taking for test preparation.

Class Focus includes a unit on each area of the curriculum. Units are divided into sections, each focusing on one of the specific expectations, or main ideas, that students must learn about in that unit. Examples, definitions, and visuals help to explain each main idea. Practice questions on the main ideas are also included. At the end of each unit is a test on the important ideas covered. The practice questions and unit tests help students identify areas they know and those they need to study more. They can also be used as preparation for tests and quizzes. Most questions are of average difficulty, though some are easy and some are hard—the harder questions are called *Challenger Questions*. The difficulty rating is based on the percentage of students that answered the question correctly when it appeared on the Diploma Exam. (Source: Alberta Education Examiner's Reports). Each unit is prefaced by a **Table of Correlations**, which correlates questions in the unit (and in the practice tests at the end of the book) to the specific curriculum expectations. Answers and solutions are found at the end of each unit.

KEY Strategies for Success on Tests helps students get ready for tests. It shows students different types of questions they might see, word clues to look for when reading them, and hints for answering them.

Practice Tests includes one to three tests based on the entire course. They are very similar to the format and level of difficulty that students may encounter on final tests. In some regions, these tests may be reprinted versions of official tests, or reflect the same difficulty levels and formats as official versions. This gives students the chance to practice using real-world examples. Answers and complete solutions are provided at the end of the section.

For the complete curriculum document (including specific expectations along with examples and sample problems), visit http://education.alberta.ca/teachers/program/science/programs.aspx.

THE KEY Study Guides are available for many courses. Check www.castlerockresearch.com for a complete listing of books available for your area.

For information about any of our resources or services, please call Castle Rock Research at 780.448.9619 or visit our website at http://www.castlerockresearch.com.

At Castle Rock Research, we strive to produce an error-free resource. If you should find an error, please contact us so that future editions can be corrected.

TABLE OF CONTENTS

NOTES

KEY Tips for Being Successful at School

⚷ *KEY* TIPS FOR BEING SUCCESSFUL AT SCHOOL

KEY FACTORS CONTRIBUTING TO SCHOOL SUCCESS

In addition to learning the content of your courses, there are some other things that you can do to help you do your best at school. Some of these strategies are listed below.

- **Keep a positive attitude:** Always reflect on what you can already do and what you already know.

- **Be prepared to learn**: Have ready the necessary pencils, pens, notebooks, and other required materials for participating in class.

- **Complete all of your assignments:** Do your best to finish all of your assignments. Even if you know the material well, practice will reinforce your knowledge. If an assignment or question is difficult for you, work through it as far as you can so that your teacher can see exactly where you are having difficulty.

- **Set small goals for yourself when you are learning new material:** For example, when learning the parts of speech, do not try to learn everything in one night. Work on only one part or section each study session. When you have memorized one particular part of speech and understand it, then move on to another one, continue this process until you have memorized and learned all the parts of speech.

- **Review your classroom work regularly at home:** Review to be sure that you understand the material that you learned in class.

- **Ask your teacher for help**: Your teacher will help you if you do not understand something or if you are having a difficult time completing your assignments.

- **Get plenty of rest and exercise:** Concentrating in class is hard work. It is important to be well-rested and have time to relax and socialize with your friends. This helps you to keep your positive attitude about your school work.

- **Eat healthy meals:** A balanced diet keeps you healthy and gives you the energy that you need for studying at school and at home.

 ## HOW TO FIND YOUR LEARNING STYLE

Every student learns differently. The manner in which you learn best is called your learning style. By knowing your learning style, you can increase your success at school. Most students use a combination of learning styles. Do you know what type of learner you are? Read the following descriptions. Which of these common learning styles do you use most often?

- **Linguistic Learner**: You may learn best by saying, hearing, and seeing words. You are probably really good at memorizing things such as dates, places, names, and facts. You may need **to write and then say out loud** the steps in a process, a formula, or the actions that lead up to a significant event.

- **Spatial Learner**: You may learn best by looking at and working with pictures. You are probably really good at puzzles, imagining things, and reading maps and charts. You may need to use strategies like **mind mapping and webbing** to organize your information and study notes.

- **Kinaesthetic Learner**: You may learn best by touching, moving, and figuring things out using manipulative. You are probably really good at physical activities and learning through movement. You may need to **draw your finger over a diagram** to remember it, **"tap out" the steps** needed to solve a problem, or **"feel" yourself writing or typing** a formula.

SCHEDULING STUDY TIME

You should review your class notes regularly to ensure that you have a clear understanding of all the new material you learned. Reviewing your lessons on a regular basis helps you to learn and remember ideas and concepts. It also reduces the quantity of material that you need to study prior to a test. Establishing a study schedule will help you to make the best use of your time.

Regardless of the type of study schedule you use, you may want to consider the following suggestions to maximize your study time and effort:

- Organize your work so that you begin with the most challenging material first.
- Divide the subject's content into small, manageable chunks.
- Alternate regularly between your different subjects and types of study activities in order to maintain your interest and motivation.
- Make a daily list with headings like "Must Do," "Should Do," and "Could Do."
- Begin each study session by quickly reviewing what you studied the day before.
- Maintain your usual routine of eating, sleeping, and exercising to help you concentrate better for extended periods of time.

CREATING STUDY NOTES

MIND-MAPPING OR WEBBING

Use the key words, ideas, or concepts from your reading or class notes to create a *mind map* or *web* (a diagram or visual representation of the given information). A mind map or web is sometimes referred to as a knowledge map.

- Write the key word, concept, theory, or formula in the centre of your page.

- Write down related facts, ideas, events, and information and then link them to the central concept with lines.

- Use coloured markers, underlining, or other symbols to emphasize things such as relationships, time lines, and important information.

- The following examples of a Frayer Model illustrate how this technique can be used to study scientific vocabulary.

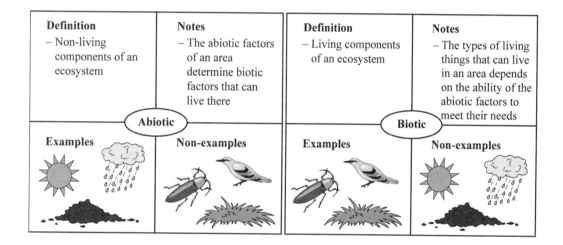

INDEX CARDS

To use index cards while studying, follow these steps:

- Write a key word or question on one side of an index card.

- On the reverse side, write the definition of the word, answer to the question, or any other important information that you want to remember.

What is the difference between
heat and thermal energy?

What is the difference between
heat and thermal energy?

Thermal energy is the total energy of the
particles in a solid, liquid, or gas.
Heat is the amount of thermal energy
transferred between objects.

SYMBOLS AND STICKY NOTES—IDENTIFYING IMPORTANT INFORMATION

Use symbols to mark your class notes. For example, an exclamation mark (!) might be used to point out something that must be learned well because it is a very important idea. A question mark (?) may highlight something that you are not certain about, and a diamond (◊) or asterisk (*) could highlight interesting information that you want to remember.

- Use sticky notes when you are not allowed to put marks in books.

- Use sticky notes to mark a page in a book that contains an important diagram, formula, explanation, etc.

- Use sticky notes to mark important facts in research books.

MEMORIZATION TECHNIQUES

- **Association** relates new learning to something you already know. For example, to remember the spelling difference between *dessert* and *desert*, recall that the word *sand* has only one *s*. So, because there is sand in a desert, the word *desert* only has on *s*.
- **Mnemonic** devices are sentences that you create to remember a list or group of items. For example, the first letter of each word in the phrase "**E**very **G**ood **B**oy **D**eserves **F**udge" helps you to remember the names of the lines on the treble clef staff (E, G, B, D, and F) in music.
- **Acronyms** are words that are formed from the first letters or parts of the words in a group. For example, **RADAR** is actually an acronym for **Ra**dio **D**etecting **A**nd **R**anging, and **MASH** is an acronym for **M**obile **A**rmy **S**urgical **H**ospital. **HOMES** helps you to remember the names of the five Great Lakes (**H**uron, **O**ntario, **M**ichigan, **E**rie, and **S**uperior).
- **Visualizing** requires you to use your mind's eye to "see" a chart, list, map, diagram, or sentence as it is in your textbook or notes, on the chalk board or computer screen, or in a display.
- **Initialisms** are abbreviations that are formed from the first letters or parts of the words in a group. Unlike acronyms, initialisms cannot be pronounced as a word themselves. For example, **BEDMAS** is an initialism for the order of operations in math (**B**rackets, **E**xponents, **D**ivide, **M**ultiply, **A**dd, **S**ubtract).

KEY STRATEGIES FOR REVIEWING

Reviewing textbook material, class notes, and handouts should be an ongoing activity. Spending time reviewing becomes more critical when you are preparing for tests. You may find some of the following review strategies useful when studying during your scheduled study time.

- Before reading a selection, preview it by noting the headings, charts, graphs, and chapter questions.
- Before reviewing a unit, note the headings, charts, graphs and chapter questions.
- Highlight key concepts, vocabulary, definitions and formulas.
- Skim the paragraph and note the key words, phrases, and information.
- Carefully read over each step in a procedure.
- Draw a picture or diagram to help make the concept clearer.

KEY STRATEGIES FOR SUCCESS: A CHECKLIST

Review, review, review: review is a huge part of doing well at school and preparing for tests. Here is a checklist for you to keep track of how many suggested strategies for success you are using. Read each question and then put a check mark (✓) in the correct column. Look at the questions where you have checked the "No" column. Think about how you might try using some of these strategies to help you do your best at school.

KEY Strategies for Success	Yes	No
Do you attend school regularly?		
Do you know your personal learning style—how you learn best?		
Do you spend 15 to 30 minutes a day reviewing your notes?		
Do you study in a quiet place at home?		
Do you clearly mark the most important ideas in your study notes?		
Do you use sticky notes to mark texts and research books?		
Do you practise answering multiple-choice and written-response questions?		
Do you ask your teacher for help when you need it?		
Are you maintaining a healthy diet and sleep routine?		
Are you participating in regular physical activity?		

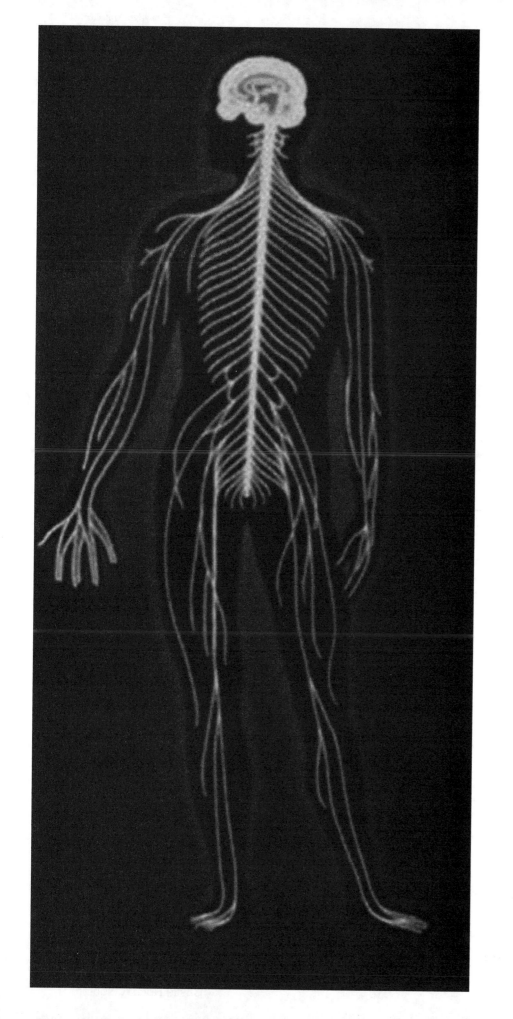

Nervous and Endocrine Systems

NERVOUS AND ENDOCRINE SYSTEMS

Table of Correlations				
Specific Expectation	**Practice Questions**	**Unit Test Questions**	**Practice Test 1**	**Practice Test 2**
Students will:				
Explain how the nervous system controls physiological processes.				
30-A1.1K describe the general structure and function of a neuron and myelin sheath, explaining the formation and transmission of an action potential, including all-or-none response and intensity of response; the transmission of a signal across a synapse; and the main chemicals and transmitters involved, i.e., norepinephrine, acetylcholine and cholinesterase	1, 2, 3, 4	1, 2, NR1, NR2, NR3	4, 5	NR2, 8
30-A1.2K identify the principal structures of the central and peripheral nervous systems and explain their functions in regulating the voluntary (somatic) and involuntary (autonomic) systems of the human organism; i.e., cerebral hemispheres and lobes, cerebellum, pons, medulla oblongata, hypothalamus, spinal cord, sympathetic and parasympathetic nervous systems, and the sensory-autonomic nervous system	6, 8, 9, 10	3, 5, 6	1, 2	7, 9
30-A1.3K describe, using an example, the organization of neurons into nerves and the composition and function of reflex arcs	5, 7, NR1	4	7	NR1
30-A1.4K describe the structure and function of the parts of the human eye; i.e., the cornea, lens, sclera, choroid, retina, rods and cones, fovea centralis, pupil, iris and optic nerve	11, 14	7	8	39
30-A1.5K describe the structure and function of the parts of the human ear, including the pinna, auditory canal, tympanum, ossicles, cochlea, organ of Corti, auditory nerve, semicircular canals, and Eustachian tube	12, 13	8	36	40
30-A1.6K explain other ways that humans sense their environment and their spatial orientation in it	15	9	NR1	

Explain how the endocrine system contributes to homeostasis.				
30-A2.1K identify the principal endocrine glands of humans; i.e., the hypothalamus/pituitary complex, thyroid, parathyroid, adrenal glands and islet cells of the pancreas	17, 18, 29	11		
30-A2.2K describe the function of the hormones of the principal endocrine glands; i.e. thyroid stimulating hormone (TSH)/thyroxine, calcitonin/parathyroid hormone (PTH), adrenocorticotropic hormone (ACTH)/cortisol, glucagon/insulin, human growth hormone (hGH), antidiuretic hormone (ADH) epinephrine, aldosterone, and describe how they maintain homeostasis through feedback	16, 19, 25	10, 15, 16		1, 6, 22, 42
30-A2.3K explain the metabolic roles hormones may play in homeostasis; i.e., thyroxine in metabolism; insulin, glucagon and cortisol in blood sugar regulation; hGH in growth; ADH in water regulation; aldosterone in sodium ion regulation	20, 27, 28, NR2, NR3, 21	12, 13	11	2, 4, 5
30-A2.4K explain how the endocrine system allows humans to sense their internal environment and respond appropriately	NR4	18		
30-A2.5K compare the endocrine and nervous control systems and explain how they act together	26	17	NR6, 42	11, 43
30-A2.6K describe, using an example, the physiological consequences of hormone imbalances; i.e., diabetes mellitus	22, 23, 24	14		3

NERVOUS AND ENDOCRINE SYSTEMS

30-A1.1K describe the general structure and function of a neuron and myelin sheath, explaining the formation and transmission of an action potential, including all-or-none response and intensity of response; the transmission of a signal across a synapse; and the main chemicals and transmitters involved; i.e. norepinephrine, acetylcholine, and cholinesterase

NEURON STRUCTURE

A neuron is a nerve cell specialized for conducting nerve signals over long distances. It has long cell extensions, called dendrites, which receive electrochemical impulses from other neurons. From the dendrites, impulses pass to the cell body containing the nucleus, then on to the axon, axon terminal, and finally to a synaptic knob. Some neurons are covered in a neurilemma, which is a membrane that helps the neuron repair itself should there be an injury. Many neurons have a white, fatty, insulating, myelin sheath covering the axon. The myelin sheath is composed of individual Schwann cells. The spaces between the Schwann cells where the axon is exposed are called nodes of Ranvier.

[handwritten: PROTECTS THE AXON, SPEEDS UP NERVE TRANSMISSION]

[handwritten: CREATES THE MYELIN SHEATH]

[handwritten: NERVE TRANSMISSION HAS TO JUMP THROUGH]

There are three kinds of neurons. Sensory neurons carry signals from the sensory organs to the central nervous system, and motor neurons carry signals from the CNS to the muscles. Signals travel within the CNS through interneurons.

Parts of a Neuron

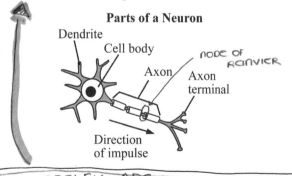

[handwritten labels: NODE OF RANVIER]

Dendrite
Cell body
Axon
Axon terminal
Direction of impulse

[handwritten boxed: REFLEX ARC
STIMULUS → SENSORY NEURONS → (TO CNS)
INTERNEURON → MOTOR NEURON → EFFECTOR (MUSCLES)]

Neurons produce electrical charges by altering the ion concentrations on either side of a neuron membrane. When a neuron is at rest, Na^+ ions are found mostly outside the axon in the extracellular fluid, while K^+ ions are found mostly within the axon in the intracellular fluid. At rest, the membrane is impermeable to sodium (Na^+), so Na^+ stays out of the axon. The membrane is slightly permeable to potassium ions (K^+), so some K^+ leaks out to the extracellular fluid (ECF). As a result, slightly more positive ions are present in the ECF than the intracellular fluid (ICF), making the ICF relatively negative with respect to the ECF. The resting membrane is thus said to be polarized. The slight difference in polarity between the two sides creates a small electrical potential of 70 mV. Because voltage is always given from the perspective of the ICF, the resting membrane potential of a neuron is –70 mV. This means that the inside of the neuron is 70 mV more negative than the outside.

Polarized Membrane (Resting)

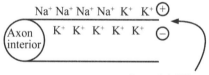

Na$^+$ Na$^+$ Na$^+$ Na$^+$ K$^+$ K$^+$ $\oplus$
(Axon interior) K$^+$ K$^+$ K$^+$ K$^+$ K$^+$ $\ominus$

Potential difference between the two sides of the membrane is 70 mV

If the dendrite of a neuron is stimulated strongly enough to reach the neuron's electrical threshold, an action potential, or nerve impulse, results. Once the neuron is stimulated, a critical change occurs. The membrane becomes permeable to sodium ions, causing Na^+ to rush into the ICF. The ICF becomes more positively charged than the ECF, reversing the original resting polarity. Sodium ions continue to pour into the axon until the ICF reaches an electrical potential of +30 mV. (Note that depending on the source, this number may vary from +30 to +40 mV.) The membrane is now said to be completely depolarized. The spike seen on a voltage graph during depolarization is called an action potential or nerve impulse.

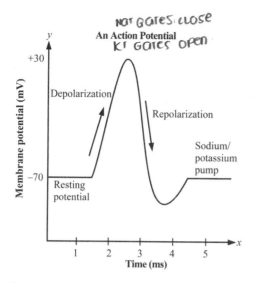

An Action Potential

Handwritten: Nat gates close / K+ gates open

In order to send another impulse, the membrane must be returned to its original resting polarity by the process of repolarization. Sodium channels in the membrane close and positive ions are actively transported out of the axon back to the ECF. In this way the ICF is returned to its relatively negative state, and the ECF to its relatively positive state. The depolarization and repolarization of one point on the membrane takes $\frac{1}{500}$ of a second.

Once a particular point on the membrane has been depolarized, the impulse travels down the axon by the process of conduction. Conduction occurs because an increase in sodium permeability at one point on the membrane causes increased permeability at an adjacent point. The action potential is conducted along the membrane as a wave of depolarization. If the axon is covered in myelin, the insulating Schwann cells prevent the entire axon from depolarizing. Instead, the action potential skips rapidly from one exposed node of Ranvier to the next. Myelinated neurons are therefore able to conduct impulses much faster than non-myelinated axons.

Handwritten: (interneurons)

Conduction of an action potential in a myelinated axon

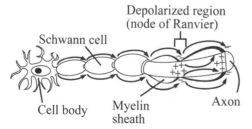

Not all stimuli cause an action potential. A stimulus above the threshold of –50 mV will initiate an action potential in a neuron. Sub-threshold stimuli simply fade out. All action potentials, regardless of the intensity of stimulus that caused them, reach a voltage of +30 mV. This is called the all-or-none response. Instead of causing a larger action potential, stronger stimuli cause an increase in the frequency of depolarization. For example, more intense pain translates to more impulses per second.

The All or None Principle

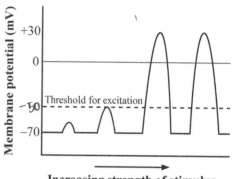

Increasing strength of stimulus

An impulse being conducted down a neuron will eventually meet a synapse. A synapse is the space between the synaptic knob of a presynaptic neuron and the dendrite of a postsynaptic neuron. The mechanism by which an impulse is passed across a synapse is called transmission. The process of transmission begins when an action potential arrives at an axon terminal. Calcium ions enter into the axon, stimulating synaptic vesicles in the synaptic knob to release neurotransmitter molecules into the synapse. *Handwritten: exocytosis* The neurotransmitters then diffuse across the synapse and bind with receptor sites on the postsynaptic dendrite, causing it to depolarize. All neurotransmitters are proteins produced by neurons. The most common neurotransmitter is acetylcholine. Others include serotonin, dopamine, GABA (gamma-aminobutyric acid), and norepinephrine. Hypersecretion or hyposecretion of neurotransmitters can have major effects on behaviour, motion, sensation, and thought patterns.

Transmission at the Synapse

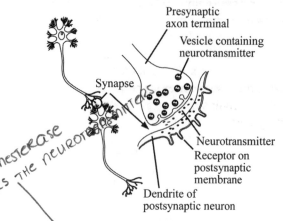

CHOLINESTERASE BREAKS THE NEUROTRANSMITTERS

REABSORBED BY endocytosis

If a neurotransmitter were to remain in a synapse it would cause the postsynaptic neuron to continuously depolarize. This is prevented by the presence of an enzyme that inactivates the transmitter. For example, a split second after the neurotransmitter acetylcholine is released into a synapse the enzyme cholinesterase is released, inactivating acetylcholine.

Practice Questions: 1, 2, 3, 4

30-A1.2K identify the principal structures of the central and peripheral nervous systems and explain their functions in regulating the voluntary (somatic) and involuntary (autonomic) systems of the human organism; i.e. cerebral hemispheres and lobes, cerebellum, pons, medulla oblongata, hypothalamus, spinal cord, sympathetic and parasympathetic nervous systems, and the sensory-somatic nervous system

30-A1.3K describe, using an example, the organization of neurons into nerves and the composition and function of reflex arcs

NERVOUS SYSTEM

The nervous system consists of the central nervous system (CNS) and the peripheral nervous system (PNS). The CNS is composed of the brain and spinal cord, while the PNS is composed of the spinal nerves that extend from both sides of the cord.

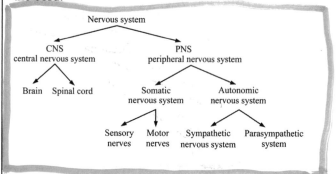

PERIPHERAL NERVOUS SYSTEM

The peripheral nervous system is made of 31 pairs of spinal nerves that extend from the spinal cord. Each spinal nerve of the somatic system contains two kinds of neurons. Sensory neurons bring sensory information into the central nervous system from sensory receptors. Motor neurons send motor commands out to muscles.

A Spinal Nerve Contains Sensory and Motor Neurons

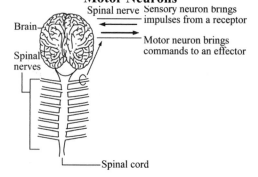

The autonomic nervous system of the PNS regulates smooth muscles of glands and organs over which a person has no conscious control. The sympathetic component of the autonomic system comes into play when there is a perceived threat. Sympathetic responses prepare the body for fight-or-flight. Blood is diverted from the gut, excretory system, reproductive system and skin to the skeletal muscles, heart, lungs, and brain. Heart rate, blood pressure and breathing rate rise, while pupils dilate. Once the threat has passed, the parasympathetic division of the autonomic system returns body systems to normal by reversing sympathetic effects. The sympathetic system is stimulated by the neurotransmitter norepinephrine, which may be referred to as adrenalin. The parasympathetic system is stimulated by the neurotransmitter acetylcholine.

CENTRAL NERVOUS SYSTEM

The central nervous system (CNS) is composed of the brain and spinal cord. The spinal cord carries sensory nerve impulses from the sensory neurons of the PNS to the brain. It also carries motor impulses from the brain to the motor neurons in the spinal nerves.

The human brain can be divided into structural and functional regions. The top portion of the brain is called the cerebrum. It is highly convoluted to increase surface area, and has a right and left hemisphere. Each hemisphere has a grey, non-myelinated cortex and a myelinated medulla.

= WRAPPED IN 3 PROTECTIVE
mcmBRanes CALLED THE
. menInGes .

The cerebrum can be divided into four major lobes. The frontal lobe controls personality and contains the motor cortex that commands voluntary motion. The parietal lobe contains the sensory cortex that processes sensation. The occipital lobe at the back of the cerebrum contains the visual cortex. The temporal lobes on the left and right sides of the cerebrum contain the auditory cortex and control hearing.

The Human Brain

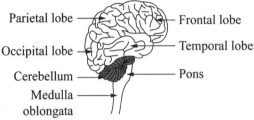

Parietal lobe
Occipital lobe
Cerebellum
Medulla oblongata
Frontal lobe
Temporal lobe
Pons

When nerve tracts from one side of the body ascend the spinal cord on the way to the brain, they cross over and enter the opposite side of the brain. As a result, the right hemisphere senses and controls the left side of the body, and vice versa. The right and left cerebral hemispheres are also specialized for slightly different tasks. The right hemisphere specializes in creative, spatial, and non-verbal expression such as art and music. The left hemisphere specializes in logic and is the home of speech, language, and mathematical ability. The right and left hemispheres are connected by the corpus callosum, which is a band of myelinated fibres that transmits information between the hemispheres.

The cerebellum, which also consists of two hemispheres, sits at the top of the brainstem and coordinates muscular movements. The pons is a relay centre for the information moving to and from the cerebrum. The medulla oblongata controls the sympathetic and parasympathetic functions of the autonomic nervous system, including breathing, heart rate, and the priority shunting of blood to different parts of the body. The pituitary gland secretes many hormones. The hypothalamus controls temperature, hunger, thirst, and monitors the endocrine system.

fluid intake

hypothalmus controls the pituitary

Nerve pathways connect stimuli with responses. The simplest nerve pathway is the reflex, which does not involve any participation by the brain. Instead, the spinal cord acts to connect a specific sensory stimulus with a specific response. Reflexes, such as the knee-jerk reflex are present at birth. A reflex begins with a sensory receptor sending an impulse along a sensory neuron of a spinal nerve, which synapses with an interneuron in the spinal cord. The interneuron then synapses with a specific motor neuron that carries motor impulses out through the spinal nerve to an effector—either a muscle or gland. Because the brain is not involved, reflex responses are rapid and often life saving.

A Reflex Arc

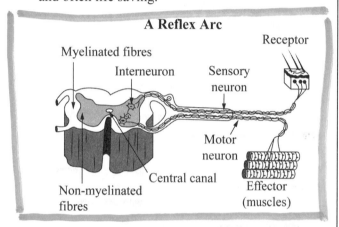

Practice Questions: 5, 6, 7, 8, 9, 10, NR1

30-A1.4K describe the structure and function of the parts of the human eye; i.e., the cornea, lens, sclera, choroid, retina, rods and cones, fovea centralis, pupil, iris and optic nerve

THE EYE

Sensory organs all stimulate sensory nerves that carry information to the CNS. For example, the eye converts light signals into action potentials in the optic nerve, which transmits the signal to the visual cortex of the brain.

Human Eye

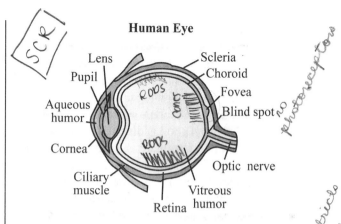

The eye has three layers: the sclera, the choroid, and the retina. The sclera is the rigid, outer protective layer of the eyeball. It is white except for the transparent part at the front, called the cornea. The middle layer is the choroid, which contains blood vessels that nourish the retina. The retina is the inner layer where the actual photoreceptors are located. Rods are photoreceptors found mostly on the periphery of the retina. Rods perceive black and white images and function only in low light levels. Cones are photoreceptors that absorb red, green, or blue light, and they function at high light levels. The highest concentration of cones occurs at the fovea, which is found directly at the back of the retina. The fovea provides the most acute vision.

Within the eyeball, certain structures focus light onto the retina. The convex surface of the cornea begins this process. Behind the cornea is the watery aqueous humor. The iris is the colored circular muscle suspended behind the aqueous humor. It dilates and constricts to control the amount of light entering the eyeball through the pupil. Suspended behind the iris is the biconvex lens made of transparent protein, which converges light rays so that they fall on the retina.

The lens is attached to ciliary muscles that change the shape of the lens in the process of accommodation. When accommodating to view distant objects the ciliary muscles tug on the lens, making it flatter. When accommodating to view near objects, the ciliary muscles relax, allowing the lens to become more spherical. Behind the lens, the eyeball is filled with clear, gelatinous, vitreous humor that maintains the eyeball's shape.

Abnormalities in the shape of the eye cause many people to require corrective lenses. Nearsighted people have eyeballs that are too long and cannot focus on distant objects because the image focuses in front of the retina instead of directly onto it. Farsighted people have eyeballs that are too short, which causes the image to focus behind the retina. People with astigmatism have a cornea or lens that does not have a smooth curvature, so one part of the visual field is in focus while other parts are not. A cataract forms when a lens becomes cloudy. Glaucoma is damage to the retina caused by excessive pressure from the buildup of aqueous humour.

[handwritten margin: hyperopia]
[handwritten margin: myopia]

Related Questions: 11, 14

30-A1.5K describe the structure and function of the parts of the human ear, including the pinna, auditory canal, tympanum, ossicles, cochlea, organ of Corti, auditory nerve, semicircular canals, and Eustachian tube

30-A1.6K explain other ways that humans sense their environment and their spatial orientation in it

THE EAR

The ear converts compressional waves in the air into compressional waves in the fluid of the inner ear. The frequency of sound waves determines the pitch of the sound, and the amplitude of the waves determines the volume of the sound. The ear has three parts: the outer ear, the air-filled middle ear, and the fluid-filled inner ear.

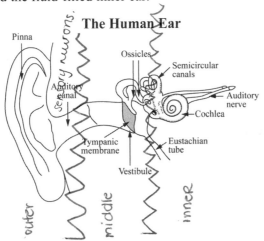

The Human Ear

Pinna
Ossicles
Semicircular canals
Auditory canal
Auditory nerve
Cochlea
Tympanic membrane
Eustachian tube
Vestibule

[handwritten labels: sensory neurons; outer; middle; inner]

The outer ear consists of the pinna and auditory canal. The middle ear consists of the structures from the tympanic membrane to the oval window. The inner ear is composed of the coiled cochlea, semi-circular canals, and the saccule and utricle. The air pressure inside the middle ear is kept equal to the air pressure in the auditory canal by the Eustachian tube, which allows air to pass between the middle ear and the back of the throat and vice versa. Microorganisms can also take this route resulting in ear infections.

The hearing mechanism depends on the accurate passage of vibrations through several parts of the ear. Sound waves are directed into the auditory canal by the pinna. The eardrum converts the sound waves into vibrations that are then carried across the middle ear by the ear bones, or ossicles, to the oval window of the cochlea. Vibrations of the oval window produce compressional waves in the fluid within the cochlea. These waves travel along the organ of Corti, a membrane covered in hair cells that function as hearing receptors. When a compressional wave deflects a hair cell, it creates an impulse in the auditory nerve that travels to the auditory cortex of the temporal lobes of the brain. The location of a deflected hair cell on the organ of Corti determines the pitch of the sound that the brain will perceive. The cochlear compressional waves are dispersed by the round window.

[handwritten: stirrup concentrates vibrations in oval window]
[handwritten: hammer, anvil, stirrup (hair bend)]
[handwritten box: BALANCE]

The three fluid-filled semi-circular canals have hair cell receptors that respond to motion. The brain uses this information to allow the body to keep its balance when moving. The saccule and utricle detect the position of the head with respect to gravity using a similar mechanism.

[handwritten: otoliths: calcium carbonate rocks.]

Hearing loss is treated by technologies such as hearing aids and cochlear implants. Hearing aids amplify and transmit sound waves to the eardrum. Cochlear implants are surgically implanted and function by stimulating the auditory nerves inside the cochlea with electrical impulses.

[handwritten: cochlea: takes sound vibrations and transmit impulses to the brain : occurs in the organ of corti]

OTHER SENSORY RECEPTORS

There are many other sensory receptors in the human body that provide the CNS with information about the internal and external environment. Thermoreceptors in the skin and in the hypothalamus respond to temperature changes. Proprioceptors provide information regarding the spatial position of the limbs. Chemoreceptors, such as the olfactory receptors that respond to smell and the taste receptors in the tongue, respond to the specific shapes of molecules. The main difference between these two receptors is that the taste receptors respond to dissolved chemical stimuli and olfactory receptors respond to airborne chemical stimuli.

Practice Questions: 12, 13, 15

30-A2.1K identify the principal endocrine glands of humans; i.e., the hypothalamus/pituitary complex, thyroid, parathyroid, adrenal glands and islet cells of the pancreas

30-A2.2K describe the function of the hormones of the principal endocrine glands; i.e., thyroid-stimulating hormone TSH/thyroxine, calcitonin/parathyroid hormone (PTH), adrenocorticotropic hormone (ACTH)/cortisol glucagon/insulin, human growth hormone (hGH),antidiuretic hormone (ADH), epinephrine, aldosterone, and describe how they maintain homeostasis through feedback

THE ENDOCRINE SYSTEM

The endocrine system, like the nervous system, allows parts of the body to communicate with each other. Endocrine glands secrete hormones into the bloodstream. Hormones are proteins or steroids that act on specific target cells to change their activity.

Peptide or protein hormones act by binding to receptors on the surface of target cells.
Steroid hormones pass through the cell and nuclear membranes of their target cells, binding to receptors within the nucleus, changing the expression of genes.

Gland	Hormone	Target Tissues	Effects
Hypo-thalamus (secreted by posterior pituitary)	ADH	Kidney tubules	Increases reabsorption of water from urine to bloodstream in response to dehydration
	Oxytocin	Uterine muscle and mammary glands	Stimulates contractions of the uterus for birth; stimulates the release of milk during breast feeding
Anterior pituitary	Thyroid-stimulating hormone (TSH)	Thyroid gland	Stimulates the thyroid to release thyroxine
	Adreno-corticotropic hormone (ACTH)	Adrenal cortex	Stimulates the adrenal cortex to release cortisol, aldosterone, and androgens in response to stress
	Growth hormone (hGH)	Bones and muscles	Causes mitosis to stimulate growth
Thyroid	Thyroxine	All body cells	Increases the rate of metabolic activity, producing ATP and heat
	Calcitonin	Bones, teeth, and gut	Decreases blood calcium by depositing Ca^{2+} in bones and teeth, and decreasing absorption from the gut
Pancreas	Insulin (from beta cells of islets of Langer-hans)	All cells, liver, and muscles	Decreases blood glucose by increasing cell permeability to glucose and conversion of blood glucose into liver and muscle glycogen
	Glucagon (from alpha cells of islets of Langer-hans)	All cells, liver, and muscles	Increases blood glucose by decreasing cell permeability to glucose and conversion of stored glycogen into glucose

Gland	Hormone	Target Tissues	Effects
Adrenal cortex	Cortisol (ACTH)	All tissues	Converts protein into glucose
	Aldosterone	Kidney tubules	Increases blood volume by increasing reabsorption Na+ and water from urine
	Testosterone (both sexes)	Many tissues	Increased muscle, bone, hair growth
Adrenal medulla	Norepinephrine *Sympathetic nervous system*	Blood vessels, heart, lungs, air passages, iris, liver	Shunts blood to core and large muscles, increases breathing and heart rates, dilates pupil, hydrolyzes liver glycogen
Parathyroid glands	Parathyroid hormone (PTH)	Bones and gut	Increases blood calcium by dissolving bones and increasing absorption from the gut

The sex hormones—testosterone, estrogen, progesterone, HCG, LH, prolactin, relaxin—will be explained in the reproduction section.

Practice Questions: 16, 17, 18, 19, 25, 29

30-A2.3K explain the metabolic roles hormones may play in homeostasis; i.e., thyroxine in metabolism; insulin, glucagon and cortisol in blood sugar regulation; hGH in growth;, ADH in water regulation; aldosterone in sodium ion regulation

30-A2.4K explain how the endocrine system allows humans to sense their internal environment and respond appropriately

30-A2.5K compare the endocrine and nervous control systems and explain how they act together

HOMEOSTASIS

Homeostasis is the process by which a stable condition is maintained. In the body, homeostasis is maintained by negative feedback mechanisms which are self-correcting systems. A monitor, usually the hypothalamus, constantly scans the blood for the levels of several body parameters. When a parameter increases beyond the normal range, the monitor responds by decreasing the parameter. Conversely, when a parameter decreases below the normal range, the monitor responds by increasing the parameter.

This self-correcting system is called negative feedback because each effect negates the previous one. For example, the metabolic rate of cells is controlled by negative feedback of the hormone thyroxine. If the hypothalamus detects a high thyroxine level, it stops releasing thyroid-stimulating hormone releasing factor (TSHRF), preventing the anterior pituitary from secreting thyroid-stimulating hormone (TSH). This stops the thyroid gland from secreting thyroxine, thus reducing metabolic rate. Eventually, low thyroxine levels will negatively feedback to the hypothalamus, causing it to release TSHRF which stimulates the anterior pituitary to release TSH, which in turn causes the thyroid gland to release thyroxine.

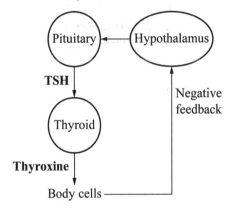

In a few cases, a blood parameter is kept constant by a pair of antagonistic hormones that counteract each other. For example, the hormone insulin decreases blood glucose when it rises too high; the hormone glucagon increases blood glucose when it falls too low. PTH and calcitonin are also antagonistic hormones.

PTH increases blood calcium, and calcitonin decreases it.

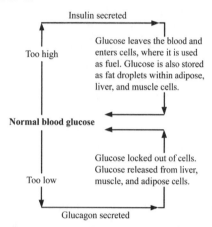

In contrast to negative feedback, positive feedback is used to magnify, not correct, an original stimulus. For example, the secretion of small amounts of the hormone oxytocin brings about labour. Positive feedback results in increasingly higher amounts of oxytocin secretion until the baby is born. The same is true of the hormone prolactin and its effect on milk supply.

COMPARING THE NERVOUS SYSTEM TO THE ENDOCRINE SYSTEM

The human body consists of somewhere around 600 trillion cells, all of which must communicate with each other to maintain homeostasis and ensure survival. Two communication systems exist in the body: the nervous system and the endocrine system.

Nervous connections are direct, communication is very rapid (within milliseconds), but the effects of nervous stimulation disappear quickly.

The endocrine system communicates using hormones rather than neurons. Hormones are chemical messengers secreted from one location and carried by the bloodstream to a target location, where they have their effect. Because the bloodstream moves much slower than nerve conduction, hormonal responses take longer to occur (minutes or hours), but their effects are sustained for as long as the hormone stays in the bloodstream.

Practice Questions: 20, 21, 26, 27, 28, NR2, NR3, NR4

30-A2.6K describe, using an example, the physiological consequences of hormone imbalances; i.e., diabetes mellitus

EFFECTS OF HORMONE IMBALANCE

There are many physiological consequences if the body is unable to maintain homeostatic hormone levels. Hypothyroidism—or too little thyroxin—causes a lower metabolic rate. A person suffering from hypothyroidism may feel tired, apathetic, cold, and may gain weight. In children, hypothyroidism results in cretinism, characterized by slowed mental and physical development. In hyperthyroidism, or Graves' disease, excess thyroxine causes a higher metabolic rate, which results in high blood pressure, sweating, irritability, sleep disturbances, and weight loss. A goitre is a swelling of the thyroid gland, often due to a lack of iodine in the diet. Iodine is needed to produce thyroxine. Without thyroxine, negative feedback produces more and more TSH, continually stimulating the thyroid, enlarging the gland often to an enormous size.

The inability to produce an adequate supply of insulin as a child is referred to as type I diabetes mellitus. Without insulin, cells are impermeable to glucose. Cells starve for fuel, resulting in fatigue and eventual coma. Indicators of inadequate insulin are high blood glucose levels and the presence of glucose in the urine. Type II diabetes mellitus usually affects older or obese individuals and is caused by an inadequate supply of insulin receptors, resulting in the same symptoms as type I.

Diabetes insipidus (unrelated to diabetes mellitus) is caused by a lack of ADH. The individual is unable to correct dehydration by reabsorbing water from the urine into the bloodstream. Water remains in the urine, resulting in copious amounts of dilute urine, thirst, and further dehydration of the blood. *less concentrated*

Imbalances in hGH secretion cause abnormalities of height. Dwarfism results when low hGH secretion as a child stunts growth of long bones. Excess hGH secretion as a child results in gigantism. *adults: acromegaly*

Practice Question: 22, 23, 24

PRACTICE QUESTIONS—NERVOUS AND ENDOCRINE SYSTEMS

Use the following information to answer the next question.

Yaws, bejel, and syphilis are three diseases known to be caused by strains of bacteria in the genus *Treponema*. Syphilis is a sexually transmitted disease, whereas yaws and bejel are not sexually transmitted. Studies of 800-year-old to 1 600-year-old skeletons from Florida, Equador, and New Mexico show that these people suffered from syphilis. Studies on 6 000-year-old skeletons from Illinois, Virginia, and Ohio show that these people suffered from yaws.

The symptoms of untreated syphilis usually disappear within 12 weeks of the initial infection. However, new symptoms may appear many years later. These include damage to neurons of the central nervous system.

– from Zabludoff, 1996

CHALLENGER QUESTION   **56.1**

1. The neurons damaged by syphilis are
   A. interneurons
   B. sensory neurons
   C. somatic motor neurons
   D. autonomic motor neurons

Source: January 2000

Use the following information to answer the next three questions.

Serotonin is a naturally occurring neurotransmitter that plays an important role in a person's mood and emotions. A shortage of serotonin has been associated with phobias, schizophrenia, aggressive behaviour, depression, uncontrolled appetite, and migraine headaches. Synthetic drugs have been developed to enhance or hinder the performance of serotonin in the brain. Some of these drugs include

I   Prozac and Zoloft, which cause serotonin to remain in the brain for longer periods of time

II   Drugs, such as Clozapine, that prevent serotonin from binding to post-synaptic membranes

III   Diet drugs, such as Redux and Fenfluramine, that stimulate nerve cells to release more serotonin

IV   Hallucinogens, such as LSD and Ecstasy, that react directly with serotonin receptors to produce the same effect as serotonin

– from Lemonick, 1997

2. The drugs numbered above that would act as competitive inhibitors to serotonin and the drugs that would slow down the rate of removal of serotonin from the synapse are, respectively,
   A. I and III
   B. II and I
   C. II and III
   D. III and IV

Source: June 2000

3. If a person were suffering from clinical depression, which of the following drugs would not reduce the symptoms of depression?

   A. LSD

   B. Zoloft

   C. Clozapine

   D. Fenfluramine

Source: June 2000

Use the following additional information to answer the next question.

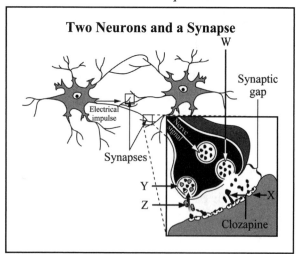

Two Neurons and a Synapse

4. The row below that identifies the structure that releases serotonin and the section of the neuron that this structure is found in is

Row	Released from structure	Found In
A.	W	axon terminal
B.	X	dendrite
C.	Y	axon
D.	Z	dendrite

Source: June 2000

Use the following diagram to answer the next question.

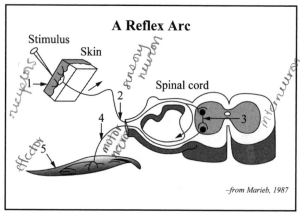

A Reflex Arc

–from Marieb, 1987

CHALLENGER QUESTION   **55.9**

Numerical Response

1. Identify the structure, as numbered above, that performs each of the functions given below.

Structure:	2	1	5	4
Function:	Transmits impulses to the central nervous system	Receives sensory stimulation	Carries out instructions from the central nervous system; is a muscle	Transmits impulses from the central nervous system to the effector

Source: January 2000

Use the following information to answer the next two questions.

A man was injured in an automobile accident. There appeared to be damage to his back, his arm, and his head.

A doctor examined the man, noted some symptoms, and hypothesized that nerve damage had occurred.

Some Possible Locations of Nerve Damage

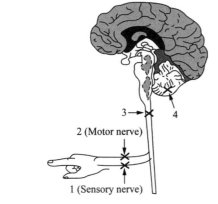

5. Which of the following rows correctly correlates possible observations about the accident victim with locations of nerve damage?

Row	Possible Observations	Locations of Nerve Damage
A.	The man could not move his wrist and could not feel sensations from his hand.	1 and 2
B.	The man could move his wrist normally but could not feel sensations from his hand.	1 and 4
C.	The man could not move his wrist but could feel sensations from his hand.	2 and 3
D.	The man could move his wrist normally and could feel sensations in his hand.	2 and 4

Source: June 2000

6. If, following the accident, the man exhibited a marked change in personality, the doctor would suspect damage to the

   A. medulla
   B. cerebrum
   C. cerebellum
   D. hypothalamus

Source: June 2000

Use the following information to answer the next question.

After accidentally hitting your thumb with a hammer, you immediately withdraw your hand. You do not feel pain for a short period of time.

7. This sequence of events may be explained by the fact that the

   A. threshold of the receptor has been so greatly exceeded that the neuron does not pass the message to the brain
   B. neural impulse is so large that the brain is unable to interpret the signal because it is beyond the range of tolerance
   C. neural processing occurred in the spinal cord first, which caused you to quickly remove your thumb from further damage
   D. sensory receptors in the thumb were damaged by the blow and are unable to initiate a stimulus to the sensory nerve

Source: January 2001

CHALLENGER QUESTION   50.8

8. Stimulation of an individual's sympathetic nervous system in response to imminent danger leads to all of the following responses **except**

    A. dilation of the pupils of the eye

    B. constriction of the bronchioles of the lungs

    C. constriction of the arterioles of the intestines

    D. dilation of the arterioles of the skeletal muscles

Source: January 2001

Use the following information to answer the next question.

Morphine is a drug obtained from the opium plant. It is routinely given to postoperative patients on a short-term basis for pain. At high doses, it causes breathing and heart contraction to become suppressed.

9. What area of the brain is affected by high doses of morphine?

    A. Pituitary

    B. Cerebrum

    C. Cerebellum

    D. Medulla oblongata

Source: January 2001

Use the following information to answer the next two questions.

Many predatory birds such as eagles have two foveas in each eye. The fovea in predatory birds is similar in structure and function to the fovea in humans. In addition, these birds have strong powers of near and far accommodation.

– from Curtis, 1983

10. If an eagle's brain were similar in structure to a human brain, impulses that begin in the retina of the eagle's eye would travel first to the

    A. frontal lobe

    B. parietal lobe

    C. occipital lobe

    D. temporal lobe

Source: January 2000

11. Strong near and far accommodation in the eye requires

    A. small blind spots

    B. a large number of rods

    C. a large number of cones

    D. highly developed ciliary muscles

Source: January 2000

Use the following information to answer the next two questions.

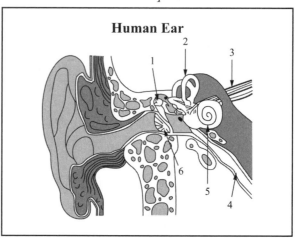

Human Ear

12. After riding the Tilt-A-Turn at an amusement park, people are often dizzy. Which of the structures numbered above is initially stimulated to cause the sensation of dizziness?

    A. Structure 1

    B. Structure 2

    C. Structure 3

    D. Structure 5

Source: June 2000

13. Which of the structures numbered on the diagram function together to convert sound waves to mechanical vibrations, and then to amplify these vibrations?

   A. Structures 6 and 1

   B. Structures 5 and 2

   C. Structures 6 and 3

   D. Structures 5 and 4

Source: June 2000

Use the following information to answer the next question.

Many scientists believe that sleep cycles are influenced by the hormone melatonin.
Two scientists have shown that the retinas in hamsters are involved in maintaining a 24-hour cycle. Their research shows that impulses sent from the retina to the brain after exposure to light influence the secretions of melatonin. Melatonin is normally produced in greater amounts at night when the eyes are exposed to less light. In humans, melatonin produces drowsiness.

– from Raloff, 1996

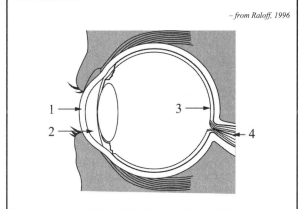

14. Melatonin secretion decreases when light stimulates receptors found in the structure labelled

   A. 1

   B. 2

   C. 3

   D. 4

Source: June 2000

15. Which two receptors respond to chemical stimuli?

   A. Olfactory receptors and thermoreceptors

   B. Proprioceptors and taste receptors

   C. Thermoreceptors and proprioceptors

   D. Taste receptors and olfactory receptors

Use the following information to answer the next question.

Oxytocin and ADH are synthesized by neurosecretory cells in the hypothalamus. These hormones are stored in the posterior pituitary. They can then be released into the bloodstream where they circulate to target cells.

Hormones of the Pituitary and Hypothalamus

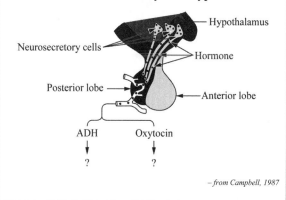

– from Campbell, 1987

16. In a human female, where are the target cells for ADH and oxytocin?

   A. In the kidney tubules and ovaries

   B. In the Bowman's capsule and the ovaries

   C. In the kidney tubules and uterine muscles

   D. In the Bowman's capsule and the uterine muscles

Source: January 2000

17. Graves' disease is caused by the overproduction of a hormone from the

   A. pancreas

   B. pituitary

   C. thyroid gland

   D. adrenal glands

18. Which of the following endocrine glands controls blood pressure in humans?

   A. Adrenal gland

   B. Pancreas

   C. Thymus

   D. Thyroid

19. A transplant of pancreatic beta cells could be used to treat

   A. High urine volume

   B. High blood glucose

   C. High blood calcium

   D. High blood pressure

20. A hemmorhage would result in

   A. the release of ADH

   B. the release of aldosterone

   C. impairment of ADH secretion

   D. impairment of aldosterone secretion

Use the following information to answer the next question.

Six Hormones

1. Insulin

2. Aldosterone

3. Glucagon

4. Thyroxine

5. Cortisol

6. Growth hormone

Numerical Response

2. Of the hormones listed, the ones that regulate blood sugar levels are ___1 3 5___.
(Record your answer as a **three-digit** number.)

Use the following information to answer the next question.

Responses Stimulated by Hormones

1. Increased metabolic rate

2. Decreased metabolic rat

3. Sodium reabsorption from the kidneys

4. Increased blood calcium concentrations

5. Increased blood glucose concentration

6. Development of long bones and muscles

Numerical Response

3. Identify the responses, as numbered above, that would result from the secretion of thyroxine, PTH, glucagon, and hGH respectively.
Response: ___1 4 5 6___
(Record your answer as a **four-digit** number.)

Use the following information to answer the next question.

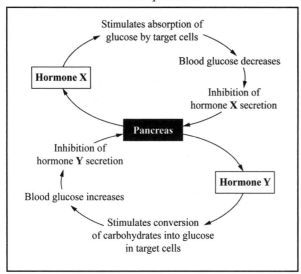

21. The names of hormones **X** and **Y** are, respectively,

  A. insulin and glucagon

  B. glucagon and insulin

  C. glycogen and insulin

  D. insulin and glycogen

Source: June 1999

22. A common symptom of hyperthyroidism or Graves' disease is exophthalmos, the protrusion of the eyeballs. Another likely symptom of Grave's disease is

  A. fatigue

  B. confusion

  C. weight loss

  D. feeling cold

Use the following information to answer the next question.

1. Blood volume increases

2. Aldosterone released from adrenal cortex

3. Increased sodium reabsorption from the urine

4. Increased reabsorption of water from the urine

Numerical Response

4. If a decrease in blood pressure is detected, a hormonal response is activated to restore blood pressure. The correct order in which the events listed occur is ___2___, ___3___, ___4___, and ___1___.

23. Gigantism is caused by overproduction of growth hormone (hGH). The effect of hGH on metabolism is

  A. increased protein synthesis

  B. excessive urine production

  C. increased blood sugar levels

  D. increased blood calcium levels

24. A person with weak and brittle bones **most likely** has a hormonal imbalance of

  A. insulin

  B. aldosterone

  C. parathyroid hormone

  D. thyroid-stimulating hormone

Use the following information to answer the next question.

Although most strains of the bacterial species *Vibrio cholerae* are harmless, the O1 strain produces a toxin that binds to cells of the small intestine, causing rapid depletion of salts and water, which, if not replaced, can be lethal in humans. This disease is known as cholera.

The transformation from harmless to harmful bacterial strains is thought to be caused by a virus that transfers the cholera toxin gene (CTX) from one bacterial strain and places it into another. Researchers can mimic this process by using current technologies.

—from Glausiusz, 1996

25. The overall effects of cholera toxin are opposite to the physiological effects of which of the following hormones?

    A. Oxytocin

    B. Thyroxine

    C. Aldosterone

    D. Epinephrine

    Source: January 2000

Use the following information to answer the next question.

Researchers have been studying the connection between maternal care and stress in rats. Those rats that received more licking and grooming as babies release lower levels of ACTH in response to stress as adults.
In humans, high levels of stress hormones are linked to an increase in heart disease, diabetes, depression, and alcoholism.

—from Strauss, 1997

Some Endocrine Glands

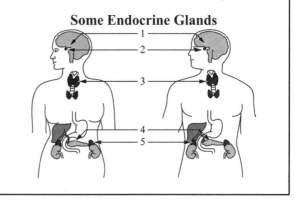

26. Humans, as well as rats, release ACTH in response to stress. The row below that identifies the gland that secretes ACTH and the target gland of ACTH in humans is

Row	Secreting Gland	Target Gland
A.	1	2
B.	1	3
C.	2	4
D.	2	5

Source: June 2000

Use the following information to answer the next two questions

A laboratory technician was asked to set up an experiment to determine the effect of thyroxine on metabolic rate. Four groups of adult male laboratory rats were used. Each group was placed in the same type of cage, which was designed to provide room for physical activity. Each of the four groups was given an adequate supply of water and one of the four diets listed below.

Diet W: rat chow, a preparation of rat food containing all essential nutrients

Diet X: rat chow containing a chemical that counteracts the effect of thyroxine in the body

Diet Y: rat chow containing dried thyroid tissue, which contains thyroxine

Diet Z: rat chow deficient in iodine
lack·

The technician was not aware of which diet she was feeding to each group of rats. The following data were obtained.

Group	Average Initial Weight (g)	Average Final Weight After Two Weeks (g)	Final Average Oxygen Consumption (mL/kg min)
I	323	392	2.5
II	328	287	10.5
III	330	400	2.0
IV	315	320	4.0

27. According to the data table, which group of rats was **most likely** the control group?
    A. I
    B. II
    C. III
    D. IV

Source: June 2000

28. The row below that correctly identifies two groups of laboratory rats and the diets they were most probably fed is

Row	Group	Diet	Group	Diet
A.	I	Z	II	W
B.	I	W	IV	X
C.	II	Y	III	X
D.	III	Z	IV	Y

Source: June 2000

29. Damage to which of the following endocrine glands would **most affect** the reaction of the body to an emergency that stimulates the sympathetic nervous system?
    A. Thyroid gland
    B. Adrenal gland
    C. Anterior pituitary gland
    D. Posterior pituitary gland

Source: January 2000

ANSWERS AND SOLUTIONS—PRACTICE QUESTIONS

1. A	7. C	14. C	NR2. 135	25. C
2. B	8. B	15. D	NR3. 1456	26. D
3. C	9. D	16. C	21. A	27. D
4. A	10. C	17. C	22. C	28. C
NR1. 2154	11. D	18. A	NR4. 2341	29. B
5. A	12. B	19. B	23. A	
6. B	13. A	20. B	24. C	

1. A

Syphilis damages neurons of the central nervous system. Interneurons are found in the CNS, specifically the core of the spinal cord. Sensory neurons, somatic motor neurons, and autonomic motor neurons all exist in peripheral nerves outside of the CNS.

2. B

II. By preventing serotonin from binding to postsynaptic membranes, these drugs are competitive inhibitors.

I. By causing serotonin to remain in the brain for longer periods of time, these drugs slow down the removal of serotonin.

3. C

Clozapine prevents serotonin from binding on the postsynaptic membranes; therefore, Clozapine will reduce the effect of serotonin. Since a shortage of serotonin has been linked to depression, it would not make sense to use this drug on a person suffering from depression.

4. A

A neurotransmitter such as serotonin is stored in a synaptic vesicle. Structure W is the vesicle releasing the neurotransmitter into the synapse. Synaptic vesicles release neurotransmitters from the axon terminals.

NR 1 2154

Structure 2 is a sensory neuron that transmits information to the spinal cord from a sensory receptor. Structure 1 is a sensory receptor in the skin that detects touch. Structure 5 is a muscle that has been stimulated to contract. Structure 4 is a motor neuron from the spinal cord.

5. A

If the man could not move his wrist, then a signal was not able to get through point 2, the motor nerve. If the man could not feel sensations in his hand, then a signal was not able to get through point 1, the sensory nerve.

If there was nerve damage at point 4, the cerebellum, the man would not be able to move his wrist normally because the cerebellum coordinates movement.

If there were damage at point 3, the spinal cord, impulses from the sensory neuron could not be relayed through the cord to the sensory cortex of the brain. Thus, the man would not likely feel sensations from his hand.

If there were damage at point 2, the motor nerve, the man would not be able to move his wrist normally.

6. B

The frontal lobe of the cerebrum is responsible for personality. A change in the victim's personality would suggest that there might be damage to the cerebrum. The medulla takes care of basic unconscious, involuntary functions relating to internal systems, such as circulation, digestion, and breathing. The cerebellum is responsible for coordinating motor activities. The hypothalamus controls the endocrine system.

7. C

A reflex is a pre-programmed stimulus response pathway that relies on the spinal cord to coordinate a response rather than the brain. The proof that this event is due to a reflex is that the hand was removed even before the cerebrum felt pain. This indicates that the spinal cord, on its own, initiated the response. During this reflex response, a pain or touch sensory receptor fires, and a sensory neuron carries the pain signal to an interneuron in the spinal cord. The interneuron interprets the incoming signal and coordinates a response, which is to pull the hand away. The interneuron synapses with a motor neuron that commands a muscle in the arm to contract and pull the hand away. Shortly thereafter, a signal is sent up through the spinal cord to the brain, which only then becomes aware of the original stimulus and feels pain.

8. B

The sympathetic nervous system prepares the body for competition, excitement, or danger—and causes what are often referred to as fight-or-flight responses. The only distractor that would not help an individual in a fight-or-flight situation is the constriction of the bronchioles of the lungs. This would decrease the air flow in and out of the lungs, reducing the flow of oxygen to the cells, reducing cell respiration and energy production. Dilation of the pupils allows more light into the eye for clearer vision. Constriction of the arterioles of the intestines and dilation of the arterioles of the skeletal muscles diverts blood to where it is most needed.

9. D

The information explains that at high doses, morphine suppresses heart contraction and breathing. Therefore, select the part of the brain that regulates heart contraction and breathing: the medulla oblongata. The pituitary influences the endocrine system, the cerebrum takes care of higher thought, and the cerebellum coordinates muscle movements.

10. C

The occipital lobe, at the back of the cerebrum, receives and coordinates visual information. The impulse that begins in the retina travels first to the occipital lobe.

The frontal lobe is associated with personality and contains the motor cortex that controls voluntary movement. The parietal lobe contains the sensory cortex that processes conscious sensation. The temporal lobe contains the auditory cortex and processes sound.

11. D

Accommodation refers to a change in the shape of the lens in order to focus on near or far objects clearly. The lens becomes rounder or flatter by relaxation or contraction of the ciliary muscles.

A blind spot exists at the point on the retina where neurons of the optic nerve gather to exit the eye. Rods are light receptors that function in very low light levels and do not perceive colour. Cones are light receptors that perceive colour and function only in bright light.

12. B

Structure 2 labels the fluid-filled semicircular canals, which detect motion. When a person moves, the movement causes the cilia of hair cells inside the semicircular canals to bend, which causes a nerve impulse to be sent to the brain. When a person feels dizzy after movement stops, it is because the fluid inside the semicircular canals continues to move like a person standing on the bus when it comes to a sudden halt.

13. A

The eardrum (tympanic membrane), structure 6, vibrates in response to sound waves. The vibration of the eardrum causes movements in the three tiny middle ear bones or ossicles, structure 1. The ossicles are designed like levers, so a small vibration in the eardrum results in a larger vibration through the middle ear bones.

14. C

Structure 3 is the retina of the eye. The retina contains the rods and cones, which are the photoreceptors that stimulate action potentials in the optic nerve. Low light levels stimulate rods on the periphery of the retina and perceive black and white. High light levels are perceived by the three types of cones which absorb red, blue, and green light.

15. D

Taste receptors (concentrated in the tongue) and olfactory receptors (concentrated in the nasal cavity) respond to chemical stimuli. Each molecule that can be smelled or tasted has a specific shape that fits into a complementarily shaped receptor in the taste buds or the olfactory epithelium in the nasal cavities.

Thermoreceptors in the skin respond to temperature changes, and proprioceptors provide a sense of spatial position of the body.

16. C

ADH stimulates the kidney tubules to be more permeable, allowing more water to diffuse from the kidney tubules back to the blood. Oxytocin causes uterine muscles to contract during labour. Oxytocin also causes the mammary glands to secrete milk into the mammary ducts.

17. C

Graves' disease is caused by the overproduction of thyroxine from the thyroid gland. It is often referred to as hyperthyroidism.

18. A

The adrenal cortex secretes aldosterone when blood pressure falls. The result is increased Na^+ reabsorption from urine to blood. Water follows by osmosis, increasing blood volume and thus blood pressure.

19. B

The beta cells in the islets of Langerhans of the pancreas are responsible for secreting insulin. Insulin is used to treat diabetes mellitus. Without insulin, blood glucose levels are high.

20. B

A decrease in blood volume, as a result of a hemorrhage, decreases the blood pressure, which stimulates the release of aldosterone from the adrenal cortex. Aldosterone increases reabsorption of Na^+ ions from urine to blood, which causes water to follow by osmosis, increasing blood volume and blood pressure. ADH would not be released because ADH responds to a drop in the water content of the blood. Because the individual did not lose water (as in vomiting or diarrhea), the constitution of the blood remains normal—there is just less of it.

NR 2   135

Glucagon increases blood glucose levels by converting glycogen to glucose. Insulin decreases blood glucose levels by converting glucose to glycogen. Cortisol increases blood glucose levels by converting proteins to glucose.

NR 3   1456

Thyroxine increases metabolic rate or the rate of cell respiration in all cells. PTH increases the blood concentration of calcium ions by dissolving bones, and increasing calcium absorption from the gut. Glucagon increases blood glucose by hydrolyzing liver glycogen to glucose and by decreasing the permeability of cells to glucose, causing the glucose to remain in the blood. Human growth hormone increases the rate of mitosis at the growth plate of long bones and in muscle cells.

21. A

The order of hormones is important, and do not confuse glucagon with glycogen.
Insulin stimulates the absorption of glucose by target cells (hormone **X**). Glucagon stimulates the conversion of glycogen into glucose in target cells (hormone **Y**).

22. C

Hyperthyroidism is the result of excess thyroxine production, which increases the metabolic rate (cell respiration). An increased metabolic rate increases the use of glucose and the production of ATP energy and heat. A high metabolic rate uses up glucose (food) at a much faster rate than normal, leading to weight loss.

Fatigue is an unlikely symptom of Graves' disease because of the increased production of ATP energy that is associated with high metabolic rate. Confusion indicates that the brain cells are not metabolizing, but Graves' disease is the result of increased metabolism, so this is an unlikely symptom. As well, the production of heat as the result of increased metabolism makes it unlikely someone with Graves' disease would feel cold.

NR 4   2341

When low blood pressure is detected, aldosterone is released. Its target cells are the kidney tubules, where aldosterone increases the reabsorption of sodium ions into the blood, thus making the blood hypertonic. Water follows the sodium from the urine into the blood by osmosis, increasing blood volume and pressure.

23. A

Growth hormone affects muscle and bone by increasing protein synthesis, which increases cell size and cell number.

24. C

Parathyroid hormone increases blood calcium levels by dissolving bones and increasing the reabsorption of calcium ions from the intestine. Too much parathyroid hormone can result in osteoporosis, leading to porous and brittle bones. High parathyroid levels are seen in pregnancy when the mother's bones are used as a source of calcium for the developing fetus.

25. C

The hormone aldosterone is released from the adrenal cortex when the level of Na^+ is too low or blood pressure or volume drops. Aldosterone causes cells lining the kidney tubules to actively transport more sodium from urine to blood. Water follows by osmosis, increasing blood volume and blood pressure.

26. D

ACTH is secreted by structure 2, the anterior pituitary. ACTH stands for adrenocorticotropic hormone. It stimulates the cortex of the adrenal gland, structure 5, to produce aldosterone (which increases blood pressure), cortisol (which increases the conversion of protein to blood glucose), and small amounts of androgens (testosterone-like compounds that have uncertain value in stress).

27. D

The control group has not been given an experimental treatment and, therefore, serves as a comparison for the groups that have been given an experimental treatment. In this case, the experimental treatments involve increasing metabolic rate (by increasing thyroxine) or decreasing metabolic rate (by decreasing thyroxine). Group IV remained about the same weight and consumed a moderate amount of oxygen. These are indications that the metabolic rate was neither increased nor decreased.

28. C

Here are the most likely diets for the groups of rats.

Group	Weight change	Oxygen consumption	Metabolic rate must be	Diet
I	Increase	Low	Low	Z—the lack of iodine reduced thyroxine production
II	Decrease	High	High	Y—the diet contained thyroxine which would increase metabolism
III	Increase	Low	Low	X—the chemical in the diet counteracted the effects of thyroxine
V	Same	Moderate	Moderate	W—a diet that would neither increase nor decrease the effects of thyroxine

29. B

The medulla of the adrenal gland secretes epinephrine and norepinephrine that have effects on the body similar to that of the sympathetic system.

The thyroid gland (**A**) produces thyroxin, which regulates metabolic rate. The anterior pituitary (**C**) and posterior pituitary (**D**) glands store and produce a variety of hormones, none of which mimic the sympathetic nervous system.

UNIT TEST—NERVOUS AND ENDOCRINE SYSTEMS

Use the following information to answer the next two questions

Two symptoms of Parkinson's disease are lack of muscular coordination and tremors, both caused by inadequate amounts of dopamine. Symptoms of Alzheimer's disease include the deterioration of memory and mental abilities, possibly caused by a decrease in acetylcholine production.

Dopamine and acetylcholine are excitatory neurotransmitters in various parts of the brain.

Use the following additional information to answer the next question.

Damage to neurons in different parts of the brain appears to cause Parkinson's and Alzheimer's diseases. Nerve growth factor (NGF), a chemical produced by peripheral nerves, promotes axon regeneration.
Studies show that neurons of the CNS are capable of regeneration when NGF is produced by genetically engineered cells that are transplanted in the CNS.

—from Greene, 1993

CHALLENGER QUESTION   **44.8**

1. What role do both dopamine and acetylcholine have when they function as excitatory neurotransmitters?

    A. They make the presynaptic membrane more permeable to K^+ ions.

    B. They make the presynaptic membrane more permeable to Na^+ ions.

    C. They make the postsynaptic membrane more permeable to K^+ ions.

    D. They make the postsynaptic membrane more permeable to Na^+ ions.

    Source: June 1999

CHALLENGER QUESTION   **53.9**

2. Would it be reasonable to use NGF to regenerate neurons in which nuclei had been destroyed?

    A. Yes, because not all cells require a nucleus to function

    B. Yes, because organelles other than the nucleus cause growth

    C. No, because the nucleus controls protein synthesis and homeostasis

    D. No, because without the nucleus to actively transport ions, the cell would die

    Source: June 1999

Use the following information to answer the next three questions.

Stimulation of a sensory neuron produces an action potential. The graph below illustrates the membrane potential of a normal neuron after stimulation.

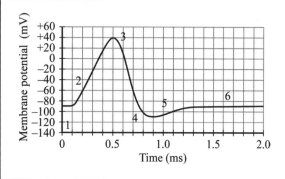

Numerical Response

1. Which part of the graph indicates the opening of sodium ion channels?
Answer: _2_

2. Which part of the graph indicates the completion of depolarization?
Answer: _3_

3. What is the membrane potential when the cell is hyperpolarized?
Answer: – _110_ mV

Use the following diagram to answer the next question.

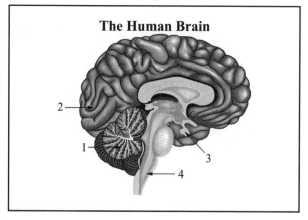

The Human Brain

3. The area of the brain that controls the sympathetic and parasympathetic nervous systems is labelled

A. 1

B. 2

C. 3

D. 4

Source: June 2001

Use the following information to answer
the next question.

A Simple Reflex Arc

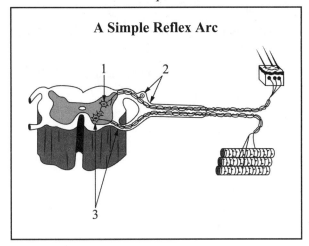

4. Structure 1 is an interneuron. Structures 2 and 3 are, **respectively**, a

   A. sensory neuron and a motor neuron

   B. motor neuron and a sensory neuron

   C. non-myelinated neuron and a myelinated neuron

   D. myelinated neuron and a non-myelinated neuron

   Source: January 1999

5. Returning involuntary body functions to normal after a period of stress is the function of which division of the nervous system?

   A. Central

   B. Somatic

   C. Sympathetic

   D. Parasympathetic

Use the following information to answer
the next question.

Mercury poisoning causes neurological damage, which leads to a deterioration of short-term memory and an inability to coordinate muscle movements.

6. The areas of the brain affected by mercury poisoning as indicated by the above symptoms are, respectively, the

   A. cerebrum and medulla

   B. cerebellum and cerebrum

   C. cerebrum and cerebellum

   D. hypothalamus and cerebellum

   Source: June 1999

Use the following information to answer
the next question.

The Human Eye

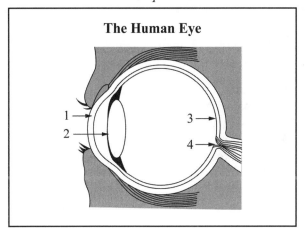

7. An area of the eye where sensory reception of light is most acute and an area where there is no such sensory reception are labelled, respectively,

   A. 1 and 2

   B. 2 and 3

   C. 3 and 4

   D. 4 and 1

Use the following information to answer the next question.

Some people experience motion sickness when they travel in a boat, airplane, or automobile. Symptoms include nausea, vomiting, dizziness, and headache. A drug can be taken to reduce these symptoms.

8. Likely, this drug inhibits the transmission of information from the

   A. cochlea to the brain

   B. organ of Corti to the brain

   C. basilar membrane to the brain

   D. semicircular canals to the brain

   Source: January 1999

Use the following information to answer the next question.

The graph below illustrates the effects of different temperatures on the responses of four different nerve fibres in the skin.

Receptors:
W—a pain receptor stimulated by cold
X—a cold receptor
Y—a heat receptor
Z—a pain receptor stimulated by heat

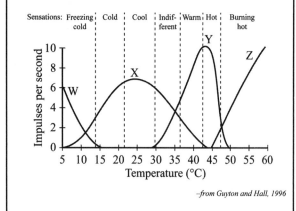

–from Guyton and Hall, 1996

9. Which of the following statements presents a valid interpretation of the information on the graph?

   A. A temperature of 5°C is less painful than a temperature of 50°C.

   B. A sensation of coolness is interpreted only when two types of receptors are stimulated.

   C. The threshold level of stimulation is higher for temperature receptors than it is for pain receptors.

   D. Temperature sensations are determined by the number of impulses per second and the specific type of receptors.

   Source: June 1999

10. During an emergency situation, the adrenal gland is stimulated to release a hormone that **directly** causes an increase in

    A. insulin levels

    B. blood glucose levels

    C. parasympathetic stimulation

    D. conversion of glucose to glycogen

    Source: January 1999

Use the following information to answer the next question.

A suspected endocrine gland was removed from a test animal, and the resulting symptoms were observed. A chemical extract of the suspected endocrine gland was then injected into the animal. The symptoms were no longer observed. Normal rats injected with the extract showed higher metabolic rates and elevated temperatures.

11. Based on these observations, the organ was

    A. the pituitary gland

    B. the thyroid gland

    C. an adrenal gland

    D. the pancreas

*Use the following information to answer
the next question.*

A tumour of the adrenal medulla is called
pheochromocytoma. This tumour causes
hypersecretion of epinephrine and
norepinephrine, and a number of other
symptoms.

12. Possible symptoms of pheochromocytoma
    include

    A. increased heart rate, increased blood
    sugar, and increased metabolic rate

    B. decreased heart rate, increased blood
    sugar, and increased metabolic rate

    C. increased heart rate, decreased blood
    sugar, and decreased metabolic rate

    D. decreased heart rate, decreased blood
    sugar, and decreased metabolic rate

    Source: January 1999

CHALLENGER QUESTION	30.2

13. A hormone that regulates glucose levels in
    the blood and a hormone that regulates Na^+
    in the blood and, indirectly, water
    reabsorption by the kidneys are,
    respectively,

    A. aldosterone and insulin

    B. glucagon and aldosterone

    C. epinephrine and glucagon

    D. insulin and antidiuretic hormone

    Source: January 1999

14. A condition that results in an enlargement of
    the thyroid gland may be caused by a diet
    deficient in

    A. iron

    B. iodine

    C. sodium

    D. potassium

    Source: January 1999

*Use the following information to answer
the next question.*

Mercury poisoning causes neurological damage,
which leads to a deterioration of short-term
memory and an inability to coordinate muscle
movements.

Mercury poisoning also affects the pituitary
gland in such a way that frequent urination
results.

15. Mercury compounds **most likely** affect the
    level of the hormone

    A. TSH

    B. ADH

    B. adrenalin

    C. aldosterone

    Source: June 1999

*Use the following information to answer
the next question.*

Chemicals found in alcohol and tea have a
diuretic effect. Diuretics cause the body to
produce greater-than-normal volumes of urine.

16. Diuretic chemicals counteract the effect
    of the hormone

    A. ADH

    B. insulin

    C. cortisol

    D. prolactin

    Source: January 2002

Use the following information to answer the next question.

During stressful experiences, interactions between the nervous and endocrine systems prepare the body to defend itself or to handle injury.

17. Which hormone is released as a direct result of sympathetic motor neuron stimulation?

A. hGH

B. Thyroxine

C. Aldosterone

D. Epinephrine

Source: June 1999

18. In response to eating a large amount of candy, negative feedback would result in

A. reduced secretion of insulin

B. increased secretion of glucagon

C. reduced permeability of cell membranes to glucose

D. increased conversion of blood glucose to liver glycogen

ANSWERS AND SOLUTIONS—UNIT TEST

1. D	4. A	10. B	16. A
2. C	5. D	11. B	17. D
NR1. 2	6. C	12. A	18. D
NR2. 3	7. C	13. B	
NR3. 110	8. D	14. B	
3. D	9. D	15. B	

1. D

Depolarization occurs when the axon membrane becomes permeable to sodium. When sodium enters the axon, the interior becomes more positive, and the exterior more negative—the reverse of the resting membrane polarity. The postsynaptic neuron is the neuron after the synapse.

The postsynaptic dendrite has receptors that, when bound to a neurotransmitter, make the membrane permeable to sodium. Making the membrane permeable to K^+ ions would not result in depolarization because K^+ ions are found in the axon interior. Increasing their permeability would cause the interior to become even more negative, or hyperpolarized.

2. C

In the given information, NGF is said to promote axon regeneration. As alternative **C** indicates, the nucleus controls protein synthesis. In other words, the nucleus is necessary to guide regeneration. NGF only promotes it. All complete cells need a nucleus to function. While it is true that mature red blood cells in mammals do not have nuclei and still function, they are considered sub-cellular and cannot regenerate themselves. Organelles other than the nucleus do cause cell growth, but these organelles still require the nucleus for direction and control. Without a nucleus, a cell will die. However, ion transport is not part of the discussion.

NR 1   2

The part of the graph labelled 2 indicates the opening of sodium ion channels. When a neuron receives a stimulus, the sodium ion channels in the membrane open. As sodium flows into the axon the interior becomes more positively charged than the exterior. The neuron is now depolarized.

The graph indicates that the cell has a resting potential of –90 mV at the part labelled 1 and a membrane potential of –40 mV at the part of the graph labelled 2. Note that depending on the source, complete depolarization potential is given as +30, +35, or +40 mV.

NR 2   3

Depolarization begins when sodium rushes into the axon, which makes the axon more positive. Depolarization is complete at +40 mV. After this point, repolarization commences.

The graph shows that in this neuron the resting potential is –90 mV. Position 4 shows a potential that is even more negative than the resting membrane potential of –90 mV. The membrane is thus hyperpolarized at –110 mV. A general description of repolarization is that extra positive ions are actively transported out of the axon to restore the negative resting membrane potential in the ICF. In actuality, repolarization is more complex. First, K^+ is actively transported out to the ECF until the normal resting polarity is restored. Then Na^+ and K^+ are exchanged using the sodium-potassium pumps in the membrane. This eventually re-establishes the correct concentrations of sodium and potassium on either side of the membrane. Active transport using the ion pumps requires large amounts of ATP, and for this reason the nervous system uses great amounts of energy.

3. D

The cerebellum (**1**) coordinates fine motor skills—essentially making the muscles work together to carry out movements. The cerebrum (**2**) is the conscious part of the brain. It is the part where thoughts, feelings, and all decisions originate. The pituitary (**3**) controls the endocrine system. The medulla (**4**) is responsible for such unconscious activities as swallowing, breathing, and heart rate.

4. A

The diagram is showing a reflex arc. Structure 2 is a sensory neuron that lead is leading from sensory receptors in a block of skin. It leads to an interneuron in the spinal cord. Structure 3 is a motor neuron that leads from an interneuron in the spinal cord to muscle cells in a muscle. Both neurons are myelinated.

5. D

The parasympathetic system is responsible for returning the body systems to normal following, for example, a stressful situation.

The sympathetic system is responsible for the stress response. The central nervous system includes the nerves of the brain and spinal cord. The somatic nervous system includes the nerves that control skeletal muscles, bones, and skin.

6. C

Mercury poisoning will affect the cerebrum, which will lead to a deterioration of the short-term memory, and the cerebellum, which will lead to an inability to coordinate muscle movements. The medulla does not control muscle coordination. The hypothalamus is not directly involved in controlling memory or muscle coordination.

7. C

Arrow 3 in the diagram points to the fovea—the most sensitive portion of the retina for light perception. The head automatically swings so that light falls on the fovea. Although it has no rod cells, it contains a high concentration of cones. Arrow 4 indicates the point where the optic nerve exits the retina. It is called the blind spot because no rods or cones are present here. Arrow 1 points to the cornea, the outer transparent layer of the eye. Arrow 2 points to the lens, which focuses incoming light on the retina.

8. D

Motion, changes in body position, and balance are sensed by the vestibule (saccule and utricle) and the semicircular canals, both present in the inner ear. Movement of fluid according to the body position stimulates nerve hair cells within these two structures and impulses are sent to the brain. Motion sickness, caused by irregular movements, can therefore be alleviated by inhibiting the transmission of nerve signals from the vestibule and semicircular canals to the brain.

The cochlea, organ of Corti, and basilar membrane are all structures that function in hearing, and therefore do not have a role in motion sickness.

9. D

As the graph illustrates, temperature sensations are determined by the number of impulses per second and the specific type of receptors. Statement **A** is incorrect because 5ºC is shown to be more painful than 50ºC. Statement **B** is incorrect because coolness seems to be a single receptor (X) sensation. Statement **C** is incorrect because no threshold levels are shown.

10. B

In an emergency situation, the adrenal medulla releases norepinephrine (adrenalin) which causes:

(i) blood sugar to rise by converting glycogen to glucose to increase the amount of readily available energy for use by muscles

(ii) an increased heart rate

(iii) an increased breathing rate

(iv) a dilation of blood vessels to increase blood flow to core, brain, and muscle tissues

(v) dilation of the iris to increase the light entering the eye

All of these responses are characteristic of stimulation of the sympathetic nervous system. The parasympathetic nervous system can be thought of as returning the body's systems to the normal state following a threat or stressful situation. Insulin is responsible for conversion of glucose to its storage form called glycogen. Increased insulin levels would be a response to activation of the parasympathetic system.

11. B

Thyroxine increases the metabolic rate (rate of cell respiration) in cells. More glucose and oxygen are used, producing more ATP energy and waste heat. The rats' symptoms suggest that the gland removed from the test animal was the thyroid, which produces thyroxine.

12. A

Epinephrine and norepinephrine are stimulators of the sympathetic nervous system. Hypersecretion of these hormones could result in increased heart rate, increased blood sugar, and increased metabolic rate.

13. B

Recall the functions of the hormones listed in the alternatives.

Hormone	Target Organ	Primary Function
Aldosterone	Kidneys (distal tubule and collecting duct)	Increases Na^+ absorption from urine, causing water to be reabsorbed indirectly by osmosis
Insulin	Body cells	Causes body cells to become permeable to glucose; liver cells convert glucose into liver and muscle glycogen
Glucagon	Liver	Stimulates liver cells to convert stored glycogen into glucose, which is released into blood
Norepinephrine	Multiple targets	Stimulates increase in blood glucose level, increases heart and breathing rate, pupils dilate, core, muscle, and brain blood vessels dilate
Antidiuretic hormone (ADH)	Kidney collecting duct	Increases the permeability of the tubules to water to increase water absorption from urine into blood

Aldosterone functions by increasing the absorption of sodium ions, which indirectly increases the reabsorption of water by the kidneys, whereas ADH directly increases the absorption of water by increasing tubule permeability to water.

14. B

The chemical structure of thyroxine includes the element iodine. Without iodine, thyroxine is not synthesized. Low thyroxine negatively feeds back to the hypothalamus increasing production of TSHRF, which increases TSH secretion from the anterior pituitary. Because the thyroid cannot produce the thyroxine, the increasingly high levels of TSH stimulate the thyroid to get larger and larger in an attempt to produce more hormone. The result is the swelling known as goiter. Goiter is common in areas where soil iodine levels are low and iodized salt is not available.

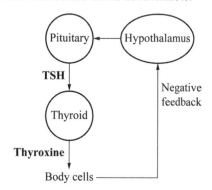

15. B

Increased urination could be caused by a drop in ADH or a drop in aldosterone. However, the pituitary gland does not secrete aldosterone, only ADH. Therefore, the mercury compounds most likely affect the release of ADH from the pituitary gland.

TSH is produced by the pituitary, but it does not have an effect on urination.

16. A

Diuretics cause an increase in the volume of urine, causing the body to excrete more water than usual. ADH is the only hormone listed that has an effect on urine production. ADH increases urine production, so diuretics block ADH secretion.

17. D

Perceptions that cause stress result in the stimulation of sympathetic motor neurons by the medulla. These impulses act to prepare the body for fight-or-flight. The adrenal medulla receives sympathetic impulses and secretes large amounts of epinephrine/norepinephrine. Note that the hormone names epinephrine/norepinephrine, adrenaline/noradrenaline are often used interchangeably. The flood of epinephrine from the adrenal medulla into the bloodstream magnifies the sympathetic effects of increased heart and breathing rate, dilation of pupils, and the shunting of blood from the periphery to the core, muscles, and brain.

18. D

The candy increases blood glucose levels, which stimulate insulin secretion from the beta cells of the Islets of Langerhans in the pancreas. Insulin reduces blood glucose by increasing cell membrane permeability to glucose, allowing glucose to enter the cells for cell respiration. Insulin also causes glucose in the blood to be stored as glycogen in the liver and muscles.

The hormone glucagon acts antagonistically to insulin. It is released when blood glucose levels fall below normal, and results in the opposite effects as insulin.

Reproduction and Development

REPRODUCTION AND DEVELOPMENT

Table of Correlations				
Specific Expectation	**Practice Questions**	**Unit Test Questions**	**Practice Test 1**	**Practice Test 2**
Students will:				
Explain how survival of the human species is ensured through reproduction.				
30-B1.1K identify the structures in the human female reproductive system and describe their functions; i.e., ovaries, Fallopian tubes, uterus, endometrium, cervix, vagina	NR1			
30-B1.2K identify the structures in the human male reproductive system and describe their functions; i.e. testes, seminiferous tubules, interstitial cells, Sertoli cells, epididyms, vasa (ductus) deferentia, Cowper's glands, seminal vesicles, prostate gland, ejaculatory duct, urethra, penis	3, NR2	1, 2, 3	13	NR4, 12, 16
30-B1.3K distinguish sperm and egg from their supporting structures; i.e., seminiferous tubules, interstitial cells, Sertoli cells, follicle, corpus luteum	7, 2		14	
30-B1.4K describe the chromosomal factors and hormonal influence on the formation of the gonads and reproductive organs in the female and male embryo and fetus; i.e., Y chromosome and role of testosterone		4	40	
30-B1.5K explain how sexually transmitted infections (STIs) can interfere with fertility and reproduction	9		15	
Explain how reproduction is regulated by chemical control systems.				
30-B2.1K describe the role of hormones, i.e., gonadotropic-releasing hormone (GnRH), follicle-stimulating hormone, luteinizing hormone (LH), estrogen, progesterone, testosterone, in the regulation of primary and secondary sex characteristics in females and males	4, 5, 6, NR3	5	6, 33	

30-B2.2K	identify the principal reproductive hormones in the female and explain their interactions in the maintenance of the menstrual cycle; i.e., estrogen, progesterone, FSH, LH	11, 12, 13, 14	7	12, 34	
30-B2.3K	identify the principal reproductive hormones in the male and explain their interactions in the maintenance and functioning of the male reproductive system; i.e. testosterone, FSH, LH	8, 10, 20, NR4	6, 10	9, 10	NR3
Explain how differentiation and development in the human organism are regulated by a combination of genetic, endocrine, and environmental factors.					
30-B3.1K	trace the processes of fertilization, implantation, and extra-embryonic membrane formation, i.e., placenta, amnion, chorion, allantois, followed by embryonic and fetal development, parturition, and lactation, and describe the control mechanisms of these events, i.e., progesterone, LH, human chorionic gonadotropin (hCG), prostaglandins, oxytocin, prolactin	15, NR5		37, 38, 39	
30-B3.2K	describe development from fertilization to parturition in the context of the main physiological events that occur in the development of organ systems during each major stage (trimester); i.e., zygote, blastocyst, gastrulation, general morphogenesis	16, 17	9, 11, NR1	17	15, 21
30-B3.3K	identify major tissues and organs that arise from differentiation and morphological development of the ectoderm, mesoderm, and endoderm in the embryo; i.e., ectoderm: nervous system, epidermis; mesoderm: skeleton, muscles, reproductive structures; endoderm: lining of the digestive and respiratory systems, endocrine glands	18			14
30-B3.4K	describe the influence of environmental factors on embryonic and fetal development	19	12		
30-B3.5K	describe the physiological or mechanical basis of different reproductive technologies; i.e. conception control, in vitro fertilization, infertility reversal	1	8		20

REPRODUCTION AND DEVELOPMENT

30-B1.1K identify the structures in the human female reproductive system and describe their functions i.e., ovaries, Fallopian tubes, uterus, endometrium, cervix, vagina

30-B1.2K identify the structures in the human male reproductive system and describe their functions i.e., testes, seminiferous tubules, interstitial cells, Sertoli cells, epididymis, vasa (ductus) deferentia, Cowper's glands,, seminal vesicles, prostate gland, ejaculatory duct, urethra, penis

HUMAN REPRODUCTIVE SYSTEMS

The Male Reproductive System

Structure	Function
Testes	Produce sperm cells and the male sex hormone testosterone
Seminiferous tubules	Hollow tubes in the testes in which spermatogenesis occurs
Interstitial cells	Surround seminiferous tubules; secrete testosterone
Sertoli cells	Support the development of spermatozoa
Epididymides	Cap of coiled tubes on the testes in which sperm cells mature and are stored until ejaculation
Vas deferens (ductus deferentia)	Smooth muscle tube; carries sperm from the epididymis to the ejaculatory duct
Cowper's gland	Secretes mucus into the semen

Structure	Function
Seminal vesicles	Secrete fructose sugar into the semen to improve sperm motility
Ejaculatory duct	Formed at the joining of the vas deferens and seminal vesicles, which conducts semen to the urethra
Urethra	Carries semen during ejaculation and urine at other times; opens at the end of the penis
Penis	Deposits semen into the female vagina during ejaculation; consists of the glans and shaft

Male Reproductive Structures

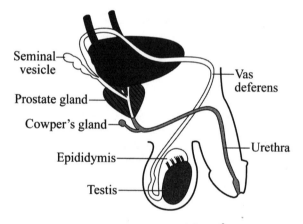

prostate gland · alkaline

The Female Reproductive System

Structure	Function
Ovaries	Site of ovum development, ovulation, and the secretion of estrogen and progesterone from follicles
Fallopian tubes (oviducts)	Lead from ovaries to the uterus; carry ova to the uterus; usual site of fertilization
Uterus	Muscular organ in which the embryo and fetus develop
Endometrium *myometrium perimetrium*	Inner lining of the uterus, develops monthly; embryo implants here; shed in menstruation
Cervix	Tightly closed bottom of uterus; dilates during birth
Vagina	Leads from the cervix to the exterior of the body; functions as a passageway for semen, as the birth canal during delivery, and as an outlet for menstrual blood

Practice Questions: 2, 3, NR1, NR2

30-B1.3K distinguish sperm and egg from their supporting structures; i.e., seminiferous tubules, interstitial cells, Sertoli cells, follicle, corpus luteum

GAMETE SUPPORT STRUCTURES

The male gametes are called spermatozoa or sperm and are produced in the paired male gonads, the testes. Testes are suspended outside the body within the sac-like scrotum. This arrangement maintains the cooler temperatures required for sperm development. The process of spermatogenesis occurs in the walls of the hollow seminiferous tubules of the testes. Here spermatogonial cells multiply to produce many diploid primary spermatocytes. Each undergoes meiosis to produce four haploid spermatids. As they mature, spermatids develop tails and motility and are stored in the epididymis until ejaculation. The Sertoli cells which also lie in the walls of the seminiferous tubules nurture and support the spermatocytes through their divisions. Interstitial cells surrounding the seminiferous tubules secrete testosterone into the bloodstream. Testosterone is needed for the full development of spermatozoa.

The female gametes are called eggs, ova or oocytes, and are produced in the ovaries, the paired female gonads. Oogenesis occurs in the hundreds of supportive follicles that exist in each ovary. Each month a few follicles are stimulated to nourish and develop the oocyte within it as it moves through the stages of meiosis. Meiosis is halted at the secondary oocyte stage when the most mature follicle bursts open, releasing its oocyte out of the ovary in the process of ovulation. The ovulated oocyte is swept down the fallopian tube where it may or may not encounter sperm and be fertilized. In addition to nourishing and developing the oocyte, the follicle also secretes the hormone estrogen. After ovulation the old follicle, the corpus luteum, secretes estrogen and progesterone until the cycle ends.

Practice Questions: 7

polar bodies carry estrid DNA

30-B1.4K describe the chromosomal factors and hormonal influences on the formation of the gonads and reproductive organs in the female and male embryo and fetus; i.e., Y chromosome and role of testosterone

DEVELOPMENT OF REPRODUCTIVE ORGANS

The sex chromosomes (pair 23) determine the gender of an individual. Females have two X chromosomes, while males have one X and one Y chromosome. In the sixth or seventh week of pregnancy, the Y chromosome stimulates the development of testes in a male fetus. Subsequent synthesis of testosterone by the testes results in the development of male primary sex characteristics. In the absence of a Y chromosome, the flooding of the embryo with estrogen from maternal blood results in the development of ovaries and female primary sex characteristics.

Practice Question: 21

30-B1.5K explain how sexually transmitted infections (STIs) can interfere with fertility and reproduction

SEXUALLY TRANSMITTED INFECTIONS AND REPRODUCTION

Sexually transmitted infections (STIs) can limit reproduction significantly. Bacterial infections such as Chlamydia and gonorrhoea can result in infertility and sterility by leading to pelvic inflammatory disease (PID), scarring of the uterus, and a reduced chance of embryo implantation. STIs can cause inflammation of the seminiferous tubules in males, which can interfere with the development of sperm.

Human papilloma virus (HPV) is a common wart virus that, when transferred to the genitalia, can cause genital warts and cellular changes that lead to the development of cervical cancer. A regular Pap test is used to detect these cellular changes. Human Immunodeficiency Virus (HIV) is transmitted sexually and may result in death. HIV can also be transmitted from mother to baby.

BACTERIAL (ANTIBIOTICS)

VIRAL STIS

Practice Question: 9

30-B2.1K describe the role of hormones, i.e., gonadotropic-releasing hormone (GnRH), follicle-stimulating hormone (FSH), luteinizing hormone (LH), estrogen, progesterone, testosterone, in the regulation of primary and secondary sex characteristics in females and males

30-B2.2K identify the principal reproductive hormones in the female and explain their interactions in the maintenance of the menstrual cycle; i.e., estrogen, progesterone, FSH, LH

30-B2.3K identify the principal reproductive hormones in the male and explain their interactions in the maintenance and functioning of the male reproductive system; i.e., testosterone, FSH, LH

REPRODUCTIVE HORMONES

Hormone	Function in Males	Function in Females
Estrogen		Development of breasts and other secondary sex characteristics; thickening and vascularisation of endometrium
Progesterone		Quiets smooth muscle contractions of uterus, maintaining endometrium
Testosterone	Stimulates primary and secondary sex characteristics: growth of testes, penis, muscles, growth of facial hair; indirectly stimulates spermatogenesis	

Hormone	Function in Males	Function in Females
Follicle Stimulating Hormone (FSH)	Acts on Sertoli cells to stimulate spermatogenesis in seminiferous tubules	Stimulates follicles in the ovaries to develop ova
Leutinizing Hormone (LH)	Stimulates interstitial cells to produce testosterone	Triggers ovulation and stimulates estrogen and progesterone secretion from corpus luteum
Gonadotropic Releasing Hormone (GnRH)	Monitors reproductive endocrine system. Stimulates synthesis and secretion of FSH and LH.	

The levels of all sex hormones are maintained by negative feedback monitored by the hypothalamus.

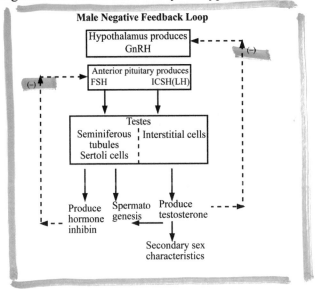

In males, when testosterone and inhibin levels are low, the hypothalamus releases GnRH, which stimulates the anterior pituitary to release FSH and LH. FSH stimulates the seminiferous tubules in the testes to undergo spermatogenesis, and causes Sertoli cells to secrete the hormone inhibin. LH stimulates the interstitial cells of the testes to secrete testosterone into the blood. Testosterone develops and maintains male secondary sex characteristics. When inhibin and testosterone levels are high, negative feedback occurs. High inhibin levels feed back to the pituitary decreasing FSH and reducing sperm production back towards normal. High testosterone levels provide feedback to the hypothalamus to inhibit GnRH, inhibiting LH and preventing overproduction of testosterone. When testosterone and inhibin levels are low, they provide feedback that increases LH and FSH levels.

Males produce gametes continuously from puberty often into old age. Millions of sperm are produced daily. Once ejaculated, a sperm lives 72 hours. By contrast, the menstrual cycle of females produces only one female gamete every 28 days. Once ovulated the egg lives for only 24 hours. Ovulation begins at puberty but drops off rapidly after peaking in the 20s. Cycles stop at menopause which occurs around the age of 50.

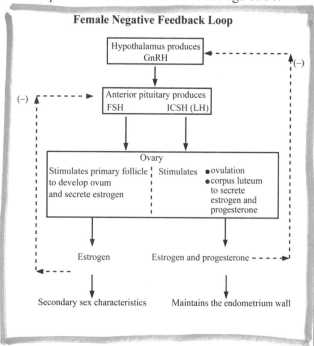

The hypothalamus controls the activities of the menstrual cycle through negative feedback of estrogen and progesterone blood levels. Day 1 of the cycle occurs on the first day of menstruation. At this time, blood estrogen and progesterone levels are low and the hypothalamus responds by secreting GnRH, which stimulates FSH and LH production by the anterior pituitary. FSH stimulates follicle cells which nurture the developing oocyte as it goes through the stages of oogenesis. While developing the oocyte, the follicle secretes estrogen. Estrogen thickens the endometrium with blood vessels and tissue, creating a suitable place for an embryo to implant and grow. On approximately day 14, LH stimulates the ovum to burst from the follicle in the process of ovulation. If sperm are present in the fallopian tube, fertilization will likely occur here. After ovulation, LH prompts the old follicle, the corpus luteum, to secrete estrogen which maintains the endometrium, and progesterone which quiets the uterine muscles in case an embryo implants. Negative feedback, however, brings the cycle to an end. High estrogen and progesterone levels from the corpus luteum feed back to the hypothalamus, inhibiting GnRH, FSH, and LH. The corpus luteum stops producing estrogen and progesterone which results in the shedding of the endometrium in menstruation. However, even as the old endometrium is being sloughed off, low levels of estrogen and progesterone are stimulating the hypothalamus to secrete GnRH and begin the cycle of egg production and endometrium development all over again.

At approximately fifty years of age, menopause begins. Follicles no longer respond to FSH and LH. Egg maturation ends, estrogen and progesterone are no longer secreted, menstruation does not occur, and secondary sex characteristics fade.

Practice Questions: 4, 5, 6, 8, 10, 11, 12, 13, 14, 20, NR3, NR4

30-B3.1K trace the processes of fertilization, implantation, and extra-embryonic membrane formation, i.e., placenta, amnion, chorion, allantois, followed by embryonic and fetal development, parturition, and lactation, and describe the control mechanisms of these events, i.e., progesterone, LH, human chorionic gonadotropin (hCG), prostaglandins, oxytocin, prolactin

30-B3.2K describe development from fertilization to parturition in the context of the main physiological events that occur in the development of organ systems during each major stage (trimester); i.e., zygote, blastocyst, gastrulation, general morphogenesis

30-B3.3K identify major tissues and organs that arise from differentiation and morphological development of the ectoderm, mesoderm and endoderm in the embryo; i.e.,

- *ectoderm; nervous system and epidermis*
- *mesoderm: skeleton, muscles, reproductive structures*
- *endoderm: lining of digestive and respiratory systems, endocrine glands*

30-B3.4K describe the influence of environmental factors on embryonic and fetal development

DEVELOPMENT OF HUMAN OFFSPRING: FERTILIZATION TO FETUS

In order for fertilization to occur, sperm deposited in the vagina must swim through the cervix, through the uterus and into the fallopian tubes. Sperm live 72 hours but an egg lives only 24 hours. If sperm are present in the fallopian tubes at the time of ovulation then thousands of sperm will surround the ovum, using the hyaluronidase in the acrosome of the sperm head to break down the ovum coat. Once one sperm penetrates and releases the contents of its nucleus into the egg, an electrochemical change prevents other sperm from entering.

Fusion of the haploid egg and sperm nuclei produces a diploid zygote that immediately begins dividing. Once division begins the zygote has become an embryo. Cleavage, a type of mitosis that increases cell number without increasing embryo size, continues until a solid ball of cells called the morula forms. During the week-long trip from the fallopian tube to the endometrium, the morula hollows out to form a blastocyst. The inner cell mass of the blastocyst will eventually form the fetus. The outer cells will form the surrounding chorionic membrane. The chorionic villi implant the blastocyst into the endometrial wall, increasing the surface area available for the absorption of nutrients. In order to prevent menstruation and subsequent spontaneous abortion, the chorion secretes the hormone hCG into the bloodstream. hCG signals the corpus luteum to continue producing estrogen and progesterone, keeping the endometrium intact.

The Blastocyst

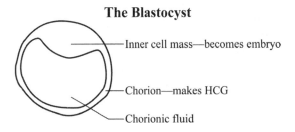

Inner cell mass—becomes embryo

Chorion—makes HCG

Chorionic fluid

Once the blastocyst is implanted in the endometrium, its cells lose their pluripotency and start to differentiate, forming the three germ layers of the gastrula. The outer ectoderm layer of the gastrula forms the epidermis, hair, and nervous system of the fetus. Mesoderm cells form bones, muscles, kidneys, and sex organs. The inner endoderm layer becomes the lining of the digestive and respiratory tracts, as well as the liver, pancreas, bladder, and endocrine glands. Gastrulation is complete by the time the embryo becomes a fetus at the end of three months.

The embryo is surrounded by supportive extra-embryonic membranes: the chorion, amnion, allantois, placenta, and yolk sac. The outer chorion membrane has villi that obtain nutrients from the endometrium. The amnion membrane is filled with amniotic fluid, which surrounds the fetus and protects it from temperature fluctuation and impact. The yolk sac functions in early embryonic circulation. The allantois will provide blood vessels for the umbilical cord and placenta.

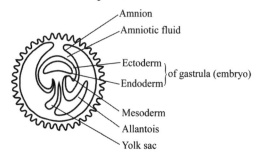

By the end of the first trimester (the first three months), the placenta has formed from the chorion and is embedded in the uterus wall. The placenta consists of maternal and fetal blood pools lying close enough together that nutrients and oxygen can diffuse from mother to the fetus, and CO_2 and wastes from the fetus can pass to the mother. An umbilical cord connects the fetus to the placenta. The placenta also functions as an endocrine gland, taking over production of progesterone and estrogen from the corpus luteum. Near the time of delivery, the placenta will also produce the hormone relaxin.

During the second trimester, organs continue to develop, and the fetus increases in size. In the third trimester, the baby continues to grow and develop. After approximately 280 days, parturition (labour) begins. Progesterone levels drop rapidly, and relaxin and oxytocin prepare the body for birth. Relaxin loosens the ligaments in the pelvis and softens the cervix while oxytocin stimulates progressively stronger uterine contractions due to positive feedback. During birth, the cervix dilates as the uterine muscles contract, eventually delivering the baby and the afterbirth (the placenta and umbilical cord). After birth, the anterior pituitary releases prolactin to stimulate the synthesis of milk by the mammary glands. The posterior pituitary releases oxytocin to stimulate the release of milk from the breast when the baby suckles.

A baby's development relies heavily on the environment inside the womb and the transfer of materials from the mother to the baby across the placenta. Poor nutrition can affect the development of the brain and other vital organs. For example, spina bifida occurs when the spinal cord fails to develop properly because of folic acid deficiencies. Many small molecules, including alcohol, nicotine, viruses, and many drugs, can also cross through the placenta to the fetus. Therefore, a woman's lifestyle choices during pregnancy can play a large role in the health of the baby throughout fetal development and after birth.

Teratogens are agents such as alcohol and certain drugs which are known to cause developmental abnormalities. Alcohol consumption is the biggest single cause of birth defects in Canada. Although an adult's liver can break down this toxin, a fetus' undeveloped liver cannot. Alcohol remains in the fetus' body for a longer period of time during which it causes mutations, slows down mental and physical development, and may cause death. Women who smoke during pregnancy give birth to babies of below-average weight. The rubella measles virus can be transferred to the fetus of an infected mother and has been known to cause deafness, blindness, and heart disease. Another natural teratogen is radiation. If a fetus is exposed to radiation, it can cause a great variety of developmental abnormalities.

Practice Questions: 15, 16, 17, 18, 19, NR5

30-B3.5K describe the physiological or mechanical basis of different reproductive technologies; i.e., conception control, in vitro fertilization, infertility reversal

REPRODUCTIVE TECHNOLOGY

Reproductive technologies can be used to decrease or increase the probability of successful reproduction. There are several conception or birth control strategies. A condom or a diaphragm can be used as a barrier for the sperm. Birth control pills prevent conception using a combination of estrogen and progesterone. These hormones negatively feed back to inhibit the hypothalamus from releasing GnRH, preventing egg development and subsequent ovulation. The pill RU 486 prevents a blastocyst from implanting in the uterus. A vasectomy is a male sterilization procedure in which the vas deferens is cut and sealed to prevent sperm from entering the semen. A tubal ligation is a female sterilization procedure in which the fallopian tubes are cut and sealed, preventing an ovulated ovum from reaching the site of fertilization.

Many technologies have been developed to assist infertile couples to reproduce. Infertility can be caused by inadequate numbers or quality of sperm or eggs. As females age, ovulation becomes less consistent and conception less likely. Injections of FSH can be used to increase the number of follicles that develop, increasing the odds of conception. This technique often leads to multiple births. In some cases, several eggs can be harvested surgically from the ovary and fertilized using *in vitro* fertilization (IVF). This process involves the fertilization of the eggs by combining them with sperm in a petri dish. An embryo formed by this process is then implanted into the mother's uterus where development continues. Male infertility (low sperm production or motility) can be related to the increasing presence of estrogenic compounds in the environment. A common treatment for males with low sperm levels is to harvest batches of immature sperm from the epididymis and then proceed with IVF.

Several technologies are available to monitor the development of the embryo and the fetus. Developmental and chromosomal problems in the fetus can be diagnosed using ultrasound, amniocentesis, and chorionic villus sampling (CVS). Ultrasound techniques bounce sound waves off the fetus to produce a rough image that can be analyzed for developmental issues. In amniocentesis, a hypodermic needle inserted into the abdomen is used to draw a sample of amniotic fluid for analysis. The fluid contains sloughed-off fetal cells that can be used for DNA analysis or to construct a karyotype. CVS provides the same information as amniocentesis, but it involves the removal of a sample of chorionic cells. CVS can be done much earlier in the pregnancy than amniocentesis.

karyotypes ✻

Practice Question: 1

PRACTICE QUESTIONS—REPRODUCTION AND DEVELOPMENT

1. Testes are responsible for the production of sperm and testosterone. Cutting and tying the vas deferens (vasectomy) blocks the passage of sperm. After a vasectomy, the hormone testosterone
   A. reaches all the body tissues because it comes from exocrine tissue
   B. reaches all the body tissues because it comes from endocrine tissue
   C. does not reach all the body tissues because it comes from exocrine tissue
   D. does not reach all the body tissues because it comes from endocrine tissue

   Source: January 2000

2. Cryptorchidism is the failure of one or both of the testes to descend from the abdominal cavity into the scrotum during human fetal development. Sterility results if both testes fail to descend. In this case, the likely cause of sterility is that
   A. lack of oxygen inhibits testosterone function
   B. gonadotropic hormones cannot stimulate the testes
   C. the testes are not connected to the external environment
   D. normal sperm do not readily develop at body temperature

   Source: January 2000

Use the following information to answer the next question.

A series of experiments initially designed to study the effects of fathers' drinking habits on fetal development produced some unexpected results.

Seventy-five male rats were injected with enough alcohol to produce a 0.2% concentration of alcohol in their blood. After 24 hours, these male rats were mated with 75 female rats not treated with alcohol. A control group of 75 untreated male rats were also mated with untreated female rats. Both sets of males copulated normally and with the same vigour.

The pregnancy rate of female rats mated with the alcohol-treated male rats was 50% lower than the pregnancy rate of female rats mated with untreated rats. Also, pup litters in the group with alcohol-treated males appeared to be smaller and individual pups weighed less. Repetition of these experiments produced similar results.

– from Fackelmann, 1994

3. Fluids in rat semen bathe the egg and sperm for several days after fertilization. This fluid contains secretions from the
   A. prostate gland only
   B. seminal vesicles only
   C. urethra and seminal vesicles
   D. Cowper's glands, prostate gland, and seminal vesicles

   Source: June 2000

Use the following information to answer the next question.

Functions of Structures in Human Females

1. Site of oogenesis

2. Site of implantation of fertilized ovum

3. Organ in which embryo develops

4. Site of fertilization

Numerical Response

1. Match each of the structures in the human female reproductive system listed below with its function as listed above.

Function: 4   3   1   2/3

Structure: Fallopian tubes   Uterus   Ovaries   Endometrium

Use the following information to answer the next question.

The Male Reproductive System and Accessory Structures

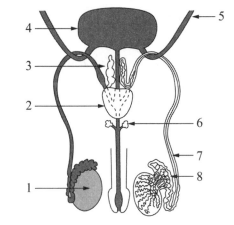

CHALLENGER QUESTION   45.4

Numerical Response

2. Identify the three structures, as numbered above, that produce the fluid secretions that make up semen.
Answer: 2   3   6
(Record your **three-digit** answer in lowest-to-highest numerical order.**)**

Source: January 1999

Use the following information to answer the next two questions.

A rare defect inherited by 19 descendants of a Dominican man named Altagracia Carrasco caused genetically male children to be considered female until age 12. At this age, hormone levels increased dramatically and caused the testes to descend from the abdomen to the scrotum and male primary and secondary sexual characteristics to develop.

In their Dominican Republic village, these people were given the name "guevedoces," which means "penis at 12 years of age."

– from Pringle, 1992

4. The "guevedoces" might have reduced fertility because the late descent of their testes would cause

A. high production of testosterone

B. high production of progesterone

C. cell development problems in their follicular cells

D. cell development problems in their seminiferous tubules

Source: June 2000

5. The sex hormone that increased in these individuals at age 12 and a secondary sexual characteristic the individuals would develop as a result are, respectively,

A. FSH and decreased body fat

B. testosterone and decreased breast size

C. testosterone and increased larynx size

D. FSH and increased muscle development

Source: June 2000

6. For the processes of spermatogenesis and oogenesis, respectively, the row that identifies the hormone that stimulates the process, the location where the process occurs, and the number of gametes produced per germ cell is

	Spermatogenesis			Oogenesis		
Row	Hormone	Location of process	Number of gametes produced	Hormone	Location of process	Number of gametes produced
A.	FSH	semi-niferous tubules	4	FSH	ovaries	1
B.	LH	epididymis	8	LH	pituitary	1
C.	testosterone	interstitial cells	4	estrogen	follicle	4
D.	FSH	testes	8	Progesterone	corpus luteum	4

Source: January 2001

7. The process of spermatogenesis occurs in the

A. vas deferens

B. prostate gland

C. seminal vesicle

D. seminiferous tubule

8. The waste of resources resulting from excessive sperm production is corrected **most directly** by

A. an FSH decrease

B. a GnRH increase

C. an inhibin increase

D. a testosterone increase

Use the following information to answer the next question.

The genital tract of both females and males can play host to many disease-causing microbes. The sexually transmitted diseases (STDs) that can result include gonorrhea, syphilis, herpes, AIDS, genital warts, and chlamydia. These diseases, if untreated, can lead to brain and nervous system deterioration, circulatory system damage, cancer, and infertility. Microbes may pass from mother to child during pregnancy and birth.

CHALLENGER QUESTION   **38.7**

9. STD microbes may be transmitted to

A. a child in the vagina

B. a zygote in the endometrium

C. an embryo through the ingestion of amniotic fluid

D. a fetus through the entry of blood from the uterine veins

Source: June 1999

Use the following information to answer the next question.

Functions of the Four Main Reproductive Hormones in Human Females

1. Stimulation of egg development

2. Inhibition of ovulation and uterine contractions

3. Stimulation of the development of secondary sex characteristics

4. Stimulation of ovulation and formation of the corpus luteum

---

3. Identify the major functions, as numbered above, of each of the hormones given below.

Function: 1   4   3   2

Hormone: FSH   LH   Estrogen   Progesterone

(Record your answer as a **four-digit** number.)

Source: January 1999

Use the following information to answer the next question.

Some Endocrine Glands and Hormones

1. Pituitary   2. Estrogen
3. Testosterone   4. Hypothalamus
5. FSH   6. Seminal vesicle
7. LH   8. Testis

---

4. To complete this statement, select the gland or hormone numbered above that best fills each blank. The production of sperm in the male is directly stimulated by the hormone ___5___, which is produced in the ___1___, and by the hormone ___3___, which is produced in the ___8___.
(Record your answer as a **four-digit** number.)

Source: June 2000

Use the following information to answer the next question.

Female Reproductive Systems

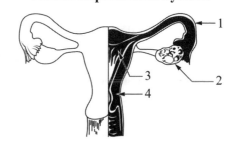

Prior to *in vitro* fertilization (IVF), oocytes must be obtained from a donor female.

---

10. To obtain oocytes for *in vitro* fertilization, the structure numbered above that must be hormonally stimulated is

A. 1
B. 2
C. 3
D. 4

Source: June 2000

*Use the following information to answer
the next question.*

**Changes That Occur in a Human Ovary
Over One Ovarian Cycle**

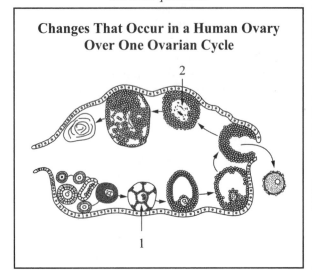

*Use the following information to answer
the next two questions.*

Clomiphene citrate is a fertility drug used to
induce ovulation in women. Clomiphene
citrate, generally taken daily from day 3 to day
7 of the menstrual cycle, decreases the naturally
circulating estrogen. The pituitary responds by
increasing production of two gonadotropic
hormones that then stimulate the ovary to ripen
and release an egg. Follicle development and
ovulation are usually monitored with a
combination of home urine tests (on day 11 or
12) and a follow-up ultrasound examination.
About 70% of women using clomiphene citrate
will ovulate and 40% of those will become
pregnant. The risk of multiple pregnancy
(usually twins) increases by 6% to 7%.

– from Bay Area Fertility and Gynecology Medical Group

11. In order for artificial implantation to be
successful, what hormone would a female
need to take to maintain the uterine lining for
implantation, and which of the structures of
the ovary numbered above would naturally
produce this hormone?

A. Estrogen and structure 1

B. Estrogen and structure 2

C. Progesterone and structure 1

D. Progesterone and structure 2

Source: June 2000

12. Without the negative feedback that results
from increasing amounts of naturally
circulating estrogen, the body responds by
secreting more

A. FSH

B. HCG

C. prolactin

D. progesterone

Source: January 2001

CHALLENGER QUESTION	46.9

13. Following clomiphene citrate treatments,
patients are advised to monitor their urine
for the presence of a hormone that will
signal ovulation. This hormone is

A. LH

B. FSH

C. HCG

D. estrogen

Source: January 2001

Use the following information to answer the next question.

Research on sheep might explain what stimulates pregnant mammals, including humans, to give birth. Through research on pregnant sheep, scientists have developed the following scheme to explain normal events as birth begins.

Influence of Fetal Hormones on the Maternal Reproductive Systems

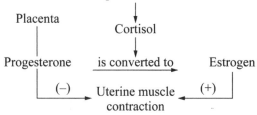

Hypothalamus of a fetal lamb

Adrenal gland of a fetal lamb

Placenta

Cortisol

Progesterone   is converted to   Estrogen

(−)   Uterine muscle   (+)
contraction

Note: The placenta produces progesterone throughout the pregnancy, but activation of the fetal hypothalamus only occurs as birth begins.

–from Discover, 1992

CHALLENGER QUESTION   45.8

14. Which of the following statements concerning human reproduction is supported by the findings of this research?

   A. Developments within the fetus determine when birth will begin.

   B. The production of fetal cortisol delays birth until gestation is complete.

   C. During early fetal development, fetal hormones do not pass into the mother.

   D. High levels of progesterone in the mother's blood are essential for birth to begin.

Source: January 2000

CHALLENGER QUESTION   59.5

15. During the first three days of development, the human embryo obtains nutrients and energy from the

   A. HCG

   B. amniotic fluid

   C. cytoplasm of the mother's egg

   D. mitochondria of the father's sperm

Source: January 2001

Use the following information to answer the next two questions.

Fetal alcohol spectrum disorders (FASD) cover a wide range of birth defects caused by maternal alcohol consumption during pregnancy. Children with FASD may have growth deficiencies, central nervous system damage, and deformed organs. Alcohol exposure is particularly damaging during the time of organ formation. Women may not be aware of their pregnancy during the first two weeks after fertilization and therefore may not avoid alcohol during this time.

16. In which stage of development do major organs begin to differentiate in humans?

   A. Fetus

   B. Zygote

   C. Embryo

   D. Gastrula

Use the following information to answer the next questions.

In vertebrates, the brain and spine develop from the neural tube of embryos. Spina bifida is a birth defect that results from incomplete closure of the embryonic neural tube. Although the cause of spina bifida is unknown, women with low levels of folic acid have a higher chance of giving birth to a baby with spina bifida.

17. Spina bifida results from a defect in the development of the
    A. ectoderm
    B. endoderm
    C. blastocyst
    D. mesoderm

Use the following information to answer the next two questions.

A series of experiments initially designed to study the effects of fathers' drinking habits on fetal development produced some unexpected results. Seventy-five male rats were injected with enough alcohol to produce a 0.2% concentration of alcohol in their blood.
After 24 hours, these male rats were mated with 75 female rats not treated with alcohol.
A control group of 75 untreated male rats were also mated with untreated female rats. Both sets of males copulated normally and with the same vigour.

The pregnancy rate of female rats mated with the alcohol-treated male rats was 50% lower than the pregnancy rate of female rats mated with untreated rats. Also, pup litters in the group with alcohol-treated males appeared to be smaller and individual pups weighed less. Repetition of these experiments produced similar results.

– from Fackelmann, 1994

18. Reduction in pregnancy rates for rodent couples in the study group could have been caused by
    A. alcohol-treated males' inability to copulate normally
    B. alcohol in the females' blood affecting egg production
    C. alcohol in the males' blood increasing pituitary hormone secretions
    D. alcohol in the semen fluids producing a poisonous environment for fertilization

Source: June 2000

19. Prolonged high concentrations of alcohol in the male would likely affect male fertility in all of the following ways **except** by
    A. reducing the rate of meiosis
    B. preventing the maturation of sperm
    C. depressing motility in sperm by damaging cells
    D. stimulating motility in sperm by increasing metabolism

Source: June 2000

Use the following information to answer the next question.

Human Embryo Six Weeks After Fertilization

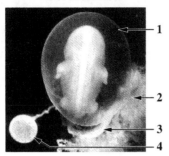

Descriptions of Embryonic Structures' Functions

A   Transports embryonic blood

B   Provides protection

C   Is the site of exchange between embryonic and maternal blood

D   Is used for nourishment in vertebrates other than mammals   YOLK SAC

– from Nilsson, 1990

CHALLENGER QUESTION   **41.7**

Numerical Response

5.   Match each embryonic structure, as numbered above, with the letter that represents its function, as listed above.

Structure: 3   1   2   4

Function: A   B   C   D

(Record your answer as a **four-digit** number.)

Source: January 2001

20. The sex of a human embryo is determined at conception by the

A.   egg

B.   sperm

C.   polar body

D.   Golgi body

ANSWERS AND SOLUTIONS—PRACTICE QUESTIONS

1. B	4. D	9. A	12. A	17. A
2. D	5. C	NR3. 1432	13. A	18. D
3. D	6. A	NR4. 5138	14. A	19. D
NR1. 4312	7. D	10. B	15. C	NR5. 3124
NR2. 236	8. A	11. D	16. C	20. B

1. B

Following a vasectomy, sperm cannot make their way through the vas deferens to the penis. However, testosterone is produced by endocrine tissue in the testes and continues to be released into the blood. As a result, after a vasectomy testosterone continues to reach all body tissues.

2. D

By failing to descend, the testes will be trapped within the body cavity and maintained at normal body temperature. Sperm production is most effective a few degrees lower than normal body temperature, which is why the testes are normally situated outside of the body cavity in the scrotum. Fewer sperm would be produced at body temperature, and many of these would be deformed. Sterility would be the result.

3. D

Semen is composed of sperm and fluids secreted by three sets of male reproductive glands. These glands are the Cowper's glands, prostate gland, and seminal vesicles.

NR 1   4312

Immature ova are present in and undergo development in the ovaries (**1**). Fertilization occurs in the fallopian tubes (**4**). The fertilized ovum then implants in the endometrium (**2**). The embryo develops in the uterus (**3**).

NR 2   236

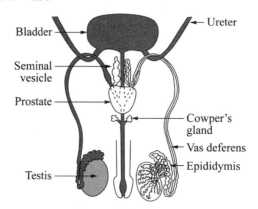

Refer to the labelled diagram above. Sperm are produced in the testes within the seminiferous tubules. They are stored within the epididymis. During ejaculation, sperm are released into the vas deferens, a tube that connects the testis to the urethra leading out of the body through the penis. As the sperm travel along the vas deferens and urethra, fluid is sequentially added from three glands. First, the seminal vesicles (**3**) add fluid containing fructose sugar (to provide energy for sperm) and prostaglandins (to promote rhythmic contractions of the female reproductive tract that push sperm toward the Fallopian tubes). Second, the prostate gland (**2**) adds alkaline fluid (to neutralize any acid within the urethra and vagina). Third, the Cowper's glands (**6**) add a milky fluid rich in mucus. Semen is therefore composed of sperm plus fluid from all three of these glands.

4. D

The guevedoces might have reduced fertility. The reason a man's testes descend into the scrotum is that sperm production is more effective a few degrees below body temperature. The sperm develop in the seminiferous tubules inside the testes, so the late descent of the testes may cause problems in these tubules.

5. C

It is the increase of testosterone production at about age 12 that stimulates the changes we associate with puberty. It is testosterone that would cause the guevedoces to acquire their male secondary sex characteristics. One of the male characteristics associated with puberty is an increased larynx or voice box.

6. A

In males, FSH stimulates sperm formation inside the seminiferous tubules. In females, FHS stimulates egg production inside the ovaries. During the process of meiosis, four sperm are produced and one egg is produced, as shown in the following diagram.

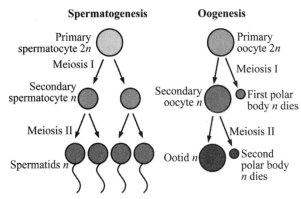

7. D

Spermatogenesis, the final stage of the formation of a mature sperm cell, occurs in the seminiferous tubules. The prostate is a single-layer gland that surrounds the urethra. It secretes an alkaline fluid that helps in the production and transport of sperm. The vas deferens connects the testis with the epididymis. The seminal vesicles are glands near the base of the bladder that help produce semen.

8. A

As sperm production in seminiferous tubules increases, the Sertoli cells produce more of the hormone inhibin. Inhibin feeds back negatively to the pituitary gland to reduce FSH secretion, which decreases spermatogenesis. Therefore, a decrease in FSH will inhibit excessive spermatogenesis, correcting the waste of resources involved in overproduction of sperm.

9. A

The genital tract here refers to the vagina. As the baby passes through the vagina at birth, it may be exposed to a variety of infectious organisms. The zygote does not pass through the genital tract. Nothing in the information provided indicates that the infections are related to amniotic fluid. As well, amniotic fluid is generated by the developing fetus. Blood from the uterine veins does not enter the fetus.

NR 3   1432

Recall the functions of the four given hormones.

Hormone	Primary function
FSH (follicle stimulating hormone)	Stimulates follicle or egg development in the ovary (**1**)
LH (luteinizing hormone)	Stimulates ovulation; stimulates development of corpus luteum (**4**)
Estrogen	Responsible for development of secondary sex characteristics; promotes thickening of the endometrium (**3**)
Progesterone	Maintains the endometrium; inhibits uterine contraction during the cycle and in pregnancy (**2**)

NR 4   5138

FSH (**5**), or follicle stimulating hormone, directly stimulates the production of sperm in males and eggs in females. FSH is produced by the anterior pituitary gland (**1**). The hormone testosterone (**3**) stimulates the development and maintenance of the male reproductive system, so it is also involved in sperm production, although indirectly. Testosterone is produced by the testis (**8**).

10. B

The structure labelled 2 is the ovary which produces eggs in response to FSH. The ovary releases the eggs in response to LH. The Fallopian tube (**1**) and the uterus (**3** and **4**) do not produce eggs.

11. D

Progesterone is needed to maintain the endometrium or uterine lining. Structure 2 is the corpus luteum—the remains of the mature follicle after ovulation. It is the corpus luteum that produces progesterone.

12. A

FSH causes a follicle to develop the oocyte within. The developing follicle produces estrogen. When the hypothalamus detects a high level of estrogen in the blood, it instructs the anterior pituitary to shut down production of FSH. If clomiphene citrate decreases the estrogen level, then the hypothalamus will not instruct the anterior pituitary to stop producing FSH. The very high level of FSH will provide a much stronger stimulus to the ovary to produce follicles (eggs).

13. A

LH, or lutenizing hormone, is produced by the anterior pituitary about halfway through a woman's monthly cycle. It stimulates ovulation and the subsequent formation of the corpus luteum. The corpus luteum produces progesterone in addition to estrogen. As the progesterone level rises in the woman's body, it has a negative feedback effect on the hypothalamus, which causes the anterior pituitary to shut down production of LH. The production of LH will rise again midway through the next cycle.

14. A

It is the activity of the hypothalamus and adrenal gland of the fetal lamb that causes the increase in estrogen necessary for the birth process. The production of fetal cortisol initiates, not delays, birth. Fetal hormones must be passing into the mother because it is the fetal cortisol that is causing the changes in the mother's hormones.

15. C

For the first few days, the developing embryo is moving down the Fallopian tube. During this time, it is a cluster of cells and is not attached to anything. It relies on the large amount of cytoplasm that was in the original egg as a source of nourishment. There will not be any amniotic fluid for a month, hCG is a hormone, and the mitochondria are not a source of energy at any time.

16. C

Major organs begin to differentiate during the embryo stage of development.

The fertilized ovum is referred to as the zygote, which then becomes a solid morula, which turns into a hollow blastocyst after seven days. After the second week, the blastocyst develops into a gastrula made of three germ layers. During weeks 3 to 8, major organs begin to differentiate within the embryo. By the ninth week, the embryo is referred to as a fetus. All of the organs are formed, although not fully developed at this time.

17. A

The central nervous system (brain and spinal cord) arise from the ectoderm; therefore, the correct answer is **A**. The mesoderm gives rise to the skeleton, muscle, and reproductive structures. The endoderm gives rise to the lining of the digestive and respiratory systems and to the endocrine glands. The blastocyst is a mass of cells from which the embryo develops. A defect in the blastocyst would result in defects of all tissues and organs, not just the central nervous system as seen in spina bifida.

18. D

The males seemed to copulate normally, and there was no alcohol in the females' blood. There is no reason to assume that alcohol in the male would increase pituitary secretions. It is possible that alcohol in the semen may make a poisonous environment for fertilization.

19. D

Although the male rats that were supplied with alcohol copulated normally, they were less likely to fertilize the females. Reducing the rate of meiosis, preventing maturation of sperm, and depressing motility of sperm would all reduce male fertility. Only stimulating motility in sperm would not reduce male fertility.

NR 5   3124

Structure 3 is the umbilical cord, which transports embryonic blood (**A**) between the placenta and the embryo or fetus. Structure 1 is the amnion, a membrane that surrounds the fetus and is filled with amniotic fluid. The fluid provides protection (**B**) from impact. Structure 2 is the placenta, a structure where maternal and fetal blood come very close together. Nutrients and oxygen from the maternal blood diffuse into the fetal blood (**C**). Wastes and CO_2 diffuse from the fetal blood into the maternal blood. Structure 4 is the yolk sac, which functions in early embryonic circulation, but has no nutritive function as it does in birds, reptiles, and other vertebrates (**D**).

20. B

The sex of a human embryo is determined at the instant of conception by the fertilizing sperm. All eggs carry an X chromosome, whereas sperm carry either an X or a Y chromosome. If an egg is fertilized by a sperm containing an X chromosome, the resulting embryo will be female. If the egg is fertilized by a sperm carrying a Y chromosome, the resulting embryo will be male.

UNIT TEST—REPRODUCTION AND DEVELOPMENT

Use the following diagrams to answer the next question.

Human Male and Female Reproductive Systems

1. Reproductive structures that have similar functions in males and females are, respectively,

   A. 1 and 11

   B. 2 and 8

   C. 4 and 9

   D. 4 and 10

   Source: June 1999

2. Collectively, the seminal vesicles, prostate gland, and Cowper's glands contribute to which of the following functions?

   A. Produce testosterone

   B. Stimulate spermatogenesis

   C. Help sperm survive in the female body

   D. Signal the pituitary to release gonadotropins

   Source: June 1999

3. The cells in the seminiferous tubules that lie alongside the developing sperm and nurture their development are known as

   A. Sertoli cells

   B. Follicle cells

   C. Interstitial cells

   D. Spermatogenic cells

Use the following information to answer the next question.

Differentiation of gender in embryos is caused by the presence of specific sex chromosomes and the secretion of hormones that result from their presence.

4. Which of the following statements about embryonic gender determination is **true**?

   A. In the absence of a Y chromosome, embryos develop ovaries.

   B. In the absence of X chromosomes, embryos form testes.

   C. The presence of an X chromosome causes the formation of ovaries.

   D. The presence of a Y chromosome causes the secretion of estrogen, which causes the formation of testes.

CHALLENGER QUESTION	55.0

5. The development of secondary sexual characteristics in the female is due to the secretion of

   A. LH, followed by the secretion of estrogen

   B. LH, followed by the secretion of progesterone

   C. FSH and LH, followed by the secretion of estrogen

   D. FSH and LH, followed by the secretion of progesterone

   Source: June 1999

6. Hormones that stimulate the production of testosterone are transported by the

A. blood

B. vas deferens

C. seminiferous tubules

D. ducts from the gland secreting the hormones

Source: June 1999

Use the following information to answer the next question.

Menopausal women often experience uncomfortable symptoms associated with changes in hormone levels. Compared with premenopausal women, women entering menopause have increased levels of FSH and LH and lower levels of progesterone and estrogen.

7. If a menopausal woman takes hormone replacement therapy consisting of estrogen and progesterone, the levels of her FSH and LH will

A. remain the same because her ovaries no longer respond to estrogen

B. cause the ovary to produce eggs, and the woman will again be fertile

C. drop because of the negative-feedback effect of progesterone and estrogen

D. rise as estrogen and progesterone levels stimulate the production of FSH and LH

Use the following information to answer the next question.

Researchers have developed a birth control vaccine that would be given once a year. This vaccine is made from a fragment of hCG attached to a protein. The vaccine causes a woman to manufacture antibodies that bind to hCG molecules (when present) in the blood. The antibodies prevent hCG from functioning and thereby affect the implantation of a blastocyst (embryo).

8. The vaccine affects the permanent implantation of a blastocyst by indirectly causing

A. disintegration of the endometrium

B. increased progesterone production

C. development of new follicles in the ovary

D. inhibition of the movement of cilia in the Fallopian tubes

Source: January 1999

9. Which of the steps of human development occurs after chorion development?

A. Fertilization

B. Implantation

C. Cleavage (division of the zygote by mitosis)

D. Organogenesis (the formation of body organs and systems)

Use the following information to answer the next question.

In rare cases, human males develop functioning mammary glands. Hormone levels are known to affect the development and function of mammary glands in both males and females.

10. In order for human males to produce milk and to eject milk, high levels of which two hormones, respectively, must be present?

A. Prolactin and relaxin

B. Relaxin and prolactin

C. Prolactin and oxytocin

D. Oxytocin and prolactin

Source: June 1999

11. In vertebrates, the early embryonic notochord is replaced by the bony vertebral column. The vertebral column arises from the

A. endoderm only

B. mesoderm only

C. ectoderm plus mesoderm

D. endoderm plus ectoderm

Mercury poisoning causes neurological damage,
which leads to a deterioration of short-term
memory and an inability to coordinate muscle
movements.

Certain mercury compounds are able to cross
the placenta and thereby affect embryological
development.

– from Hedegard, 1993

CHALLENGER QUESTION	41.9

12. Exposure to mercury compounds during
embryological development would **most
likely** disrupt the

  A. production of amniotic fluid

  B. development of the neural tube

  C. production of ovarian hormones

  D. development of the umbilical cord

Source: June 1999

In order to initiate *in vitro* fertilization,
a woman must undergo hormonal therapy to
release numerous mature eggs and to prepare
the uterine lining. The eggs are removed using
a laparoscope and fertilized in a petri dish.
The developing embryos are inserted back into
the woman for implantation to take place.

In vitro Fertilization

Numerical Response

1. Match the parts of the diagram numbered
above that represent the terms given below.

Number:	1	5	4	3
Term:	Oocyte	Blastocyst	First mitotic division	Fertilization

(Record your answer as a **four-digit**
number.)

Source: June 2000

ANSWERS AND SOLUTIONS—UNIT TEST

1. C	4. A	7. C	10. C	NR1. 1543
2. C	5. C	8. A	11. B	
3. A	6. A	9. D	12. B	

1. C

The vas deferens (**4**) carries sperm from the testis to the accessory glands. The Fallopian tube (**9**) carries an ovum from the ovary towards the uterus. Both carry gametes.

2. C

The glands named in the question produce secretions that are added to the sperm, forming semen. The seminal vesicles secrete fructose sugar that fuels the mitochondria of the spermatozoa. The ATP energy produced permits contraction of the sperm flagellum, allowing the sperm to swim towards the egg. The prostate gland produces alkaline secretions that prevent the sperm from being killed by the high acidity of the vagina. Cowper's gland produces mucus that provides lubrication and provides a medium for the swimming action of sperm cells. All three glands then contribute to helping sperm survive in the female body.

3. A

Seminiferous tubules are hollow tubular structures that lie coiled inside each testis. The wall of each seminiferous tubule is lined with diploid spermatogonial cells that multiply to form primary spermatocytes which undergo meiosis to produce haploid spermatids. Lying beside these cells are the Sertoli cells that respond to stimulation by FSH, initiating spermatogenesis, and nurturing the spermatocytes as they divide.

4. A

All fetuses without a Y chromosome will become female because of the high estrogen level provided by the maternal blood. The estrogen stimulates the development of the ovaries in the embryo. The Y chromosome carries a gene that causes the early XY embryo to secrete testosterone from the neural crest. This results in formation of testes and other male primary sex characteristics.

5. C

Female secondary sex characteristics are caused by estrogen. In the first part of the menstrual cycle FSH stimulates follicle development and the follicle secretes estrogen. In the second half of the cycle, LH stimulates the old follicle, called the corpus luteum to secrete estrogen and progesterone. Therefore, **C** is the best of the answers provided.

6. A

All hormones are secreted directly into the blood; none are carried by tubes or ducts. The term endocrine gland means ductless gland. Once hormones are in the bloodstream, blood pressure carries them to all cells.

7. C

In a normal menstrual cycle, the secretion of FSH from the anterior pituitary results in the secretion of estrogen from the developing follicle. Later, the secretion of LH from the anterior pituitary results in secretion of estrogen and progesterone from the old follicle, the corpus luteum. The question states that in menopause FSH and LH levels are high, but estrogen and progesterone levels are low. This indicates that even though the follicle and corpus luteum are being stimulated by FSH and LH, they are no longer responding. The low levels of estrogen and progesterone have negatively fed back causing more and more FSH and LH to be secreted. If the woman undergoes hormone replacement therapy, the increase in circulating estrogen and progesterone will negatively feed back to the hypothalamus and pituitary, reducing the secretion of FSH and LH.

8. A

The vaccine inhibits hCG (human chorionic gonadotropin) from performing its normal function. The hormone hCG is produced by the chorion as soon as it develops. It is secreted into the bloodstream and signals the corpus luteum to continue producing estrogen and progesterone, even though negative feedback of the high estrogen and progesterone levels seen in the last part of the cycle should be causing estrogen and progesterone to plummet, the endometrium to fall, and menstruation to begin. The hCG produced by the embryo's chorion will override negative feedback and cause the corpus luteum to continue to secrete estrogen and progesterone. The endometrium will remain intact, preventing menstruation and subsequent miscarriage from occurring. With the secretion of hCG the embryo is in a way, saving its own life.

With hCG inhibited, the high levels of estrogen and progesterone seen in the third week of the menstrual cycle negatively feed back to the hypothalamus. LH secretion stops, preventing the corpus luteum from secreting the progesterone and estrogen that keeps the myometrium quiet and the endometrium intact. The endometrium would then disintegrate and be shed in menstruation.
The implanted embryo would be washed away, producing a miscarriage.

9. D

The chorion, the outer membrane of the developing embryo forms as the morula becomes a blastocyst. The chorion, the outer wall of the hollow blastocyst, has villi that extend into the wall of the endometrium, implanting the embryo firmly. The only event that is yet to occur is organogenesis.

10. C

The hormone prolactin stimulates lactation, the synthesis of milk. Oxytocin causes contraction of the smooth muscles in the ducts leading from the mammary glands, releasing the flow of milk into the nipple.

11. B

The vertebral column is made of bone. No mention is made of the spinal cord lying within the vertebral column. Bone arises from mesoderm cells.

12. B

Notice the effect of mercury poisoning described in the information preceding the question: deterioration of short-term memory and inability to coordinate muscle movements. The relationship to the neural tube should be clear. There is no relevant connection here between mercury and the amniotic fluid, and the ovaries are not directly implicated. Also, no mention is made of any ovarian hormones.

NR 1   1543

The numbered structures and processes are the oocyte or egg (**1**), the sperm (**2**), fertilization (**3**) to form a zygote that then immediately begins mitosis (**4**), and, after a few days, implants in the uterus as a hollow blastocyst (**5**).

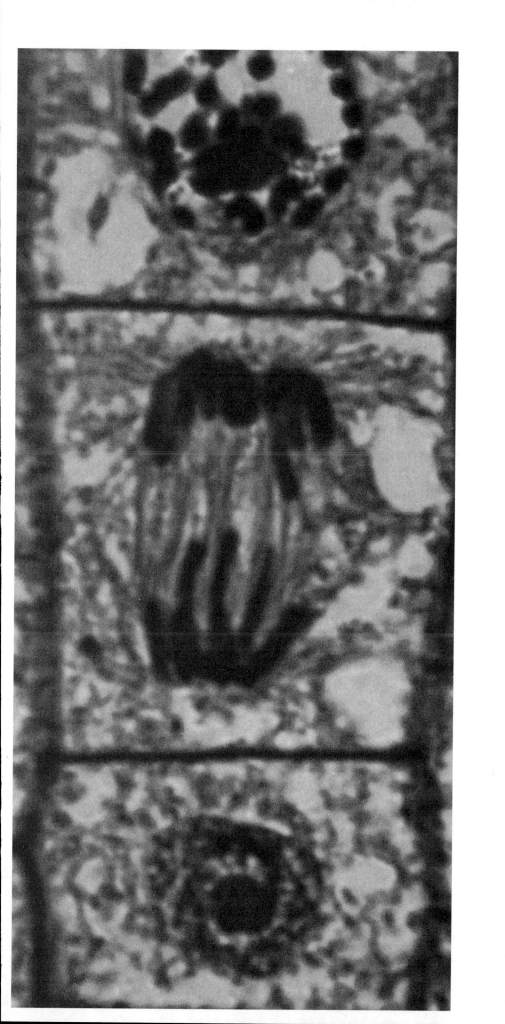

Cell Division, Genetics, and Molecular Biology

CELL DIVISION, GENETICS, AND MOLECULAR BIOLOGY

Table of Corrrelations				
Specific Expectation	**Practice Questions**	**Unit Test Questions**	**Practice Test 1**	**Practice Test 2**
Students will:				
Describe the processes of mitosis and meiosis.				
30-C1.1K define and explain the significance of chromosome number in somatic and sex cells; i.e., haploidy, diploidy, and polyploidy	1, 33			
30-C1.2K explain, in general terms, the events of the cell cycle; i.e., interphase, mitosis, and cytokinesis	17, 18, NR2	6, 12	16	
30-C1.3K describe the process of meiosis (spermatogenesis and oogenesis) and the necessity for the reduction of chromosome number	23, 24, NR3	2, 7, 8, 15		17, 24
30-C1.4K compare the process of mitosis and meiosis	14, 15, 19	11, 13	35	NR6
30-C1.5K describe the processes of crossing over and nondisjunction and evaluate their significance to organism inheritance and development	21, 22	16	23, 24	19
30-C1.6K compare the formation of fraternal and identical offspring in a single birthing event	31		25	18
30-C1.7K describe the diversity of reproductive strategies by comparing the alternation of generations in a range of organisms	16, 20	NR1	NR3	34, 35

Explain the basic rules and processes associated with the transmission of genetic characteristics.				
30-C2.1K describe the evidence for dominance, segregation and the independent assortment of genes on different chromosomes, as investigated by Mendel	25, 26	18, 22	27	27, NR5
30-C2.2K compare ratios and probabilities of genotypes and phenotypes for dominant and recessive, multiple, incompletely dominant, and codominant alleles	34, 35, 36, NR6, NR7, NR9	17, 19, 20, 25, NR6, NR7, NR8	20, 21, 26, 31, NR2	26, 32
30-C2.3K explain the influence of gene linkage and crossing over on variability	9, 10	9, NR2	NR5	
30-C2.4K explain the relationship between variability and the number of genes controlling a trait	27, 39	NR4		28, 29, 30, 31
30-C2.5K compare the pattern of inheritance produced by genes on sex chromosomes to that produced by genes on autosomes, as investigated by Morgan and others	37, 38, NR8	23, 24	29, NR4	
Explain classical genetics at the molecular level.				
30-C3.1K summarize the historical events that led to the discovery of the structure of the DNA molecule, including the work of Franklin and Watson and Crick	28	14		
30-C3.2K describe, in general, how genetic information is contained in the sequence of basis in DNA molecules in chromosomes and how the DNA molecules replicate themselves	6, 7, 29,	4, 5, NR3	28, 30	
30-C3.3K describe, in general, how genetic information is transcribed into sequences of bases in RNA molecules and is finally translated into sequences of amino acids in proteins	2, 4, 8, 30, NR1, NR4	3, NR5	3, 18	10, 13, 25, 37
30-C3.4K explain, in general, how restriction enzymes cut DNA molecules into smaller fragments and how ligases reassemble them	3		41	
30-C3.5K explain, in general, how cells may be transformed by inserting new DNA sequences into their genomes	11, 13, NR5	10		
30-C3.6K explain how a random change (mutation) in the sequence of bases results in abnormalities or provides a source of genetic variability	5, 12	1	19, 32	23
30-C3.7K explain how base sequences in nucleic acids contained in the nucleus, mitochondrion and chloroplast give evidence for the relationships among organisms of different species	32	21		

CELL DIVISION, GENETICS, AND MOLECULAR BIOLOGY

30-C1.1K define and explain the significance of chromosome number in somatic and sex cells; i.e., haploidy, diploidy and polyploidy

30-C1.2K explain, in general terms, the events of the cell cycle; i.e., interphase, mitosis and cytokinesis

CHROMOSOMES AND THE CELL CYCLE

The characteristics of each individual are coded for by sections of DNA called genes. Each gene codes for one trait, such as hair color. Chromosomes are long strings of genes lined up in a specific sequence. The more genes in a species the greater the number of chromosomes needed. Humans have approximately 20 000 genes which fit onto 23 chromosomes. However, because humans are sexually reproducing organisms, the normal human chromosome number is 46.

The guarantee of sexual reproduction is that each parent will contribute information towards each trait. Thus, both mother and father provide the zygote with a full set of 23 chromosomes in their egg and sperm. The zygote, and the offspring that forms from it have two complete sets of genetic information. Whether the offspring will actually express the mother's gene (e.g. dark) or father's (e.g. light) depends on the rules of dominance and recessiveness. Two chromosomes in a nucleus that have the same gene sequence and come from each parent are called a homologous pair.

All cells that have homologous pairs are said to be diploid or have the *2n* chromosome number, which in humans is 46. All cells that have derived from the zygote by mitosis are also *2n*.

If all zygotes have the diploid number of chromosomes then egg and sperm cannot; they must have only 23. Diploid cells in the ovary or testis undergo meiosis to produce cells with the haploid or *n* chromosome number, which in humans, is 23. When a *2n* ovary or testis cell undergoes meiosis to halve the chromosome number, only one chromosome of each homologous pair is allowed to enter a gamete. Whether that chromosome is maternal or paternal is completely random. Each haploid sperm will therefore be a unique combination of the man's maternal and paternal chromosomes.

Each haploid egg will be a unique combination of the woman's parents' chromosomes. When a sperm and egg unite in fertilization, the diploid chromosome number is restored in the zygote and every cell that is derived from it in mitosis.

The 20 000 genes expressed in an offspring are a unique combination that is never repeated in any individual except identical twins.

Mitosis is cell division that produces two cells that are genetically identical to each other and to the mother cell. Mitosis occurs when an organism grows, or needs to repair itself. The rate of mitosis is mostly dependent on an individual's age.

When one is very young the rate of mitosis is far greater than the rate of cell death. Extremely rapid rates of mitosis are typical of cancers.

The Cell Cycle: Interphase, Mitosis and Cytokinesis

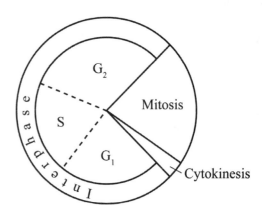

The period from one cell division to the next is called a cell cycle, which is divided into three stages: interphase, mitosis, and cytokinesis. One cell cycle can be hours or years long depending on the type of cell. Cells spend most of each cell cycle in interphase, during which the cell carries out its normal functions and grows larger. Interphase can be divided into three phases: G1, S, and G2. During Gap 1 (G1 phase), the cell grows. Chromosomes are not visible during interphase; at this point they are long strings of uncondensed DNA called chromatin. During the S, or synthesis phase, the cell begins to prepare for cell division by replicating the DNA. The 46 strings of chromatin (23 from each parent) are replicated. Each chromatin string and its replicate become buttoned together by a centromere, and are referred to as sister chromatids. In Gap 2 (G2 phase) the cell continues growing until its volume to surface area ratio becomes too large, and cell division becomes necessary.

The goal of mitosis is to separate the 46 sets of sister chromatids into two complete sets—one chromatid from each pair of sister chromatids should go to each daughter cell. Mitosis has 4 stages: prophase, metaphase, anaphase, and telophase. Prophase begins when the nuclear membrane and nucleolus disappear, making room for an organizing spindle which appears shortly. The DNA which to this point was invisible chromatin, suddenly becomes visible as it supercoils (condenses) to form solid chromosomes which are much easier to move around the cell. Two sister chromatids joined by a centromere make one chromosome. During prophase two centrioles can be seen migrating toward the cell poles. As the centrioles move apart, spindle fibres form, stretching between the centrioles to form a spindle. In metaphase the chromosomes migrate to the metaphase plate and line up along the cell equator. A spindle fibre attaches to each centromere. In anaphase, the centromeres divide so each sister chromatid has its own centromere. Because the definition of a chromosome is any DNA held together by a centromere, each sister chromatid is now its own chromosome. As anaphase continues the spindle fibres attach to the centromeres and proceed to pull the sister chromatids apart, forming a cluster of chromosomes at each pole.

The last phase of mitosis is telophase, during which a nuclear membrane reforms around each of the two clusters of chromosomes. Chromosomes decondense to form chromatin and become invisible again. Mitosis is then complete.

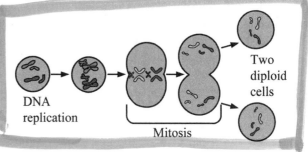

At this point the mother cell is still intact but has two nuclei. The cell cytoplasm is split into two separate cells in the process of cytokinesis. In animal cells, cytokinesis occurs when the cell pinches in the middle to form a cell furrow. In plant cells, the cytoplasm splits when a cell or division plate forms down the middle of the cell. Once cytokinesis is complete, the two identical daughter cells enter interphase, beginning a new cell cycle.

Practice Questions: 1, 17, 18, 33, NR2

30-C1.3K describe the process of meiosis (spermatogenesis and oogenesis) and the necessity for the reduction of chromosome number

30-C1.4K compare the processes of mitosis and meiosis

30-C1.5K describe the processes of crossing over and nondisjunction and evaluate their significance to organism inheritance and development

30-C1.6K compare the formation of fraternal and identical offspring in a single birthing event

30-C1.7K describe the diversity of reproductive strategies by comparing the alternation of generations in a range of organisms

MEIOSIS

The somatic cells of each human parent participating in sexual reproduction have the diploid (*2n*) chromosome number of 46, composed of 23 homologous pairs of chromosomes. If each parent contributed a full set of 46 chromosomes to their offspring, the offspring would have 92 chromosomes, resulting in an abnormal polypoloid organism. In order to participate in sexual reproduction each parent needs to undergo meiosis, a type of reduction division that produces gametes – cells with half the normal chromosome number. If normal human cells have the diploid or *2n* chromosome number which is 46, then gametes will have the haploid or *n* chromosome number which is 23. In meiosis, one chromosome from each homologous pair must find its way into each gamete so that each parent contributes a gene for every trait that the offspring has.

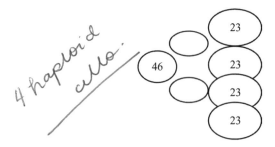

4 haploid cells.

When meiosis occurs in females it takes place in the ovaries and is called oogenesis. When it occurs in males it takes place in the seminiferous tubules of the testes and is called spermatogenesis. Meiosis is very much like two consecutive mitotic divisions. Four cells are produced for each mother cell that enters meiosis; however, the cells produced are haploid gametes with the *n* chromosome number. The chromosome number is reduced by eliminating DNA replication in the interphase before the second division. The second difference between meiosis and mitosis is that in meiosis, the homologous chromosomes and their sister chromatids come together in the first prophase forming a tetrad. Synapsis (crossing-over) occurs at this time where identical and non-idental chromatids of the tetrad twist around each other, and exchange segments, producing new gene combinations.

Because sexual reproduction thrives on the introduction of variation, synapsis is considered to be very adaptive.

Cells that enter the first division of meiosis are called primary oocytes or spermatocytes.

The first division of meiosis (meiosis I) starts with prophase I, which features the dissolving of the nuclear membrane and formation of the spindle. When the chromatin condenses, the chromosomes appear as thick X-shaped forms. Each is actually a tetrad made of a homologous pair and their identical sister chromatids. Synapsis occurs and chromosomes enter metaphase I, lining up along the equator and attaching to spindle fibres. In anaphase I, one homologous chromosome and its identical sister chromatid is torn away from the other homologue and its sister chromatid. Telophase I isolates the two nuclear clusters into new nuclear membranes, and cytokinesis forms the two secondary oocytes or spermatocytes. The first division of meiosis is complete. Because haploid cells are by definition cells that have only one chromosome from each homologous pair, secondary oocytes and spermatocytes are considered to be haploid.

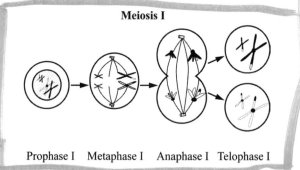

Meiosis I

Prophase I   Metaphase I   Anaphase I   Telophase I

After meiosis I, both cells now enter a short interphase where the S phase (DNA replication) does not occur. In prophase II, chromosomes again condense appearing as single chromosomes which are actually composed of two identical sister chromatids held together by their centromere. In metaphase II, all chromosomes line up on the equator, centromeres divide and attach to spindle fibres. As anaphase II continues, spindle fibres tear sister chromatids apart, pulling one chromatid toward each pole, ensuring that each daughter cell has an exact copy. In telophase II nuclear membranes form around the new nuclei and when cytokinesis is complete, four haploid gametes result. The male cells are referred to as spermatids, and the female cells, as ootids.

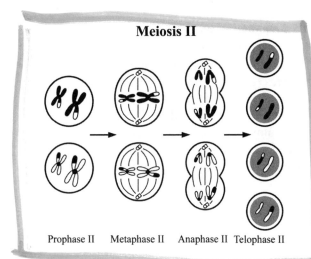

Meiosis II

Prophase II   Metaphase II   Anaphase II Telophase II

Other than the location in which each process occurs (testis and ovary) there are a few differences between spermatogenesis and oogenesis. In spermatogenesis, all four products of meiosis become functional sperm and all four cells are of the same small size. Because sperm only donate their chromosomes to the zygote, the size of the sperm cell is not important. The larger the egg is in relation to the sperm, the more successful reproduction is likely to be. The reason for this is that even though both sperm and egg provide half the chromosomes, the egg provides all the cytoplasmic organelles, nutrients, and energy to support the zygote and early embryo. To obtain a large egg, unequal cytokinesis occurs at the end of the first meiotic division of oogenesis, producing one large secondary oocyte and a tiny polar body that is reabsorbed. The single secondary oocyte goes on to complete the second meiotic division where again, unequal cytokinesis results in a very large ootid (egg) and a second polar body, that is reabsorbed.

Another difference between the two processes is that meiosis I begins in females embryonically and continues up to the secondary oocyte stage during follicle development. Meiosis II is not actually completed until the time of fertilization. Spermatogenesis begins at the time of puberty and continues at a constant rate from that point on. Oogenesis ends at midlife in menopause, while spermatogenesis continues, with some decrease, into old age.

The genetic variation needed for successful natural selection and evolution is achieved through synapsis, random assortment of chromosomes during meiosis, and random mutations that can occur at any time. Note that only mutations of reproductive tissue (testes and ovaries) can affect future generations.

Nondisjunction is a type of chromosomal mutation that results when chromosomes do not separate normally in meiosis. If nondisjunction occurs in meiosis I, the resulting gametes will be $n + 1$, $n + 1$, $n - 1$, and $n - 1$. If nondisjunction occurs in meiosis II, the products will be $n + 1$, $n - 1$, n, and n.

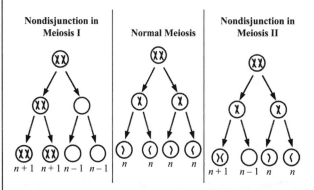

If an $n + 1$ gamete joins with a normal gamete in fertilization, a trisomy will occur in the fetus. Down's syndrome, which involves a degree of mental disability, is caused by a trisomy of chromosome pair 21. If an $n - 1$ gamete fuses with an n gamete, the result will be a monosomy in the offspring's cells. Klinefelter's and Turner's syndrome are caused by nondisjunctions of sex chromosomes during meiosis. Klinefelter's syndrome is a trisomy that occurs when an XX egg is fertilized by a Y sperm. Turner's syndrome (monosomy X) results when an X sperm or egg fuses with a gamete that is missing a sex chromosome.

Karotype: Down Syndrome (Trisomy 21)

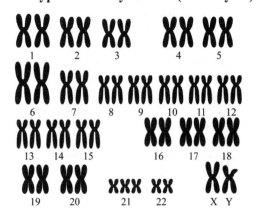

TWINS

Monozygotic (identical) twins form from a single zygote. One egg and one sperm form a zygote then morula. The morula is disrupted and splits into two masses, each of which is still totipotent and develops into 2 embryos, identical because they are the products of mitosis from single zygote. Monozygotic twins may not share a chorion, amnion, or placenta.

Dizygotic (fraternal) twins form from two different zygotes. Two eggs and two sperms form two embryos, each with its own chorion, amnion, and placenta. Because they are from two different gametes, they are as different as any two siblings from that set of parents.

ALTERATION OF GENERATIONS

Alternation of Generations is a reproductive strategy employed by plants to maximize reproduction. Animals have only one multicellular form – our present body composed of diploid cells. A haploid phase exists as short-lived single-celled gametes. In humans, there is no multicellular haploid stage.

Plants, however, have two different multicellular forms: a diploid form called a sporophyte, and a haploid form called a gametophyte. Two haploid gametes ($1n$) fuse in fertilization to form a diploid zygote ($2n$). The zygote undergoes mitosis to become a multicellular diploid sporophyte. The diploid sporophyte undergoes meiosis to produce haploid spores (n). The haploid spores undergo mitosis to create a multicellular haploid gametophyte (n). The gametophyte produces haploid gametes (n) through mitosis, which then start the reproductive cycle again. Because the haploid gametophyte generation alternates with the diploid sporophyte generation this reproductive strategy of plants is referred to as alternation of generations.

Alternation of Generations—Moss Life Cycle

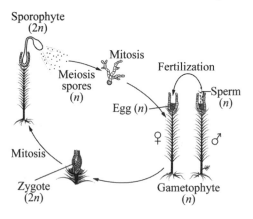

Practice Questions: 14, 15, 16, 19, 20, 21, 22, 23, 24, 31, NR3

30-C2.1K describe the evidence for dominance, segregation and the independent assortment of genes on different chromosomes, as investigated by Mendel

30-C2.2K compare ratios and probabilities of genotypes and phenotypes for dominant and recessive, multiple, incompletely dominant, and codominant alleles

30-C2.3K explain the influence of gene linkage and crossing over on variability

30-C2.4K explain the relationship between variability and the number of genes controlling a trait; e.g., one pair of genes, as for Rh factor, versus two or more pairs of genes, as for skin colour and height

30-C2.5K compare the pattern of inheritance produced by genes of the sex chromosomes to that produced by genes on autosomes, as investigated by Morgan and others

PRINCIPLES OF HEREDITY

During the 1800s, the German monk and gardener Gregor Mendel discovered that traits are determined by distinct physical factors that are now called genes. He realized there were alternate forms of genes that gave rise to different forms of the trait. These alternate gene forms are called alleles. For example, there are green and yellow alleles of the gene for the trait of seed color. When pure-breeding plants with alternate forms of a trait were crossed, Mendel observed that one form disappeared and that all the offspring were of the other form. However, when these offspring were bred together, the trait that had disappeared in the first generation of offspring reappeared in the second generation offspring. He deduced that the information that disappeared was actually present in the first generation of offspring but had been hidden. His conclusion was that each individual carries two unit factors (genes) for each trait and that one can hide the other.

Today we recognize the two unit factors as being the genes donated by sperm and egg. The allele that is hidden is said to be recessive. The allele that expresses is said to be dominant. In the case of pea seed color the green allele is dominant to the yellow allele. The term phenotype is used to describe an observable trait. The term genotype refers to the two alleles present in each individual. The genotype of the individual determines the phenotype. Individuals with homozygous dominant or heterozygous genotypes will show the dominant phenotype. Only individuals with a homozygous recessive genotype will show a recessive phenotype. In the case of pea seed color, *GG* and *Gg* genotypes result in the green phenotype. The *gg* genotype results in the yellow phenotype.

Mendel reasoned that in order for there to be two copies of each gene in an offspring, gametes could only contain one copy of each gene. The two copies of each gene must separate during gamete formation – a principle he referred to as the Law of Segregation. Knowledge of meiosis eventually confirmed that gametes are haploid because homologous pairs separate during meiosis.

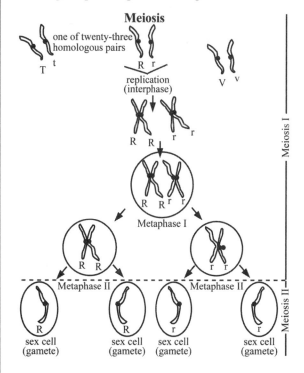

When parents mate or are crossed, a Punnett square can be used to predict the phenotypic ratios in the offspring. A cross between a homozygous (pure-breeding) dominant (AA) organism and a homozygous (pure-breeding) recessive (aa) organism will result in an F_1 generation of offspring with the dominant phenotype and heterozygous genotype (Aa). If these heterozygous offspring are crossed, the F_2 generation will show the dominant and recessive phenotypes in a ratio of 3:1. The following diagram illustrates the genotypes of these crosses and resultant phenotypic ratios.

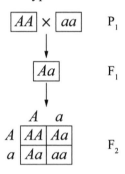

Mendel devised a method called a test cross to determine if an organism showing the dominant phenotype was homozygous (BB) or heterozygous (Bb) by crossing it with an organism showing the recessive phenotype (bb). If any of the offspring showed the recessive trait (genotype bb), the organism in question had to be heterozygous.

Some genes have more than two possible forms (multiple alleles). For example, there are three different alleles that determine blood type in humans: I^A, I^B, and i. The alleles I^A and I^B show codominance (phenotype AB). The allele i is recessive to both I^A and I^B. These alleles form the following phenotypes and genotypes:

- phenotype A—$I^A I^A$ or $I^A i$

- phenotype B—$I^B I^B$ or $I^B i$

- phenotype AB—$I^A I^B$

- phenotype O—ii

Another form of allele interaction is incomplete dominance. If both alleles are present in the genotype, and neither is dominant, then the phenotype will be a mixture of the two. For example, if a pure-breeding red flower and a pure breeding white flower are crossed and the F_1 offspring are all pink, then incomplete dominance exists. A cross of two of the F_1's would produce an F_2 generation with a ratio of 1 red (RR) to 2 pink (RW) to 1 white (WW). Mendel also completed crosses involving two different traits (dihybrid crosses) and found that they also produced characteristic ratios. P_1 parents pure-breeding for two traits were crossed, producing an F_1 generation of all dihybrids. When two of the F_1 dihybrid offspring were crossed as the P_2, the F_2 offspring occurred in the phenotypic ratio of 9:3:3:1.

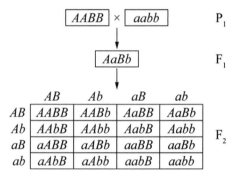

Mendel explained these results by stating that the gene for each trait was inherited independently of the other gene (Law of Independent Assortment). The alleles for each gene assort independently as long as they are located on different chromosomes.

Some traits are polygenic, meaning that two or more genes determine a single trait. Examples are skin colour and height. Polygenic traits produce a wider variability in phenotypes than single gene traits. Some genes are epistatic, meaning that two genes interact to form different phenotypes. The environment also plays a role in whether or not genes are expressed. Most genes are affected by the environment that exists inside or outside the body, such that a phenotype may or may not be produced even though the corresponding genotype exists.

Inherited conditions can be mapped through the generations using a diagram called a pedigree. The pedigree indicates the generation of an individual, whether they are male or female, the position of the individual within the family, the mate of the individual, and whether or not they are affected by the condition.

Sample Pedigree

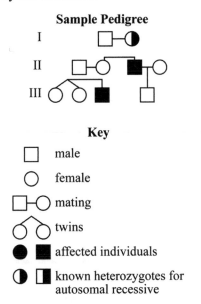

Key

☐   male

○   female

☐─○   mating

⚭ twins

● ■   affected individuals

◑ ◪   known heterozygotes for autosomal recessive

SEX LINKAGE

Most genes are found on the 22 pairs of autosomes (non-sex chromosomes). The twenty-third pair are sex chromosomes that determine an individual's gender. Females have two X chromosomes. Males have an X and a Y chromosome. X and Y chromosomes are not homologous; genes that are found on the X chromosome are not found on the Y. Phenotypes associated with genes on autosomes are found equally in males and females. Genes that are found on sex chromosomes (sex-linked genes) produce phenotypes that are found in different ratios in males and females.

X-linked genes are found only on X chromosomes; the Y chromosome does not contribute to X-linked traits. X-linked recessive traits such as hemophilia and color-blindness are more likely to show up in males than females because males do not have a second X chromosome that could counteract a recessive allele on an X chromosome. A cross of a male without hemophilia ($X^H Y$) and a woman who is a carrier for hemophilia ($X^H X^h$) would not produce any hemophiliac daughters.

	X^H	Y
X^H	$X^H X^H$	$X^H Y$
X^h	$X^H X^h$	$X^h Y$

The phenotypic ratio of the offspring is predicted to be 50% normal females 25% normal males 25% hemophiliac males.

Conversely, because females have two X chromosomes, X-linked dominant traits are more likely to show up in females. A cross between a male with hypertrichosis ($X^{CH} Y$) and a normal female ($X^{ch} X^{ch}$) would not produce any sons with hypertrichosis.

	X^{CH}	Y
X^{ch}	$X^{CH} X^{ch}$	$X^{ch} Y$
X^{ch}	$X^{CH} X^{ch}$	$X^{ch} Y$

Phenotypes of offspring: 1/2 affected females 1/2 normal males

A father will always pass his X chromosome to his daughters. His Y chromosome is always passed on to his sons. A mother will always pass an X chromosome to either sex of her offspring. A carrier is an individual who has an allele that does not appear in the phenotype. Because females have two X chromosomes, females can be hidden carriers of an X-linked recessive allele. When carrying out a cross involving a sex-linked gene, both the sex chromosomes and the alleles on the sex chromosomes must be indicated.

Determining the type of inheritance operating can be difficult, but there are indicators of each type. A condition is autosomal if there is no significant difference between the genders in the frequency of a phenotype. A condition is sex-linked if there is a significant difference in the incidence of the condition in males and females. A condition is autosomal recessive if unaffected parents are producing an affected child.

**Pedigree of a Family
with Cystic Fibrosis**

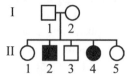

A condition is autosomal dominant if the condition is found in each generation. This may be difficult to determine if little information is given.

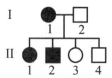

If significantly more males than females have the condition then the condition is X-linked recessive.

X-Linked Recessive Pedigree

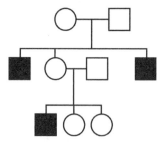

If significantly more females than males are affected then the condition is X-linked dominant.

X-Linked Dominant Pedigree

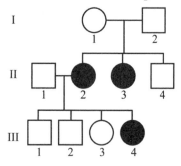

GENE LINKAGE AND CHROMOSOME MAPPING

Because there are 20 000 human genes on only 23 chromosome pairs, many genes are linked together on each chromosome. When two genes are linked on the same chromosome, independent assortment cannot occur because the linked alleles are not free to separate from each other.

For example, if two genes are not linked on the same chromosome, a cross of *AaBb* × *AaBb* should produce 4 types of gametes from each parent, and a phenotypic ratio of 9:3:3:1 in the offspring. If, however, these two genes are linked on the same chromosome, (*A* linked with *B*, and *a* linked with *b*) then only *AB* and *ab* gametes can be produced, halving the number of phenotypes that can occur in the offspring. Because not all gamete combinations can be made, gene linkage greatly reduces variability in gametes and offspring.

While gene linkage limits variability, crossing-over (synapsis) of linked genes during prophase I of meiosis restores variability, increasing the number of gamete and offspring types possible. Offspring that result from crossing-over are referred to as recombinants. The percentage of crossovers is related to the distance between two genes on a chromosome. The farther away two genes are from each other, the greater the probability of a cross-over event and the higher the number of recombinant offspring that would occur. Therefore, the crossover percentage (recombination frequency) can be used as a map distance between any two genes that are linked on the same chromosome.

$$\text{Crossover percentage} = \frac{\text{Number of recombinants}}{\text{Total number of offspring}} \times 100\%$$

If a cross occurred between an A and B gene linked on the same chromosome, and 40 out of 200 offspring were recombinants, the map distance between the A and B gene would be 20 map units (cM). When given the recombination frequencies between several genes linked on the same chromosome, it is possible to determine the sequence of genes on the chromosome.

Gene pairs	Recombination (or crossover) frequency between each pair of genes	Distance between the two genes in map units
L & R	6	6 cM
R & H	20	20 cM
L & H	26	26 cM

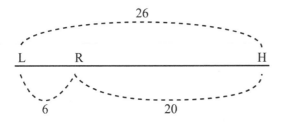

Practice Questions: 9, 10, 25, 26, 27, 34, 35, 36, 37, 38, 39, NR6, NR7, NR8, NR9

30-C3.1K summarize the historical events that led to the discovery of the DNA molecule, including the work of Franklin and Watson and Crick

30-C3.2K describe, in general, how genetic information is contained in the sequence of bases in DNA molecules in chromosomes and how the DNA molecules replicate themselves

30-C3.3K describe, in general, how genetic information is transcribed into sequences of bases in RNA molecules and is finally translated into sequences of amino acids in proteins

DNA STRUCTURE

In the 1940s, the work of Griffith, Avery, MacLeod, and McCarty led scientists to question the prevailing theory that proteins were the hereditary material. The results of experiments done by Hershey and Chase confirmed that DNA was the hereditary material.

Chargaff discovered the relationship between the amounts of the nitrogenous bases in a molecule of DNA. In the DNA of any species, the amount of adenine always equals the amount of thymine, and the amount of guanine always equals the amount of cytosine. The conclusion was that adenine was paired with thymine, and guanine was paired with cytosine. Scientists then focused on determining how the DNA molecule functions. In the 1950s, Franklin used X-ray diffraction to determine that the DNA molecule had a helical structure. Using Franklin's findings, Watson and Crick then constructed a 3-D model of DNA that illustrated the double helix structure and the relationship between the nitrogenous bases.

The acronym DNA stands for deoxyribonucleic acid. DNA is found in the nucleus, and has a double helix structure made of two strings of nucleotides joined in the middle by hydrogen bonds. A nucleotide consists of a deoxyribose sugar, a phosphate group, and a nitrogenous base attached to the sugar. DNA is like a ladder, with the two sugar-phosphate backbones as the sides of the ladder and the base pairs form the rungs. The bases of one DNA strand pair with their complementary bases on the other strand. The purine nitrogenous base adenine (A) always pairs with the pyrimidine thymine (T), and the purine guanine (G) always pairs with the pyrimidine cytosine (C). The amounts of A and T in DNA should be equal, as should the amounts of C and G.

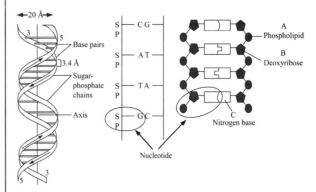

The order of the four bases on the DNA molecule provides the genetic information to build needed proteins out of the many amino acids that are ingested in the diet.

It is extremely important that every cell in the body have a complete set of DNA and can produce the same proteins. When young, human cells are always dividing in the process of mitosis to keep up with growth and repair. To make sure every new cell produced in mitosis has an identical set of DNA, the DNA must undergo replication prior to cell division. This involves the precise copying of 3 billion base pairs spread over 46 chromosomes. Replication begins when the enzyme gyrase unwinds the double helix of chromosome.

The enzyme helicase then unzips the double helix by breaking the hydrogen bonds between the base pairs. This produces two template strands.

The enzyme DNA polymerase builds a new strand by escorting complementary DNA nucleotides floating in the nucleus into position opposite each template strand. Each template strand is joined to its complementary strand with hydrogen bonds, forming two identical DNA molecules.

Because the two new molecules of DNA are each made of one old (template) strand and one new strand, DNA replication is considered to be semi-conservative.

DNA replication occurs prior to mitotis and meiosis I, and ensures that the DNA in the daughter cells will be identical to that of the mother cell.

Semi-Conservative Replication of DNA

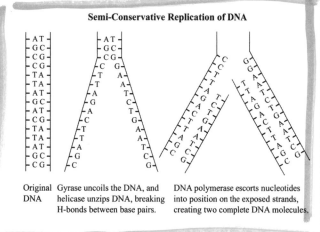

Original DNA | Gyrase uncoils the DNA, and helicase unzips DNA, breaking H-bonds between base pairs. | DNA polymerase escorts nucleotides into position on the exposed strands, creating two complete DNA molecules.

PROTEIN SYNTHESIS

The body requires thousands of different proteins in order to function: enzymes, pigments, hormones, muscle filaments, cartilage, neurotransmitters, ion pumps, and hair are but a partial list. Each protein is made of a different number, type, and sequence of amino acids joined together by peptide bonds. The twenty different amino acids that are used to form proteins are ingested in the diet and travel to the cytoplasm of cells where they wait to be incorporated into a particular protein. A gene is a section of chromosomal DNA that directs the assembly of one specific protein. The DNA code indicates which amino acids to use to build a specific protein, how many amino acids to use, and in what sequence to arrange them. As it turns out, only one strand of DNA is important and is called the active strand. Starting from the beginning of the active strand, every three nitrogenous bases forms a triplet code, or codon, that codes for one particular amino acid.

Protein synthesis seems complex because of the problem of geography. The DNA gene for a protein is part of a chromosome, and chromosomes are in the nucleus. The site of protein assembly (the ribosome) is in the cytoplasm. The amino acids that are the raw materials needed for protein assembly are also floating throughout the cytoplasm. For this reason a helper molecule, RNA (ribonucleic acid) is used to bring the individual elements together to produce the protein. RNA is similar to DNA, but there are three important differences: the sugar in RNA is ribose, not deoxyribose; RNA has the base uracil in place of the DNA base thymine; and RNA is single-stranded, not double-stranded like DNA. Messenger RNA (mRNA) will function to make a copy of the DNA in the nucleus and bring it to the ribosome in the cytoplasm. Transfer RNA (tRNA) will function to pick up requested amino acids from the cytoplasm and bring them to the ribosome for assembly.

Protein synthesis is divided into two phases: transcription and translation. In transcription, which occurs in the nucleus, the base sequence on DNA is copied complementarily onto a molecule of messenger RNA (mRNA).

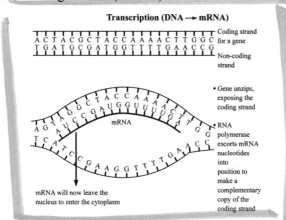

Transcription (DNA → mRNA)

Coding strand for a gene

Non-coding strand

• Gene unzips, exposing the coding strand

mRNA

• RNA polymerase escorts mRNA nucleotides into position to make a complementary copy of the coding strand

mRNA will now leave the nucleus to enter the cytoplasm

To accomplish transcription, the DNA in the region of the gene unwinds and unzips, exposing the active strand of the gene. RNA polymerase escorts complementary RNA nucleotides into position opposite the active strand. Once transcription is complete, the mRNA molecule slides out of the nucleus into the cytoplasm where it enters a ribosome.

Within the ribosome, the second phase of protein synthesis, translation, begins. The ribosome translates, or reads, the instructions on the mRNA. It reads three nitrogenous bases (one triplet codon) on the mRNA at a time. The ribosome then determines which amino acid that particular codon is requesting. This can be done using the mRNA Codon Translation Table in the appendix. Because the needed amino acids are floating around in the cytoplasm, the ribosome sends a transfer RNA molecule to transfer the amino acid into the ribosome. One end of the tRNA molecule has an anticodon that complementarily matches the codon on the mRNA currently being read by the ribosome. The other end of the tRNA is attached to the requested amino acid. The tRNA molecule brings the amino acid into the ribosome and, after dropping it off, returns to the cytoplasm. The ribosome then reads the next codon on the mRNA, following the same sequence of translation.

When the second amino acid has been dropped off in the ribosome, a peptide bond forms with the first one, beginning the creation of a polypeptide.

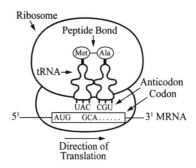

Once all the codons on the mRNA molecule have been translated, the ribosome releases the final polypeptide chain, which coils into its particular 3-D shape, and becomes a functional protein. That protein may be secreted out of the cell (e.g. a hormone) or used within the cell (e.g. an enzyme).

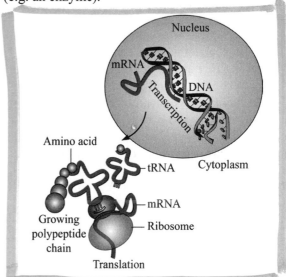

As an example, assume the hormone insulin is the protein that will be assembled. Insulin is made of 51 amino acids each in a specific order. The gene (DNA base sequence) for insulin is on chromosome eleven in human cells. First, the strands of the insulin gene separate, exposing the sequence of bases on the active strand. mRNA nucleotides come in and attach in a complementary fashion to the exposed DNA bases.

Assume that the first DNA triplet is TAC. This is transcribed as the mRNA codon AUG. Once transcription of the gene is complete the insulin mRNA slides away from chromosome eleven and squeezes through a nuclear pore to reach the cytoplasm where it parks alongside a ribosome. The ribosome begins to translate the coded message that exists in the form of codons (three bases on the mRNA). The first codon of the insulin mRNA is AUG. The mRNA Codon Translation Table indicates that the amino acid being requested is methionine. Methionine, like all amino acids, is floating around the cytoplasm. The ribosome sends out a tRNA molecule to fetch methionine and bring it to the ribosome. The only tRNA that can do this is one that has the anticodon to the mRNA codon being read. Therefore, a tRNA with the anticodon UAC on one end and the amino acid methionine attached to the other end moves from the cytoplasm into the ribosome, where it drops off the methionine and then wanders back to the cytoplasm.

The transcription and translation of the first amino acid in insulin is now complete. The ribosome now begins the translation of the second mRNA codon. When the second amino acid is brought by a tRNA into the ribosome, it will be joined to methionine by a peptide bond, beginning the peptide chain that will, eventually become the protein insulin. The translation of mRNA codons continues until the ribosome reads a termination codon, indicating that the protein, composed of 51 amino acids, is complete.

In summary, in order for the amino acid methionine to become part of the insulin protein being synthesized, the DNA base triplet TAC is transcribed complementarily onto mRNA as the codon AUG. The ribosome translates the mRNA codon AUG and requests that a tRNA with the anticodon UAC bring methionine to the ribosome.

Practice Questions: 2, 4, 6, 7, 8, 28, 29, 30, NR1, NR4

30-C3.4K explain, in general, how restriction enzymes cut DNA molecules into smaller fragments and how ligases reassemble them

30-C3.5K explain, in general, how cells may be transformed by inserting new DNA sequences into their genomes

BIOTECHNOLOGY

The DNA of all species is made of nucleotides with the same 4 bases: A,G,T, and C. Thus, the DNA of any species can be translated by any other species. Therefore, the genes from any species can be cut and pasted into another species to allow the recipient organism to make proteins different from the proteins that it could have made naturally. Recombinant DNA is DNA that has been modified in this way. Restriction enzymes are used in recombinant DNA technology, acting as chemical scissors that are used to cut DNA. Each type of restriction enzyme recognizes a specific DNA sequence and cuts at this recognition site in a precise way, producing gene segments that have sticky ends made of a sequence of unpaired bases. If two different DNA molecules are cut with the same restriction enzyme, they will have complementary sticky ends. Cut up segments of DNA will seek out each other's complementary sticky ends. Ligase enzyme is used to paste them together. The new introduced gene functions as any other gene would. It is transcribed and translated in protein synthesis, producing a protein that could not have been produced by this organism in nature.

Scientists can use these molecular tools in the process of genetic transformation by inserting a foreign gene into a bacterial genome. The most commonly transformed organisms are bacteria. Bacteria carry an extra circle of chromosomal DNA called a plasmid. Assume that it is desirable to place a foreign gene into a bacterial plasmid. The plasmid, as well as the gene of interest isolated from another organism, can be cut with a specific restriction enzyme. The two DNA molecules will have complementary sticky ends that can be joined together with a ligase enzyme and then reintroduced into the bacteria.

The bacteria will then transcribe and translate the plasmid as it would normally, synthesizing the protein coded for by the introduced gene.

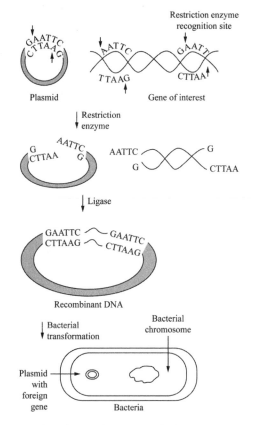

An example of transformation is the insertion of a human insulin gene into the genome of *E.coli* bacteria—this is the source of much of the insulin in use today. The advantage is that bacterial cells are easy to grow, and will secrete copious amounts of human insulin that can be extracted from the growth medium and sold inexpensively. An additional advantage is that because recombinant insulin is a human protein, adverse reactions such as allergies, cannot occur.

Bioengineering and the production of recombinant life forms is now a common occurrence in the pharmaceutical and agricultural industries.

Practice Questions: 3, 11, 13, NR5

30-C3.6K explain how a random change (mutation) in the sequences of bases results in abnormalities or provides a source of genetic variability

30-C3.7K explain how base sequences in nucleic acids contained in the nucleus, mitochondrion and chloroplast give evidence for the relationships among organisms of different species

MUTATION

Since information needed to synthesize proteins is encoded in the sequence of bases on DNA, changes in their sequence might have consequences for the organism. Mutations, or changes in the base sequence, can occur spontaneously or can be induced by mutagenic agents such as radiation or toxic chemicals. Mutations happen continuously, mostly during DNA replication, but in most cases DNA repair mechanisms correct the errors. Point mutations involve only one gene and consist of the substitution, addition, or deletion of bases. Depending on the position of the mutation, it may or may not result in the translation of a different amino acid, which may or may not result in an altered shape and function of the final protein.

Not all mutations are negative. Many genetic variations that the environment acts upon in natural selection are the result of mutation. It is the environment of the organism that determines whether the mutation is positive or negative. If in a particular environment the mutation increases the organism's chances of survival and reproduction, the mutation is considered positive, and will likely increase in frequency in the gene pool. Without variability in a population, the population is susceptible to extinction should the environment change.

Chromosomal mutations occur when either the chromosome number is changed (e.g., nondisjunction causing Down's syndrome) or when entire sections of a chromosome are translocated or inverted. These mutations almost always have severe and negative effects. Mutations of non-reproductive (somatic) cells cannot be inherited by offspring.

Populations can diverge into different species as mutations accumulate, particularly if accompanied by reproductive or geographic isolation. Scientists can determine the relatedness of species by examining their genomes. Species that are closely related have genomes that are more similar than species that are more distantly related. This is because genomes of two species with a recent common ancestor would have had less time for mutations to accumulate. However, nuclear genomes are often large and complex to analyze; therefore, mitochondrial or chloroplast genes are often examined instead.

Practice Questions: 5, 12, 32

PRACTICE QUESTIONS—CELL DIVISION, GENETICS, AND MOLECULAR BIOLOGY

1. The chromosome number in human sex cells is

 A. diploid

 B. triploid

 C. haploid

 D. tetraploid

Use the following information to answer the next two questions.

Some people have condemned the use of food preservatives because they may cause cancer. A researcher has found contradictory evidence that suggests that two widely used food preservatives actually increase levels of natural cancer-fighting agents in laboratory animals. The preservatives BHA and BHT increase the activity of a gene that controls the production of an enzyme. This enzyme helps destroy cancer-causing substances (carcinogens) before they trigger the development of tumours.

– from Pearson et al, 1983

CHALLENGER QUESTION 50.1

2. The **most direct** relationship between a gene and an enzyme is that

 A. an enzyme causes a gene to destroy carcinogens

 B. the sequence of nucleotides in a gene determines the structure of an enzyme

 C. each gene contains the code needed to construct many different types of enzymes

 D. the sequence of amino acids in an enzyme is unrelated to nucleotide sequence in a gene

Source: January 2000

Use the following additional information to answer the next question.

Some Events that Occur Following BHA or BHT Exposure

1. The polypeptide folds into an enzyme shape.

2. tRNAs transport amino acids to the ribosomes.

3. A polypeptide is released from the ribosomes.

4. mRNA leaves the nucleus and attaches to ribosomes in the cytoplasm.

CHALLENGER QUESTION 57.9

Numerical Response

1. The sequence of events that results in the production of the cancer-fighting enzyme is 4 , 2 , 1 , and 3 .
(Record your answer as a **four-digit** number.)

Source: January 2000

Use the following information to answer the next question.

Although most strains of the bacterial species *Vibrio cholera* are harmless, the 01 strain produces a toxin that binds to cells of the small intestine, causing rapid depletion of salts and water, which, if not replaced, can be lethal in humans. This disease is known as cholera.

The transformation from harmless to harmful bacterial strains is thought to be caused by a virus that transfers the cholera toxin gene (CTX) from one bacterial strain and places it into another. Researchers can mimic this process by using current technologies.

– from Glausiusz, 1996

3. The sequence of events that would enable researchers to incorporate the CTX gene into bacterial DNA would be to

  A. first open the bacterial DNA with ligase enzymes, then position the CTX gene in the DNA, and then join the DNA by restriction enzymes

  B. first open the bacterial DNA with restriction enzymes, then position the CTX gene in the DNA, and then join the DNA by ligase enzymes

  C. first position the CTX gene in the DNA, then open the DNA with ligase enzymes, and then join the DNA by restriction enzymes

  D. first position the CTX gene in the DNA, then open the DNA with restriction enzymes, and then join the DNA by ligase enzymes

Source: January 2000

Use the following information to answer the next question.

A study published in the journal *Pediatrics* indicates that breast-fed infants have a substantially decreased risk of developing diarrhea compared with infants fed formula. Another study reported that although a majority of infants harbour populations of bacteria that would cause diarrhea in adults, breast-fed infants do not get sick. The bacterium *Clostridium difficile* produces a toxin that irritates the lining of the colon, causing diarrhea. Breast milk contains a protein called secretory component that binds to the toxin, thus causing the toxin to be ineffective.

– from J.T., 1997

4. The protein secretory component is produced in breast milk when

  A. DNA is translated

  B. DNA is replicated

  C. mRNA is translated

  D. mRNA is replicated

Source: June 2000

Use the following information to answer the next question.

Cystic fibrosis is a recessive Mendelian trait in the human population. A symptom of cystic fibrosis is the production of large amounts of mucin protein. New studies indicate that although the cystic fibrosis condition is present at birth, increased mucin production is preceded by an infection with the bacterium *Pseudomonas aeruginosa*. Individuals who are not affected by cystic fibrosis produce a natural antibiotic, defensin, that kills the *Pseudomonas aeruginosa* and eliminates the stimulus for increased mucin production. Defensin is destroyed by a high chloride content in the tissues of individuals with cystic fibrosis as a result of faulty chloride-channel proteins.

–from Sternberg, 1997

5. The allele that causes cystic fibrosis **most likely** results in a faulty amino acid sequence for the

   A. channel proteins

   B. mucin molecules

   C. defensin molecules

   D. Pseudomonas bacteria

   Source: June 2000

6. Which of the following rows correctly describes a DNA molecule?

Row	Components	Backbone	Molecules that form the links between two strands
A.	amino acids, sugars, and bases	sugars and bases	amino acids
B.	amino acids, sugars, and bases	sugars and amino acids	bases
C.	phosphates, sugars, and bases	sugars and bases	phosphates
D.	phosphates, sugars, and bases	sugars and phosphates	bases

Source: January 2001

Use the following information to answer the next question.

A section of template DNA contains the following proportions of bases:

adenine–20%   thymine–30%
cytosine–10%   guanine–40%

7. The proportions of three of the mRNA nucleotides produced from this DNA are

   A. 20% adenine, 30% uracil, and 10% cytosine

   B. 40% cytosine, 20% adenine, and 30% uracil

   C. 20% uracil, 40% cytosine, and 10% guanine

   D. 20% thymine, 30% adenine, and 10% guanine

   Source: January 2001

Use the following information to answer the next question.

"It begins in your gut and quickly spreads to your heart and head. Your confidence is swept away with dark foreboding as your heart races and your stomach becomes nauseous."

This description was given by a person experiencing a "panic attack" induced by the injection of cholecystokinin (CCK). CCK is a molecule with different functions in different parts of the body. In the brain, it acts as a neurotransmitter that normally regulates memory and recall. It also arouses the emotional and motivational regions of the brain. A gene that encodes CCK has been located.

– from Hall, 1996

8. After mRNA has been produced, the production of CCK is the result of

   A. translation

   B. replication

   C. transcription

   D. recombination

   Source: June 1999

Use the following information to answer the next two questions.

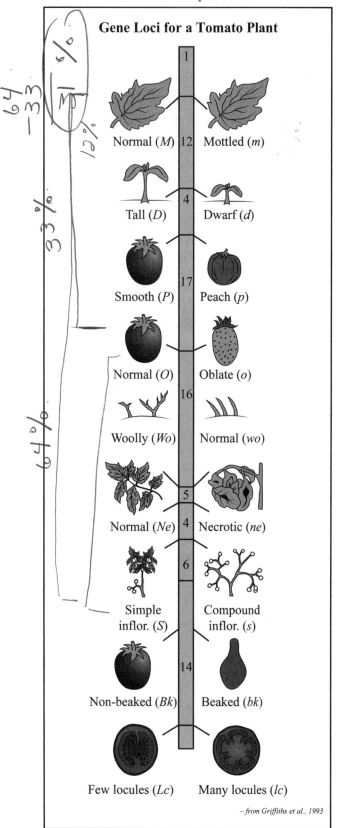

Gene Loci for a Tomato Plant

Normal (*M*) | 12 | Mottled (*m*)

Tall (*D*) | 4 | Dwarf (*d*)

Smooth (*P*) | 17 | Peach (*p*)

Normal (*O*) | | Oblate (*o*)

Woolly (*Wo*) | 16 | Normal (*wo*)

Normal (*Ne*) | 5 4 | Necrotic (*ne*)

Simple inflor. (*S*) | 6 | Compound inflor. (*s*)

Non-beaked (*Bk*) | 14 | Beaked (*bk*)

Few locules (*Lc*) | | Many locules (*lc*)

– from Griffiths et al., 1993

---

9. During meiosis, which of the following pairs of genes given above has the greatest chance of being separated by crossing over?

A. (*m*) and (*d*)

B. (*ne*) and (*p*)

C. (*m*) and (*lc*)

D. (*p*) and (*o*)

Source: January 2001

Use the following additional information to answer the next question.

Cross-over frequencies for some genes on a tomato plant:	
Genes	**Cross-Over Frequency**
normal leaf (*M*) and tall plant (*D*)	12%
normal leaf (*M*) and normal tomato (*O*)	33%
normal leaf (*M*) and simple inflorescence (*S*)	64%
tall plant (*D*) and normal tomato (*O*)	21%
tall plant (*D*) and simple inflorescence (*S*)	52%

10. The cross-over frequency between genes *O* and *S* is

A. 6%

B. 29%

C. 31%

D. 97%

Source: January 2001

---

11. In one type of cloning, the nucleus of a cell taken from the blastula stage of an embryo is inserted into an enucleated egg cell (an egg cell with its nucleus removed). The nucleus of a cell taken from a more mature embryo would be **less suitable** for this type of cloning because such a nucleus would

   A. be too large to fit inside an enucleated egg cell

   B. be specialized because differentiation would have begun

   C. lack some of the genes needed to develop into a total organism

   D. undergo only meiosis, whereas cells of early embryos would undergo only mitosis

Use the following information to answer the next two questions.

Researchers have found a gene known as *p53*. It codes for a protein that binds to specific areas of DNA and activates them. This causes the production of a set of proteins that halts cell division or, in some cells, activates the cell's suicide program (apoptosis). The *p53* gene is activated when a cell is damaged and/or undergoes a DNA mutation.

Research on the *p53* gene was initially done with cancer cells obtained from a laboratory animal. These cells were grown in a petri dish. A cell with two normal *p53* alleles was found to have normal cell division. Cells with one normal and one mutated *p53* allele were also found to have normal cell division. Cells that had mutations in both *p53* alleles were unable to control cell division and were associated with cancer.

– from Seachrist, 1996

12. The initial research findings described above

   A. demonstrate that the activated *p53* gene causes cancer in lab animals

   B. demonstrate that the *p53* protein causes the formation of cancer cells

   C. indicate that the normal *p53* gene is responsible for preventing cancer in all mammals

   D. indicate that the normal *p53* gene is responsible for preventing cancer under laboratory conditions

Source: January 2001

13. Gene therapy that might stop uncontrolled cell division due to the mutant *p53* allele would require

   A. one functional *p53* allele to be successfully inserted into cancer cells

   B. two functional *p53* alleles to be successfully inserted into cancer cells

   C. one functional *p53* allele to be successfully removed from cancer cells

   D. two functional *p53* alleles to be successfully removed from cancer cells

Source: January 2001

Use the following information to answer the next two questions.

Chromosome Content of Human Cells During a Series of Events

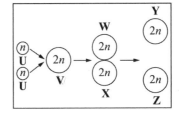

14. In humans, what process must occur before cell V forms cells W and X?

   A. Mitosis

   B. Meiosis

   C. Recombination

   D. Nondisjunction

Source: January 2000

15. In humans, what process must have occurred to obtain the cells at **U**?

A. Mitosis

B. Meiosis

C. Fertilization

D. Differentiation

Source: January 2000

Use the following information to answer the next question.

Phases of Mitosis

1. Anaphase
2. Metaphase
3. Prophase
4. Telophase

Numerical Response

2. The phases of mitosis, listed in the sequence in which they occur, are __3__ , __2__ , __1__ , and __4__ .
(Record your answer as a **four-digit** number.)

Source: January 2000

Use the following information to answer the next question.

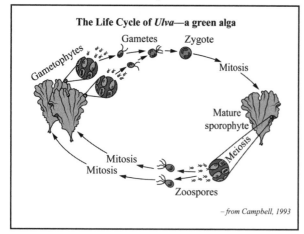

The Life Cycle of Ulva—a green alga

– from Campbell, 1993

16. Which structures in the life cycle of the *Ulva* are haploid (monoploid)?

A. Zoospores and the zygote

B. The sporophyte and the zygote

C. Zoospores and the gametophytes

D. The sporophyte and the gametophytes

Source: January 2000

Use the following information to answer the next three questions.

Investigators were interested in determining the role chromosomes play in the formation of the mitotic spindle. Using extracts of eggs from the African frog *Xenopus laevis*, they monitored spindle assembly in a test tube. The researchers replaced the chromosomes with beads coated with random sequences of DNA. The beads served as substitute genetic material, but centrosomes (centrioles) were absent. As well, a part of the centromere was missing.

Simplified Diagram of Normal Mitotic Cell

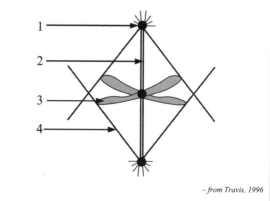

– from Travis, 1996

17. Which of the structures numbered above was replaced by the beads in the experimental setup?

A. 1

B. 2

C. 3

D. 4

Source: June 2000

Use the following additional information to answer the next question.

The investigators observed that the genetic material on the beads condensed and microtubules began to form. Within 90 minutes, the microtubules formed a spindle-like structure that lined up the beads along the centre of the cell.

–from Travis, 1996

18. Based on the results of this research, the structure or molecule that does **not** appear to be necessary for mitosis is

   A. DNA

   B. a spindle

   C. centrosomes

   D. microtubules

Source: June 2000

19. Similarities between mitosis and meiosis include the

   A. number of divisions

   B. number of cells produced

   C. location where each process occurs

   D. chromosome number of the original mother cell

Use the following information to answer the next question.

Species such as the lodgepole pine undergo both sexual and asexual lifecycles. Other species, such as humans, undergo only sexual reproduction.

20. Which of the following statements about sexual and asexual reproduction in lodgepole pines and humans is true?

   A. Both lodgepole pines and humans produce haploid gametophytes.

   B. Lodgepole pines produce diploid zygotes, humans do not.

   C. Both lodgepole pines and humans produce haploid gametes.

   D. Both lodgepole pines and humans produce diploid sporophyte.

Use the following information to answer the next two questions.

Amniocentesis is a common prenatal procedure used to obtain cells to test for genetic abnormalities that lead to disorders such as Down syndrome, cystic fibrosis, and hemophilia. The test is usually offered between the 15th and 18th weeks of pregnancy to women who have an increased risk of having children with genetic abnormalities.

21. Down syndrome is a trisomy disorder that can be caused by the presence of three copies of chromosome 21. Which of the following chromosome combinations identifies Down syndrome?

   A. 46 chromosomes consisting of 45 autosomes and 1 sex chromosome

   B. 46 chromosomes consisting of 44 autosomes and 2 sex chromosomes

   C. 47 chromosomes consisting of 45 autosomes and 2 sex chromosomes

   D. 47 chromosomes consisting of 44 autosomes and 3 sex chromosomes

Source: June 2000

22. A genetic abnormality such as Down syndrome can be diagnosed by using the cells obtained during amniocentesis to create a

A. karyotype

B. therapeutic gene

C. DNA fingerprint

D. recombinant vector

Source: June 2000

Use the following information to answer the next two questions.

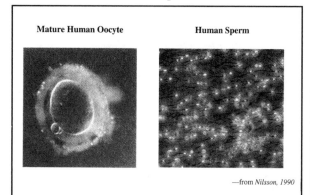

Mature Human Oocyte   **Human Sperm**

—from *Nilsson, 1990*

23. The difference in size between the human oocyte and sperm is **mostly** due to the

A. difference in magnification of the two photographs

B. distance that the sperm must travel in order to reach the oocyte

C. amount of cytoplasm present in the oocyte as compared with that in the sperm

D. number of chromosomes in the nucleus of the oocyte as compared with the number in the sperm

Source: January 2001

24. The nucleus of a human oocyte would normally be

A. diploid and contain 23 chromosomes

B. diploid and contain 46 chromosomes

C. haploid and contain 23 chromosomes

D. haploid and contain 46 chromosomes

Source: January 2001

Use the following information to answer the next question.

In garden peas, the allele for tall plant height (T) is dominant over the allele for short plant height (t), and the allele for axial flower position (A) is dominant over the allele for terminal flower position (a). The alleles for plant height and flower position assort independently.

25. A plant heterozygous for both traits was crossed with a plant homozygous recessive for both traits. What percentage of the offspring produced would be expected to display at least one of the dominant traits?

A. 25%

B. 50%

C. 75%

D. 100%

Source: June 1999

26. Alternate forms of the same gene are known as

A. alleles

B. gametes

C. genotypes

D. heterozygotes

Source: June 2001

Numerical Response

3. How many spermatids are produced by a primary spermatocyte following meiotic division?

_____

(Record your answer as a whole number.)

Use the following information to answer
the next question.

In the hypothetical pedigree below, shaded
individuals have sickle cell anemia and are
homozygous for the defective allele Hb^S.
The normal allele is Hb^A. Carriers of the Hb^S
allele are not identified in the pedigree.

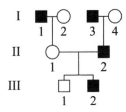

27. Individual III-1 has blood type A.
His genotype could be

A. $I^A i\ Hb^A Hb^S$

B. $I^A I^A\ Hb^S Hb^S$

C. $I^A I^B\ Hb^A Hb^S$

D. $I^A I^B\ Hb^A Hb^A$

Source: June 2001

28. Rosalind Franklin's X-ray diffraction study of
DNA helped to determine all of the following
facts except that

A. DNA is a helix

B. DNA is double stranded

C. the distance between DNA strands
is constant

D. DNA consists of the nitrogen bases
adenine, guanine, cytosine, and thymine

29. Which of the following rows correctly
matches a DNA triplet with its corresponding
mRNA codon, requested amino acid, and
tRNA anticodon?

Row	DNA triplet	mRNA codon	Amino acid	tRNA anti-codon
A.	TCG	AGC	Serine	UCG
B.	CAT	GUA	Valine	CAT
C.	GAT	CTA	Aspartate	GAU
D.	UGU	ACA	Threonine	UGU

30. Fraternal twins result from fertilization of

A. one oocyte by two spermatazoa

B. two oocytes by two spermatazoa

C. two oocytes by the same spermatazoan

D. one oocyte by one spermatazoan
following by splitting of the morula

Use the following information to answer
the next question.

The following DNA sequences were obtained
from four different species.

• Species W: TCCACTA

• Species X: ACTGGAT

• Species Y: TCATACC

• Species Z: CCTCGAG

31. Based on the given DNA sequence, which
two species are the **most closely** related?

A. Species W and Y

B. Species X and Z

C. Species W and Z

D. Species X and Y

Use the following information to answer the next question.

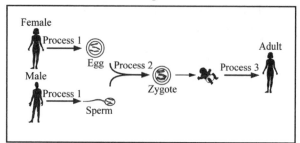

32. The activity that is associated with process 3 is
    A. division of diploid cells to produce haploid cells
    B. division of diploid cells to produce diploid cells
    C. halploid cells combine to form diploid cells
    D. halpoid cells combine to form haploid cells

Use the following information to answer the next question.

Events Involved in Translation

1. The ribosome reads the mRNA codon, GCU.

2. The tRNA carrying alanine enters the ribosome.

3. The tRNA-with a CGA anticodon is activated.

4. A peptide bond forms between alanine and the previous amino acid.

Numerical Response

4. The order of the given events in which they would occur during translation is ___, ___, ___, and ___.
(Record your answer as a **four-digit** number.)

Use the following information to answer the next question.

1. Complementary bases of sticky ends align.

2. Ligase is added to glue sticky ends together.

3. Both DNA samples are combined in a test tube.

4. A bacterial plasmid is opened using restriction enzyme.

5. Isolation of the human insulin gene using the same restriction enzyme.

Numerical Response

5. The order in which scientists would perform these steps to insert the human insulin gene into a bacterial genome is ___, ___, ___, ___, and ___.
(Record your answer as a five-digit number.)

Use the following information to answer the next four questions.

Two different genes control the expression of kernel colour in Mexican black corn: black pigment gene *B* and dotted pigment gene *D*. Gene *B* influences the expression of gene *D*. The dotted phenotype appears only when gene *B* is in the homozygous recessive state. A colourless variation occurs when both genes are homozygous recessive.

After pure-breeding black-pigmented plants were crossed with colourless plants, all of the offspring were black-pigmented.

– from Griffiths et al., 1993

33. The genotypes of the parents of these F$_1$ offspring could be
    A. *BBDD × bbdd*
    B. *BbDD × bbdd*
    C. *Bbdd × bbDD*
    D. *bbDD × Bbdd*

Source: June 2000

CHALLENGER QUESTION   51.3

34. Plants of the F_1 generation are suspected of being heterozygous for both genes. A test cross of colourless plants with the heterozygote plants should produce a phenotypic ratio in the offspring of

A. 1:0

B. 3:1

C. 2:1:1

D. 1:1:1:1

Source: June 2000

Numerical Response

6. What is the probability of dotted offspring being produced from the test cross described in the previous question?

_____

(Record your answer as a value from 0 and 1, rounded to **two decimal** places.)

Source: June 2000

7. If the total number of offspring produced in the test crosses was 1 024 plants, how many plants would you expect to be black-pigmented?

_____

(Record your answer as a **whole** number.)

Source: June 2000

Use the following information to answer the next two questions.

In humans, the allele for normal blood clotting, H, is dominant to the allele for hemophilia, h. The trait is X-linked.

35. A female hemophiliac marries a man who is not a hemophiliac. The row that indicates the probability of this couple having a child that is a hemophiliac and the sex that the child would be is

Row	Probability	Sex of Affected Child
A.	0.25	male
B.	0.25	either female or male
C.	0.50	male
D.	0.50	either male or female

Source: June 2000

Numerical Response

8. A woman who is not a hemophiliac has a father who is a hemophiliac. If this woman marries a man who is a hemophiliac, what is the probability of them having a hemophiliac son?

_____

(Record your answer as a value from 0 and 1, rounded to **two decimal** places.)

Source: June 2000

Use the following information to answer the next question.

A high percentage of purebred dogs have genetic defects. Some examples of these defects follow.

1. Hip dysplasia, a defect in the hip joints that can cripple a dog, occurs in 60% of golden retrievers.

2. Hereditary deafness, due to a recessive autosomal disorder, occurs in 30% of Dalmatians.

3. Retinal disease, which may cause blindness, occurs in 70% of collies.

4. Hemophilia, an X-linked recessive disorder, is common in Labrador retrievers. Dwarfism is also common in this breed of dog.

– from Lemonick, 1994.

A healthy female Labrador retriever has won several ribbons for her appearance in dog shows. She was mated with two healthy male Labrador retrievers. In the two litters produced, some of the offspring had hemophilia and others were normal.

CHALLENGER QUESTION   **55.4**

36. If the female is bred to one of her male offspring that does not have hemophilia, then the probability of the female offspring of this cross having hemophilia is

A. 0%

B. 25%

C. 75%

D. 100%

Source: January 2001

Use the following information to answer the next two questions.

Tay-Sachs disease is a hereditary disease that kills 1 in 360 000 individuals in the general population, but 1 in 4 800 among the Ashkenazi (Eastern European) Jews. The disease disrupts or halts proper formation of lysosomes and increases fat deposition around the nerve sheath. Individuals that are homozygous for the defective allele have Tay-Sachs disease and die at an early age. Studies suggest that heterozygous individuals have a higher survival rate against tuberculosis than the rest of the population. Biochemical tests can be done to determine if parents are carriers.

– from Cummings, 1994

37. What type of inheritance is demonstrated in Tay-Sachs disease?

A. Autosomal recessive

B. Autosomal dominant

C. Sex-linked recessive

D. Sex-linked dominant

Source: January 2001

Numerical Response

9. A young couple decided to have genetic screening done to determine if they were carriers of Tay-Sachs disease. If both individuals were carriers, what percentage of their offspring would be predicted to have protection from tuberculosis but not have Tay-Sachs disease?

_____%

(Record your answer as a **whole** number percentage.)

Source: January 2001

Use the following information to answer the next question.

Punnett Square for a Dihybrid Cross to Investigate Coat Colour in Mice

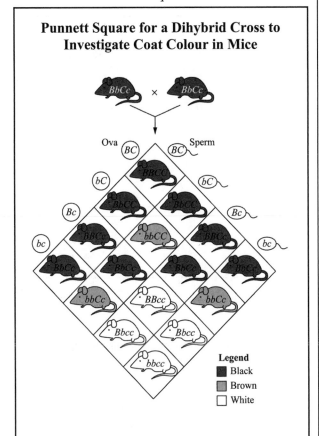

Coat colour in mice is controlled by the interaction of two genes. Three phenotypes result: black coat, brown coat, and white coat.

– *from Campbell, 1993*

38. In the dihybrid cross between the two black mice, the *C* allele codes for

A. black colour

B. brown colour

C. colour absent

D. colour present

Source: January 2001

ANSWERS AND SOLUTIONS—PRACTICE QUESTIONS

1. C	10. C	19. D	28. D	NR7. 512
2. B	11. B	20. C	29. A	35. C
NR1. 4231	12. D	21. C	30. B	NR8. 0.25
3. B	13. A	22. A	31. B	36. A
4. C	14. A	23. C	32. B	37. A
5. A	15. B	24. C	NR4. 1324	NR9. 50
6. D	NR2. 3231	25. C	NR5. 45312	38. D
7. C	16. C	26. A	33. A	
8. A	17. C	NR3. 4	34. C	
9. C	18. C	27. A	NR6. 0.25	

1. C

Human gametes contain one copy of every chromosome and have half the normal amount of genetic material as somatic (body) cells. Therefore, human gametes are haploid.

2. B

The sequence of nucleotides in one gene determines the order of amino acids that makes up one protein (for example, the enzyme lipase).

NR 1   4231

4—The DNA of a gene transcribes a strand of mRNA, which is moved from the nucleus to the ribosomes.

2—The ribosome reads the mRNA and causes the correct sequence of tRNAs to bind with the mRNA. Amino acids are attached to the tRNAs, so the amino acids are being transported to the ribosomes.

3—When the polypeptide is a functional enzyme, it is released from the ribosome.

1—The polypeptide is the sequence of amino acids. As it is formed, it folds itself into a specific shape that will make it a functional enzyme.

3. B

During genetic engineering, a section of bacterial DNA is opened using a restriction enzyme. Restriction enzymes can be thought of as being like scissors. The same restriction enzyme is used to cut out a gene that will be inserted into the bacterial DNA. Ligase enzymes are then used to fasten the pieces of DNA together. Ligase acts like a molecular glue.

4. C

When a protein is made, mRNA is translated by a ribosome into a chain of amino acid called a polypeptide. When the polypeptide coils, it becomes a functional protein, such as secretory component. DNA is replicated every time a cell undergoes mitosis, but this has nothing to do with the synthesis of a protein.

5. A

It seems that the faulty chloride-channel proteins result in a high level of chloride ions. These ions destroy the natural antibiotic defensin, which allows the bacteria to increase in number. This increase results in excessive mucin production. So, the original problem is that a faulty amino acid sequence is unable to correctly form the chloride-channel proteins.

6. D

The following diagram shows the structure of DNA and the molecules that make it up.

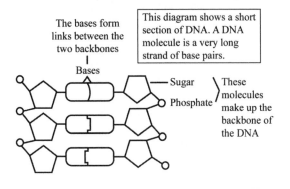

The bases form links between the two backbones

This diagram shows a short section of DNA. A DNA molecule is a very long strand of base pairs.

Bases

Sugar

Phosphate

These molecules make up the backbone of the DNA

7. C

DNA transcribes to mRNA in the following manner:

DNA base	Complementary mRNA base
Adenine	Uracil
Thymine	Adenine
Cytosine	Guanine
Guanine	Cytosine

It is important to remember that in RNA, uracil, not thymine, is opposite to adenine.

DNA template	mRNA nucleotides transcribed
Adenine 20%	Uracil 20%
Thymine 30%	Adenine 30%
Cytosine 10 %	Guanine 10%
Guanine 40%	Cytosine 40%

8. A

Recall protein synthesis. The sequence of production of CCK requires transcription of the appropriate DNA code into mRNA, then translation from mRNA to an amino acid sequence at the ribosomes. Replication refers to the creation of an identical set of DNA which occurs just prior to mitosis (and the first meiotic division). Transcription has to occur first. Recombination can refer to two processes. When crossing over occurs in prophase I of meiosis, and gene segments switch between homologous chromosomes, this is referred to as recombination because it creates new combinations of genes. Recombination can also refer to the cutting and pasting of a foreign gene into a genome.

9. C

Crossing over occurs during prophase I of meiosis. At that time, sections of homologous chromosomes are exchanged. Genes that are close together on a chromosome are likely to be exchanged together or remain together. Genes that are far apart are more likely to become separated during crossing over, with one gene being exchanged and the other being left behind. So, to answer this question, select the genes that are farthest apart. The genes *m* and *lc* are separated by 78 map units, so they have the greatest chance of being separated by crossing over.

10. C

The easiest way to determine the cross-over frequency between *O* and *S* is to construct a gene map. Cross-over frequency is an indication of the distance between genes.

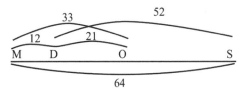

The cross-over frequency between *O* and *S* can be calculated by subtraction.
$64 - 21 - 12 = 31$.

The cross-over frequency between *O* and *S* is 31%.

11. B

The blastula is the product of repeated mitosis of the fertilized egg cell. At the blastula stage, all cells are essentially the same. Each cell can adopt any fate, so these cells are termed pleuripotent.

In order for cloning to work, the cell from which the nucleus is derived must be pleuripotent and not differentiated, otherwise the resulting developing embryo would be missing some cell types. The size of the nucleus in a living cell normally does not change during development. Genes are not removed or added from a cell during development. All cells have the same genes. What makes one cell different from another is the number and combination of genes that are expressed or silent. Cells in the early embryo undergo only mitosis, not meiosis. (Recall that meiosis is used for the production of gametes).

12. D

When the $p53$ gene was normal, the cells in the petri dish divided normally. That means the cells were not cancerous. This study was done with the cells from one kind of laboratory animal. The $p53$ gene did seem to prevent cancer under those conditions. However, to conclude that $p53$ prevents cancer in all mammals is not supported by this evidence.

13. A

Since the $p53$ gene stops cancer, it should not be removed from cells to stop uncontrolled division. From the information given, it appears that only one normal $p53$ allele is needed to control cell division, so if one functional $p53$ allele is inserted successfully into the cancer cells, uncontrolled cell division might be stopped.

14. A

Mitosis is the cellular process in which replicated chromosomes are distributed amongst two daughter nuclei to create two diploid ($2n$) nuclei. Meiosis results in n cells. Recombination usually refers to the process (during prophase I of meiosis) in which crossing over occurs to produce new gene combinations. Nondisjunction refers to an error in cell division in which daughter cells end up containing only one chromosome of a pair (monosomy) or three of a pair (trisomy). There is no reason to assume that nondisjunction has occurred between cell V and cells W and X.

15. B

The cells at U are n, or haploid, so they must have resulted from meiosis. Cells formed during mitosis are always diploid or $2n$. (The exception to this rule is in alternation of generation in plants where a haploid spore undergoes mitosis to form a multicellular haploid gametophyte). Fertilization, which is the fusion of two gametes, produces a $2n$ cell, and differentiation results in specialized $2n$ cells.

NR 2   3214

3—Prophase is the first phase in which chromosomes are visible. The nuclear membrane disappears as does the nucleolus. The two centrioles begin to form asters and migrate to the poles.

2—During metaphase, the spindle forms from the asters and the chromosomes line up on the cell equator.

1—During anaphase, chromatids are pulled by spindle fibres to opposite poles.

4—During telophase, chromosomes unwind (decondense) to become chromatin and the nuclear membrane and nucleolus reform.

16. C

Haploid cells containing unpaired chromosomes result from meiosis. Examples in humans are sperm and eggs. In the life cycle of *Ulva*, zoospores result from meiosis, so it can be concluded that zoospores are haploid.
The gametophyte develops from the zoospore through mitosis, which involves production of genetically identical cells, so the gametophyte must also be haploid.

17. C

Label 3 refers to the chromosome in the diagram and the text states that the beads coated with DNA replaced the chromosomes.

18. C

It appears from the description that centrosomes (centrioles) were not part of the experiment and therefore mitosis can progress normally.
The genetic material containing DNA formed the microtubules that became the spindle. All of these structures were needed for mitosis.

19. D

Cells entering mitosis or meiosis all begin as diploid ($2n$) cells. The chromosome number of the original mother cell is the same for cells undergoing either mitosis or meiosis.

Meiosis involves two consecutive divisions producing four cells, while mitosis only has one division, producing two cells. In terms of the location where the process occurs, meiosis never occurs in somatic (body) cells. Only primary spermatocytes or oocytes in the testes or ovaries can undergo meiosis. Mitosis occurs in all body cells, increasing the size of the organism and repairing injury. Mitosis does however occur briefly in the ovary and testes. Diploid germ cells (spermatogonial and oogonial cells) go through a period of mitosis to maximize the number of primary spermatocytes and oocytes that will enter meiosis.

20. C

The process of meiosis in both lodgepole pines and humans produces haploid gametes.

Gametophytes are only produced in lodgepole pines from spores through the process of mitosis. Both lodgepole pines and humans produce diploid zygotes through the process of fertilization. Diploid sporophytes are only produced in lodgepole pines through the process of mitosis.

21. C

Normally a person has 46 chromosomes, made up of 22 pairs of autosomes and one pair of sex chromosomes. Down syndrome is caused by trisomy 21. Autosome pair 21 has three copies rather than the normal two. In Down syndrome, the one pair of sex chromosomes is normal.

22. A

During amniocentesis, amniotic fluid is withdrawn. Inside the amniotic fluid, there are sloughed-off cells from the fetus. The cells can be grown in a petri dish and a karyotype created using the following process. A cell in the petri dish is photographed as it goes through metaphase of mitosis. The photo can be cut up to separate the chromosomes. Homologous pairs can be matched by their size, position of the centromere, and their banding pattern. Homologous pairs are pasted down side by side from the largest pair (pair 1) to the smallest pair (pair 22). The remaining two chromosomes are the sex chromosomes which form chromosome pair 23. This karyotype can be used to determine if a monosomy or trisomy has occurred, and will indicate the gender of the fetus. Individual genes cannot be seen.

23. C

The sperm is a means of delivering the genetic material to the oocyte. It has very little cytoplasm. The oocyte, on the other hand, contains the same amount of nuclear DNA as the sperm, but it also contains a large amount of cytoplasm. The large amount of cytoplasm is needed because the fertilized egg must have enough energy and cell organelles to survive through many cell divisions before it can start to gain energy from the mother's endometrium.

24. C

A mature human oocyte would be a secondary oocyte. A secondary oocyte has already completed meiosis I. During meiosis I, a homologous pair of chromosomes would have separated, one homologue entering each secondary oocyte. Because the secondary oocyte no longer has both homologues (maternal and paternal), the cell is considered to be haploid, with a chromosome number of 23. Note that each chromosome at this stage is actually two sister chromatids joined by a centromere. Because counting centromeres is a means of counting chromosomes, each pair of sister chromatids equals one chromosome.

25. C

A homozygous recessive plant can only produce the gamete *ta*. When crossed with a heterozygous plant, as shown in the Punnett square below, 50% of the offspring will display the tall trait and 50% will show the axial flower trait. Of the offspring, 75% show at least one of those two traits.

	TA	*Ta*	*tA*	*ta*
ta	*TtAa*	*Ttaa*	*ttAa*	*ttaa*
Displayed Traits	tall axial	tall terminal	short axial	short terminal

26. A

The term allele means a form of a gene. Sometimes when sources discuss ABO blood types, they will mention the type A gene or the type O gene, which is incorrect. It is correct to say that the gene for ABO blood types has three possible alleles: an I^A allele, an I^B allele, and an i allele. Type A, B, and O are phenotypes, not genotypes. Another example relates to the gene for height in pea plants: the height gene has a tall allele and a short allele. It is incorrect to say the tall gene and the short gene.

NR 3   4

Four spermatids are formed when a primary spermatocyte undergoes both divisions of meiosis. Spermatids are haploid (*n*).

27. A

Since III-1 has blood type A, he could have the genotype $I^A I^A$ or $I^A i$ for blood type. Since he has a father who has sickle cell anemia ($Hb^S Hb^S$) and a mother who does not ($Hb^A Hb^A$ or $Hb^A Hb^S$) and he himself does not have sickle cell anemia, he must have received the normal allele from his mother and the disease allele from his father, so his genotype is ($Hb^A Hb^S$). Only option **A** is an answer that has a possible blood type and is heterozygous for sickle cell anemia.

28. D

The fact that DNA consists of the nitrogenous bases adenine, guanine, cytosine, and thymine was known prior to the work of Franklin.

29. A

mRNA codons are complementary to DNA triplets. tRNA anticodons are complementary to mRNA codons. The requested amino acid is found using an mRNA Codon Translation Chart. The mRNA codons and tRNA anticodons will have U (uracil) instead of the T (thymine) found in DNA.

The row with serine is the only row with a sequence that follows the base pairing rules.

The row with valine has a thymine (T) in the tRNA anticodon, which is not possible because uracil (U) replaces T in RNA. The same is true for the mRNA codon in the row with aspartate. The row with threonine has uracil in the DNA molecule, which is not possible because thymine is present in DNA.

30. B

Fraternal twins are not identical. They may be of the same or different sex, and they are only as similar as any two siblings. They occur when two oocytes are ovulated. If each oocyte is fertilized by different sperm cells, two independent embryos form, each with its own placenta.

31. B

Species X and Z are the most closely related of the species given. They have DNA sequences that have 4 of 7 nucleotides in common.

Species X: A C T G G A T
Species Z: C C T C G A G

Species W: T C C A C T A
Species Y: T C A T A C C

Species W: T C C A C T A
Species Z: C C T C G A G

Species X: A C T G G A T
Species Y: T C A T A C C

32. B

The division of diploid cells to produce more diploid cells is growth, process 3. When haploid cells or sperm and eggs combine to form a diploid cell, this is fertilization, process 2.

In process 1, the male and female are producing gametes. The male and female consist of diploid cells. Their gametes are haploid.

NR 4   1324

Translation is the second phase of protein synthesis. The messenger RNA molecule (made in transcription) enters a ribosome. The ribosome translates mRNA codons into a request for a specific amino acid (step 1). Translation can be done using an mRNA translation chart.
Amino acids are located floating in the cytoplasm, attached to transfer RNA molecules. The ribosome must signal the correct tRNA molecule to bring in its amino acid. The tRNA molecule with the anticodon to the codon currently being read is activated (step 3) and signalled to enter the ribosome, bringing its attached amino acid with it (step 2). When the tRNA drops off its amino acid, a peptide bond will join it to any amino acids that have been brought in previously, continuing the synthesis of a polypeptide chain (step 4). Once the tRNA has dropped off its amino acid, it returns to the cytoplasm.

NR 5   45312

To insert the human insulin gene into a bacterial genome, the first step is to open up the DNA of the bacterial plasmid using a restriction enzyme (**4**). The insulin gene is also freed from its chromosome (**5**). The two sources of DNA are then brought together (**3**). The sticky ends of the unpaired bases will align complementarily with each other, splicing the new insulin gene into position in the bacterial plasmid (**1**). Ligase glues the sticky ends together so the splicing is permanent (**2**).
The plasmid is then reinserted into a bacterial cell. The ribosomes in the bacterial cell will translate the insulin gene, producing human insulin.
This process is referred to as recombination or transformation.

33. A

The colourless plant must be *bbdd*. Since the black-pigmented plants are pure-breeding, they are homozygous, *BB*. This is confirmed by the fact that all of the offspring were black. The offspring could all be *Bb* and appear black only if the black parent always gave a *B*. Hence, the black parent must have been *BB*. The dotted phenotype only appears if the individual is *bb*, so there will be no dotted offspring if the parents are *BBDD* and *bbdd*.

34. C

There will be 2 black, 1 dotted, 1 colourless, as shown below. The colourless individual (*bbdd*) can only produce the gamete *bd*. The heterozygote (*BbDd*) can produce the gametes *BD*, *Bd*, *bD*, and *bd*.

Parental Gametes	*BD*	*Bd*	*bD*	*bd*
bd	*BbDd*	*Bbdd*	*bbDd*	*bbdd*
Phenotype	black	black	dotted	colourless

NR 6   0.25

From the Punnett square for the previous question, dotted offspring occur 1 out of 4 times.

NR 7   512

If the test cross is between a heterozygote (*BbDd*) and a colourless plant (*bbdd*), 50% of the offspring will be black. See the Punnett square for question 34.
50% of 1 024 is 512.

35. C

Hemophilia is a sex-linked disorder in which the affected allele is on the X chromosome. If the woman has hemophilia, her genotype is $X^h X^h$. Since the man does not have hemophilia, his genotype is $X^H Y$. For all female children, his sperm contains the chromosome X^H. Therefore, none of his female children will have hemophilia, although they will all be carriers. For male children, his sperm contains the Y chromosome. Since the woman always provides an egg with the affected allele (X^h), all of the male children will have hemophilia.

NR 8   0.25

Since the woman's father is a hemophiliac but she is not, she must have the heterozygous genotype. The symbolic representation of the woman is $X^H X^h$ and that of the man she marries is $X^H Y$. A cross of $X^H X^h$ and $X^H Y$ results in a 50% chance that these parents will have a hemophiliac child. The probability that they will have a hemophiliac son is $0.50 \times 0.50 = 0.25$.

36. A

A Punnett square shows this cross. She is healthy but has had offspring with hemophilia, so she is a carrier. Her genotype is $X^H X^h$. The healthy male she is mated with has a genotype $X^H Y$.

Parental Gametes	X^H	X^h
X^H	$X^H X^H$	$X^H X^h$
Y	$X^H Y$	$X^h Y$

None of the female offspring will have hemophilia. However, half of the female offspring will be carriers.

37. A

Assume that the Tay-Sachs condition is autosomal, meaning the gene for it is on one of the first 22 pairs of chromosomes (the autosomes) and not on one of the sex chromosomes. If the disease were X-linked, males could not be heterozygous because the gene would be absent on the Y chromosome. Also, if it were X-linked recessive it would be far more common in males. Since individuals have to be homozygous for the defective allele to get Tay-Sachs and heterozygous individuals do not have the disease, inheritance is autosomal recessive.

NR 9   50

Since both parents are carriers, they are both heterozygous for this autosomal recessive trait. Give them the genotypes *Tt* × *Tt*.

	T	t
T	TT	Tt
t	Tt	tt

The individuals with protection from tuberculosis are those that are heterozygous; that is, 50% of the offspring.

38. D

All of the offspring that have at least one uppercase *C* have coat colour, either brown or black. If the offspring have two recessive lower case *c*'s, then the offspring has no coat colour. A gene that controls the expression of another gene—whether or not the coat colour gene is expressed—is called an epistatic gene.

UNIT TEST—CELL DIVISION, GENETICS, AND MOLECULAR BIOLOGY

CHALLENGER QUESTION   **47.8**

1. As cells age, there is an increase in DNA damage and a decrease in DNA repair processes. The **initial** effect is

   A. a decrease in ATP synthesis

   B. an increase of cancerous cells

   C. the production of altered proteins

   D. the production of abnormal mRNA

   Source: January 1999

---

2. During spermatogenesis, the cell division stage that separates the X and Y chromosomes is called the

   A. mitosis of spermatogonia

   B. mitosis of primary spermatocytes

   C. meiosis of primary spermatocytes

   D. meiosis of secondary spermatocytes

3. DNA is structurally different from RNA in that DNA

   A. contains uracil and is composed of double strands whereas RNA contains thymine and is composed of single strands

   B. contains adenine and is composed of single strands whereas RNA contains uracil and is composed of double strands

   C. contains guanine and is composed of single strands whereas RNA contains adenine and is composed of double strands

   D. contains thymine and is composed of double strands whereas RNA contains uracil and is composed of single strands

4. Analysis of a DNA sample showed that 15% of the nitrogen-base molecules present were adenine molecules. This sample would likely contain

   A. 15% thymine

   B. 15% uracil

   C. 85% thymine

   D. 85% uracil

Use the following information to answer the next question.

In DNA replication, the two strands of the double helix separate and a new strand forms along each old one. Each new DNA molecule has one old and one new strand.

---

5. Which of the following rows gives the name of an old DNA strand, the site of DNA replication, and the term that describes replication?

Row	Name of Old Strand	Site	Term
A.	template	nucleus	semi-conservative
B.	template	cytoplasm	conservative
C.	active	nucleus	semi-conservative
D.	active	cytoplasm	conservative

Use the following information to answer the next question.

Studies showed that the phase that involves pulling chromosomes to the two poles of mitotic cells can be delayed for up to 4.5 h by pulling a chromosome out of line from the centre of the cell.

–from Travis, 1996

6. The phase that is delayed and the phase in which the chromosomes line up at the equator are, respectively,

   A. telophase and anaphase

   B. metaphase and prophase

   C. interphase and telophase

   D. anaphase and metaphase

   Source: June 2000

7. During human gametogenesis, the respective number of ova and spermatozoa produced from 100 secondary oocytes and 100 secondary spermatocytes is

   A. 50 ova and 100 spermatozoa

   B. 100 ova and 100 spermatozoa

   C. 100 ova and 200 spermatozoa

   D. 200 ova and 200 spermatozoa

8. Which of the following characteristics describes a similarity between the processes of spermatogenesis and oogenesis?

   A. Size of cells produced

   B. Location where the processes occur

   C. Number of functional gametes produced

   D. Chromosome number in cells produced

Use the following information to answer the next question.

The use of marker genes and the analysis of crossover frequencies of genes have enabled geneticists to map the location of many genes on human chromosomes. Blue colour vision and blue colourblindness (tritanopia) are controlled by a gene on chromosome 7. The gene for the production of trypsin (a digestive enzyme) and the gene responsible for cystic fibrosis are also found on chromosome 7. Some crossover frequencies of these genes are shown below.

Pair of Genes	Crossover Frequency
Marker gene–cystic fibrosis	18%
Marker gene–tritanopia	13%
Cystic fibrosis–trypsin	6%
Trypsin–tritanopia	1%

–from Rimoin et al., 1996

9. Which of the following gene maps shows the correct sequence of these genes on chromosome 7?

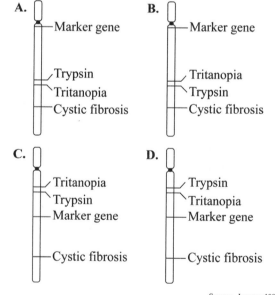

Source: January 1999

Use the following information to answer the next question.

A bacterium has been found that produces a form of plastic called polyhydroxybutyrate (PHB). Genes from this bacterium have been transferred into a weed called *Arabidopsis thaliana*. These weeds now produce a biodegradable plastic.

– from Poirier, et al., 1997

---

10. The technology of transferring a gene from a bacterium into a green plant is based on the principle that

   A. all genes carry the same genetic information

   B. all genes have the same basic chemical components

   C. the genotypes of the bacterium and green plant are the same

   D. the phenotype of an organism is not altered when one gene is exchanged for another

   Source: June 1999

11. Which of the following statements about asexual reproduction is **false**?

   A. Offspring produced by asexual reproduction have the same number of chromosomes as the parent.

   B. Offspring produced by asexual reproduction are genetically different from the parent.

   C. Offspring are produced by mitosis in asexual reproduction.

   D. Bacteria and yeast reproduce asexually.

12. During mitosis, the chromosomes

   A. are located at the cell equator during prophase

   B. are located at the cell equator during telophase

   C. move toward the poles of the cell during anaphase

   D. move toward the poles of the cell during metaphase

   Source: January 1999

13. One aspect of meiosis that is different from mitosis is that normally, by the end of meiosis, there are

   A. two diploid cells

   B. four diploid cells

   C. two haploid cells

   D. four haploid cells

   Source: January 1999

14. According to Watson and Crick's model of DNA, which of the following rows correctly depicts base pairing in DNA?

Row	Strand 1	Strand 2
A.	ATCGCAT	TAGCGAT
B.	ATCGCAT	TAGCGTA
C.	ATCGCAT	UAGCGUA
D.	AGCTCAT	UCGACUT

Use the following information to answer the next question.

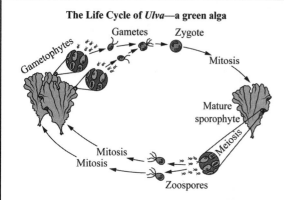

The Life Cycle of *Ulva*—a green alga

Gametes Zygote

Gametophytes

Mitosis

Mature sporophyte

Meiosis

Mitosis
Mitosis

Zoospores

–from Campbell, 1993

Source: January 2000

The green algae species *Ulva spinulosa* has a haploid chromosome number of 8.

Numerical Response

1. For each of the following structures, enter the appropriate chromosome number.

_____ _____ _____

Zoospores Gametophytes Sporophyte

(Record your answer as a **four-digit** number.)

Use the following information to answer the next question

A cross of **Drosophila** was made to determine the relative distance between gene A and gene B. The following progeny phenotypic ratios were observed.

Phenotype	Number of Progeny
Parental phenotype 1	145
Parental phenotype 2	45
Recombinant phenotype 1	5
Recombinant phenotype 2	5

Numerical Response

2. According to this information, what is the relative distance between gene A and gene B?
Answer: _____
(Record your answer as a whole number.)

Use the following information to answer the next question.

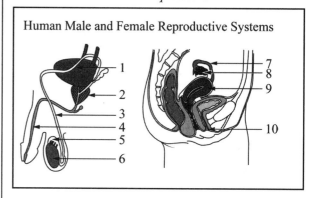

Human Male and Female Reproductive Systems

1
2
3
4
5
6

7
8
9

10

15. Meiosis occurs in the male and female structures numbered, respectively,

A. 6 and 9

B. 6 and 8

C. 5 and 9

D. 5 and 8

Source: June 1999

16. Certain disorders result if an extra chromosome is present in all nucleated cells of the body (trisomy) or if a chromosome is missing from all nucleated cells of the body (monosomy). These disorders arise because of nondisjunction, a malfunction that occurs during

A. DNA replication

B. RNA transcription

C. telophase of mitosis

D. anaphase of meiosis

Source: January 1999

Use the following information to answer the next two questions.

In pea plants, tall (T) is dominant over short (t), and round seed (R) is dominant over wrinkled seed (r). The Punnett square below shows a cross between a heterozygous tall-heterozygous round-seed pea plant and a short-heterozygous round-seed pea plant. Different types of offspring are represented by numbers.

	TR	*Tr*	*tR*	*tr*
tR	1	2	3	4
tr	5	6	7	8

17. Which two types of offspring are pure breeding for both plant height and seed shape?

   A. 1 and 6

   B. 2 and 5

   C. 3 and 8

   D. 4 and 7

   Source: January 1999

18. Which two types of offspring, when crossed, could be expected to produce a population in which 50% of their offspring would be tall and 100% would produce round seeds?

   A. 1 and 8

   B. 2 and 4

   C. 3 and 7

   D. 5 and 6

   Source: January 1999

Use the following information to answer the next question

1. Gyrase uncoils DNA

2. Template strands are exposed

3. DNA ligase joins fragments together

4. DNA helicase breaks hydrogen bonds between bases

5. DNA polymerase escorts complementary nucleotides into position opposite template strands

Numerical Response

3. List the above events in the order in which they occur in DNA replication.

   ___, ___, ___, ___, and ___.

   (Record your answer as a **five-digit** number.)

Use the following information to answer the next question.

F_1 Blood Type Cross	
$I^A I^B$	$I^A i$
$I^A I^B$	$I^A i$

19. The genotypes of the parents to whom this Punnett square applies are

   A. heterozygous B and homozygous A

   B. heterozygous O and homozygous A

   C. homozygous B and heterozygous A

   D. heterozygous B and heterozygous A

Use the following information to answer the next question.

There is some evidence that two genes, $BRCA_1$ and $BARD_1$, suppress certain types of cancer. If either of these genes is defective, ovarian and/or breast tumours may develop. The mutant form of $BARD_1$ is considered to be recessive.

Studies have shown that the proteins encoded by the $BRCA_1$ and $BARD_1$ genes differ from one another, but that they probably link up. In doing so, they somehow prevent tumour growth. The abnormal genes may result in the production of faulty proteins that will not link.

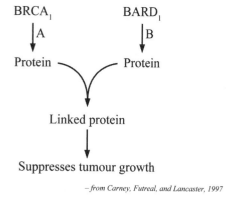

– *from Carney, Futreal, and Lancaster, 1997*

20. Four individuals undergo carrier screening for the two genes, and the following results are observed. Which of the following individuals is **most likely** to develop ovarian and/or breast tumours?

Row	Individual	$BRCA_1$	$BARD_1$
A.	1	heterozygous	homozygous dominant
B.	2	heterozygous	heterozygous
C.	3	homozygous normal	homozygous normal
D.	4	heterozygous	homozygous recessive

Source: June 1999

21. Species with more DNA base sequences in common are **more closely** related because

A. mutations are less likely to occur in species with a common ancestor

B. similar mutations occurred in both species since the time they diverged from a common ancestor

C. less time has passed for mutations to accumulate since the two species diverged from a common ancestor

D. more time has lapsed between the time mutations occurred and the time the two species diverged from a common ancestor.

Use the following information to answer the next question.

Piebald spotting is a rare human disorder. Although this disorder occurs in all races, piebald spotting is most obvious in people with dark skin. A dominant allele appears to interfere with the migration of pigment-producing cells; thus, patches of skin and hair lack pigment, allowing "spots" to form.

Pedigree Chart for Piebald Spotting

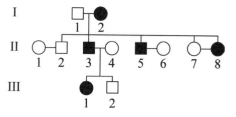

Numerical Response

4. What is the probability that any offspring produced by individuals II-5 and II-6 would have piebald spotting?
(Record your answer as a value from 0 to 1 rounded to **two decimal** places.)

Source: June 1999

Use the following information to answer the next question

A protein fragment contains the following amino-acid sequence:
Pro-Arg-Tyr-Cys-Gly-Ala

Numerical Response

5. How many nucleotides are present in the DNA sequence that encodes for the given protein fragment?

_____

(Record your answer as a **two-digit** number.)

Use the following information to answer the next two questions.

Cystic fibrosis is the most common genetic disorder among Caucasians, affecting one in 2 000 Caucasian children. The cystic fibrosis allele results in the production of sticky mucus in several structures, including the lungs and exocrine glands. Two parents who are unaffected by the disorder can have a child with the disorder.

A girl and both her parents are unaffected by the disease. However, her sister is affected by cystic fibrosis.

Numerical Response

6. These parents, who are unaffected by cystic fibrosis, are planning to have another child. What is the percentage probability that their next child will be affected by cystic fibrosis?
___%
(Record your answer as a whole number percentage.)

Source: January 1999

22. Which of the following terms **best** describes the allele for cystic fibrosis?

A. X-linked   B. Recessive

C. Dominant   D. Codominant

Source: January 1999

Use the following information to answer the next question.

Hypophosphatemia is one of the few genetic diseases caused by a dominant allele carried on the X chromosome. It causes a severe deficiency of phosphate ions in the blood.

– from Rimoin, et al., 1996

CHALLENGER QUESTION	57.0

23. A female with hypophosphatemia whose father had the disease but whose mother did not will likely transmit the disorder to

A. her sons only

B. her sons and her daughters equally

C. all of her daughters but none of her sons

D. all of her daughters and 50% of her sons

Source: January 1999

Use the following information to answer the next question

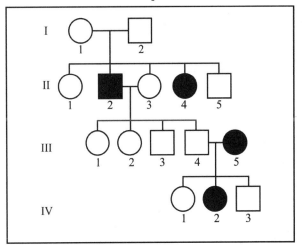

Numerical Response

7. If individual II-4 and a man with the same genotype have children, what is the percentage probability of having an affected child?

_____%
(Record your answer as a **whole** number percentage.)

Use the following information to answer the next question.

Scientists believe that a mutant form of an autosomal gene called BRCA$_1$ may be associated with 5% to 10% of all cases of breast cancer. About 80% of women who inherit the gene in its defective form are likely to develop a cancerous breast tumour. Men who carry the faulty gene rarely develop breast cancer, but they may pass the gene to their offspring.

A couple have two children, a girl and a boy. The mother has a single mutant gene for breast cancer; the father is not a carrier of the mutant BRCA$_1$ gene.

– from Richards, 1996

CHALLENGER QUESTION	57.0

24. What is the probability that their daughter has inherited the mutant BRCA$_1$ gene?

A. 75%

B. 50%

C. 25%

D. 0%

Source: June 1999

Use the following information to answer the next question.

"Alligator men" or "fish women" were exhibited for their physical abnormalities in fairs or circuses earlier this century.
These people probably suffered from X-linked ichthyosis, which produces symmetric dark scales on the body. The disease occurs in 1 in 6 000 males and much more rarely in females. Ichthyosis is likely a recessive disorder.

– from Cummings, 1994

Numerical Response

8. If an "alligator man" were to marry a woman homozygous for the normal condition, what is the percentage probability that their children would have ichthyosis?
_____%
(Record your answer as a **whole** number percentage.)

Source: June 1999

ANSWERS AND SOLUTIONS—UNIT TEST

1. D	8. D	NR1. 8816	19. A	23. B
2. C	9. A	NR2. 5	20. D	NR7. 100
3. D	10. B	15. B	21. C	24. B
4. A	11. B	16. D	NR4. 0.50	NR8. 0
5. A	12. C	17. C	NR5. 18	
6. D	13. D	18. A	NR6. 25	
7. C	14. B	NR3. 14253	22. B	

1. D

The role of DNA is to inform cell ribosomes how to build specific proteins. An increase in DNA damage will ultimately lead to the production of altered proteins. However, the question asks for the initial effect of DNA damage. During protein synthesis DNA triplets are first transcribed into mRNA codons.

2. C

The question refers to spermatogenesis which is the process of meiosis that produces haploid sperm. When the primary spermatocyte begins the prophase I, a tetrad forms consisting of the sex chromosomes and their sister chromatids (XXYY). In anaphase I, the homologues separate, XX enters one secondary spermatocyte, and YY enters the other.

3. D

Recall that DNA is a double-stranded helix composed of a sugar-phosphate backbone and the four nitrogenous bases A (adenine), T (thymine), G (guanine), and C (cytosine). RNA is single-stranded and is also made of a sugar-phosphate backbone and four nitrogen bases A, U (uracil), G, and C.

4. A

Chargaff's rule states that the amount of adenine in DNA equals the amount of thymine, and the amount of guanine equals the amount of cytosine. Therefore **A** is correct. Uracil is not found in DNA, only in RNA.

5. A

The goal of DNA replication is to produce two molecules of DNA that are exactly the same as the original molecule. All DNA (except for mitochondrial DNA) exists inside the nucleus. First, DNA is unzipped to expose the two old or template strands. A new complementary strand is built opposite each template strand. Each of the two new complementary strands and the template strands opposite them are fused together to create a new DNA molecule that is half old and half new. For this reason replication is considered to be semi-conservative.

6. D

Prophase and metaphase have been completed if the chromosomes are at the centre of the cell. According to the studies referred to, if a chromosome is pulled out of line, the phase in which chromosomes move to the poles will be delayed. The phases that are delayed are the phases that follow metaphase. Anaphase is the phase that involves pulling the chromosomes to the poles. Following anaphase is telophase, which cannot occur until anaphase has been completed.

7. C

After one meiotic division in spermatogenesis, two equal sized secondary spermatocytes exist. Each of these enter the second meiotic division, dividing to produce two spermatids. In oogenesis, unequal cytokinesis in meiosis I results in one large secondary oocyte and one tiny polar body that is reabsorbed. When a secondary oocyte undergoes meiosis II, unequal cytokinesis occurs again forming a large ootid and another tiny polar body which is reabsorbed. Therefore, one secondary oocyte results in one ovum. One secondary spermatocyte results in two spermatozoa.

8. D

The purpose of meiosis, whether it occurs in males or females, is to create cells that have half the normal diploid number of chromosomes. Therefore, the products of both oogenesis and spermatogenesis have the haploid (n) chromosome number. The size and number of functional gametes is not the same in that one large ovum is produced and four tiny sperm cells are produced. The site is also different in that oogenesis occurs in the ovary and spermatogenesis in the testis.

9. A

Recall that crossover frequency is directly proportional to the map distances between genes that are linked on the same chromosome. Using the frequencies provided in the preamble, the following map can be generated:

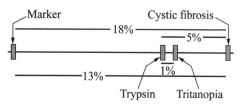

This order and arrangement of genes on the map corresponds to the chromosome shown in **A**.

10. B

DNA is essentially the same in all living organisms and is composed of the four nitrogenous bases, phosphates and the sugar deoxyribose. The similarity in the structure of DNA makes DNA quite transferable between organisms of different kinds. Genes do not all carry the same information, genotypes of bacteria and plants are not the same, and the phenotype of an organism may be altered if one gene is exchanged for another.

11. B

Asexual reproduction produces offspring that are identical to the parent cell. Only one set of genes is involved. Mitosis is therefore a form of asexual reproduction, as is binary fission which occurs in prokaryotes.

12. C

During prophase, the chromosomes are located in the cell nucleus. The nuclear membrane dissolves and the chromosomes begin to move to the cell equator. During metaphase, chromosomes line up along the cell equator. During anaphase, spindle fibres pull the chromosomes toward the poles of the cell. During telophase, chromosomes reach the poles of the cell and a new nuclear membrane forms.

13. D

Whereas the purpose of mitosis is to produce more cells identical to the parent cell (diploid parent cell gives rise to diploid daughter cells), the purpose of meiosis is to create haploid cells (gametes) from a normal diploid cell. Meiosis occurs in two divisions: (meiosis I and II) that result in a final product of four haploid cells.

14. B

In DNA, adenine must bond with thymine, and guanine must bond with cytosine.

The last two bases of the two strands in row A are not complementary. Uracil (U) is not present in DNA, only in RNA.

NR 1   8816

The zoospores are formed by meiosis and are haploid. They contain one copy of every chromosome; therefore, there are 8 chromosomes. The gametophytes are formed by mitosis of the spores, which maintains the chromosome number of 8. The sporophyte is formed by fertilization of the haploid gametes. Therefore, the sporophyte contains two copies of every chromosome, and the chromosome number is 16.

NR 2   5

The recombinants are offspring that have phenotypes that are possible only because of crossing over (synapsis). According to the list, recombinants make up 5% of the offspring. The recombination frequency is equal to the cross over percentage, which is equal to the map distance between the two genes.

$$\text{Cross over percentage} = \frac{\text{Number of recombinants}}{\text{Total number of offspring}} \times 100\%$$
$$= \frac{5+5}{200} \times 100\%$$
$$= 5\%$$
$$= 5 \text{ map units}$$

15. B

Meiosis occurs in the testis in males and in the ovaries in females. Reject **A** because number 9 indicates the uterus. Reject **C** because of the epididymis, where sperm mature and are stored, and the uterus. Reject **D** because number 5 indicates the epididymis. In this question, knowledge of the structure and function of the male and female reproductive organs is needed.

16. D

Nondisjunction occurs during an abnormal meiosis and describes the failure of homologous chromosomes to separate during anaphase I, or sister chromatids to separate during anaphase II. An error in either DNA replication or RNA transcription would probably, at most, alter one gene or gene product, not an entire chromosome. A mistake during mitosis would not result in nondisjunction. Probably, a mistake at telophase of mitosis would result in loss of one or both of the daughter cells following mitosis.

17. C

	TR	*Tr*	*tR*	*tr*
tR	TtRR 1	TtRr 2	ttRR 3	ttRr 4
tr	TtRr 5	Ttrr 6	ttRr 7	ttrr 8

Pure-breeding individuals are homozygous for the respective allele and can donate only one kind of allele to the offspring in their gametes.
Therefore, in order for a plant to be pure breeding for both plant height and seed shape, the plant must be homozygous for both the height and shape alleles. Only individuals 3 and 8 are homozygous for both genes

18. A

Determine the genotypes required in the parents separately for each allele. For 100% of the offspring to have round seeds, one parent must have two *R* alleles. Therefore, 2 and 4 as well as 5 and 6 can be ruled out because the genotypes for the round alleles do not include 1 parent with two RR alleles. You can then test the remaining choices (1 and 8; 3 and 7) for the tall phenotype.

- 1 and 8 $\Rightarrow$ $Tt \times tt \rightarrow$ progeny:

  $\frac{1}{2}$ Tt (tall), $\frac{1}{2}$ tt (short)

- 3 and 7 $\Rightarrow$ $tt \times tt \rightarrow$ progeny: all tt (short)

By process of elimination it can be determined that from the choices given, only a cross between 1 and 8 would result in progeny with 100% round seeds and 50% tall.

NR 3   14253

In DNA replication, the process begins with DNA helicase uncoiling the DNA molecule (**1**) and then breaking the hydrogen bonds between the bases (**4**). Gyrase unzips the DNA into two template strands (**2**). DNA polymerase escorts DNA nucleotides into position opposite the exposed template bases, creating a complementary strand from each template strand (**5**). The template and complementary strand are glued together by ligase, forming two complete and identical molecules of DNA (**3**).

19. A

Note that the blood type gene has three possible alleles: I^A, I^B, and i. There are numerous ways to solve this question, the easiest is by the process of elimination. Note that because I^A and I^B are codominant, the heterozygous B genotype is not $I^B I^A$, but $I^B i$. A cross of $I^A I^A \times I^B i$ will produce the right answer.

	I^A	I^A
I^B	$I^A I^B$	$I^A I^B$
i	$I^A i$	$I^A i$

Alternative **B** contains heterozygous O, which does not exist. A cross of homozygous B with heterozygous A will produce some $I^B i$ offspring, so reject **C**. A cross of heterozygous B with heterozygous A will produce $I^A I^B$, $I^A i$, $I^B i$, and ii offspring, so reject **D**.

20. D

Let A represent the BRCA allele and B represent the BARD allele. Look for the occurrence of any recessive genes. Individual 4 is heterozygous for BRCA (Aa) and homozygous recessive for BARD (bb). This individual has three out of four recessive genes and so is most likely to develop tumours. Individual 1 has only one recessive gene: Aa, BB. Individual 2 has two recessive genes: Aa, Bb. Individual 3 has no recessive genes: AA, BB.

21. C

Species that are distantly related have genomes that are less similar than species that are closely related. The genomes of two species with a recent common ancestor would have had less time for genomic mutations to accumulate; therefore the genomes will show fewer differences.

NR 4   0.50

Piebald spotting is caused by a dominant allele (P), so individual II-6 is homozygous recessive (pp). The question requires knowledge of the genotype of individual II-5. Look at the parents I-1 and I-2. Parent I-1 is obviously pp. Parent I-2 carries at least one dominant allele: PP or Pp. Both individuals II-2 and II-7 are pp, so they must have received a recessive allele from each parent; therefore, parent I-2 must be heterozygous (Pp). This means that individual II-5 must also be heterozygous (Pp).

	P	p
p	Pp	pp
p	Pp	pp

The Punnett square indicates the possible offspring of II-5 (Pp) and II-6 (pp). A dominant allele will be found in half of their offspring, or 50%. The probability that any offspring will have piebald spotting is 0.50.

NR 5   18

The protein fragment consists of 6 amino acids. Each triplet (group of three bases) on the DNA molecule codes for one amino acid. One nucleotide consists of a base, a sugar, and a phosphate. Because 18 bases are needed to code for the protein segment, 18 nucleotides are needed as well.

AN EDUCATION THAT WILL PREPARE YOU FOR FUTURE CHALLENGES

Like whether to study in Manoa or Maui

STUDENTS FROM OTHER ENGINEERING SCHOOLS MIGHT ASK YOU FOR MONEY

If you win a Schulich engineering scholarship, you probably won't mind. After all, they're Canada's largest engineering scholarships. This year we'll offer 10 awards of up to $56,800 each, and 16 more of up to $34,200 each. You could receive one for your academic excellence, or for your entrepreneurial or volunteer achievement. Learn more at **schulich.ucalgary.ca**

SCHULICH
School of Engineering

UNIVERSITY OF
CALGARY

LEVIATHANIC, MASSIVE, GOOGOLPLEXIAN, GINORMOUS, WHOPPING, BROBDINGNAGIAN, HUGANTIC, COLOSSAL...

Just some of the words used to describe these scholarships

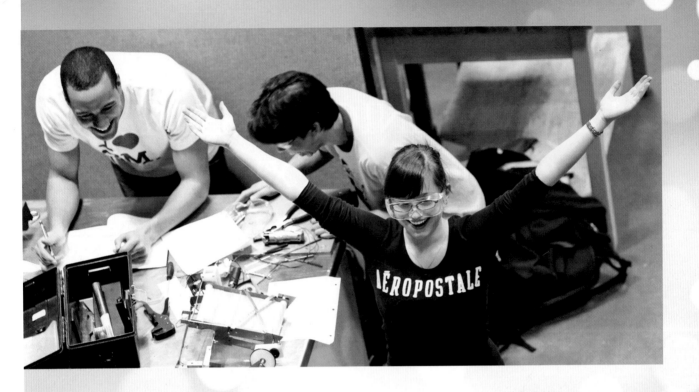

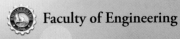

GET READY.

Did you know police officers use physics?

A truck with a mass of 1200 kg was involved in a collision with another vehicle. Based on the damage done to the two vehicles and the distance that they travelled after the collision, it was determined that the truck was going 39.0 km/h at the moment of the collision. The truck left skid marks 10.0 m long, from the point where the driver applied the breaks to the point of impact. From the road conditions and type of tire, it is estimated that the force of friction slowing the vehicle was 9840 N.

If the speed limit was 50.0 km/h, was the truck speeding prior to hitting the breaks?

Find the solution at
JoinEPS.ca/physics

Want a career that's always in demand?

Get a career in accounting or finance

All businesses rely on people who understand numbers.
No matter what the business, people who understand the numbers are always in demand. When you earn a CGA designation, there's no telling where you can go! Earning it will get you to that next career level – opening doors and offering you an ever-expanding range of career options. In fact, there are thousands of CGAs in hundreds of industries all over the world making great money and leading balanced lives. When you're ready, you can even apply some of your university or college credits toward your CGA designation. It's like being ahead before you begin. Put your future in focus.

cga-alberta.org

CGA® CERTIFIED GENERAL ACCOUNTANTS

We see more than numbers.

LEADERSHIP | FLEXIBILITY | PORTABILITY | GROWTH | SUCCESS

NR 6   25

Because unaffected parents can have an affected child, we know that the CF allele is recessive. It is autosomal, not X-linked recessive, because the father would have had to have been affected if it were X-linked. Because neither parent is affected, they could each be *NN* or *Nn*. However, since one of their children is affected (*nn*), both parents must be heterozygous (*Nn*).

	N	*n*
N	*NN*	*Nn*
n	*Nn*	*nn*

Two heterozygous parents have a 25% probability of producing a non-carrier child (*NN*), a 50% probability of producing a carrier (*Nn*), and a 25% probability of producing an affected child (*nn*). Therefore, 25% is correct.

22. B

If two normal parents can have a child affected with cystic fibrosis, then both parents must be carriers of the alleles that cause cystic fibrosis.

If *CF* = normal and *cf* = cystic fibrosis allele:

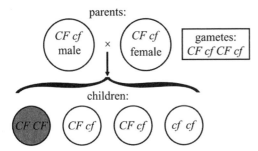

If both parents can be carriers of the cystic fibrosis allele but not have the disease themselves, then the disease allele must be recessive. If the disease were X-linked (meaning the gene for cystic fibrosis is on the X chromosome), the father would have been affected by the disease, whether the allele was recessive or dominant. That is, knowing that males have only one X chromosome, the father's genotype would have been $X^{cf}Y$, and he would have had the disease. Both parents as carriers would also have been affected with the disease if the allele were either dominant or codominant. Recall that codominant means that both alleles are expressed.

For example, roan cattle have both red and white hairs (giving them the "roan" color) due to expression of the allele coding for red hair as well as expression of the allele coding for white hair.

23. B

A breeding diagram is constructed below using the information provided.

X^H—hypophosphatemia allele
X^h—normal allele

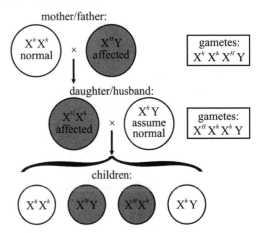

- 50% are affected with hypophosphatemia, 50% are normal

- 50% of her sons and 50% of her daughters are expected to have the disease

NR 7   100

The darkened individuals have the condition and are therefore said to be affected. Begin by determining what kind of inheritance is occurring—autosomal recessive, autosomal dominant, X-linked recessive, or X-linked dominant. Neither parent in generation I is affected, yet some of the children (generation II) are affected. Therefore, the condition is recessive, and each parent has donated one recessive allele to II-4. To determine if the condition is autosomal recessive or X-linked recessive, consider the frequency of the condition in the two genders. More females have the condition, which often indicates that the condition is X-linked dominant. This cannot be the case here because the condition is recessive.

If the condition were X-linked recessive, many more males with the condition would be seen. Also, individual II-4 would have received one recessive allele from her father's X chromosome, and she would have to have the recessive phenotype. Therefore, it can be assumed that the condition is autosomal recessive. Individual II-4 is homozygous recessive, having received one recessive allele from each unaffected parent. If she has children with a man with the same genotype, there is 100% certainty that all offspring will be homozygous recessive and therefore affected.

24. B

The inheritance of the condition is autosomal because no reference is made to an unequal distribution of the allele between genders. The $BRCA_1$ allele is recessive because of the reference to a carrier. One cannot be a hidden carrier of a dominant allele because a dominant allele always expresses. If the mother has a single mutant gene, she is a heterozygous. The father is not a carrier, so he is homozygous dominant.

	B	*B*
B	*BB*	*BB*
b	*Bb*	*Bb*

A basic Punnett square shows that 50% of the offspring have a recessive gene and 50% are homozygous dominant (unaffected). Since the condition is autosomal, there is no difference in the proportion of males or females that inherit the condition. There is a 50% chance their daughters will inherit the gene, just as there is a 50% chance that their sons will inherit the gene.

Ichthyosis is an X-Slinked recessive disorder. An alligator man would be X^iY. The homozygous normal woman would be X^IX^I. The Punnet square indicates that none of the children will have the condition, although both females will be carriers of the recessive allele.

	X^I	X^I
X^i	X^IX^i	X^IX^i
Y	X^IY	X^IY

Population and Community Dynamics

POPULATION AND COMMUNITY DYNAMICS

<table>
<tr><td colspan="5" align="center">**Table of Correlations**</td></tr>
<tr><td>**Specific Expectation**</td><td>**Practice Questions**</td><td>**Unit Test Questions**</td><td>**Practice Test 1**</td><td>**Practice Test 2**</td></tr>
<tr><td colspan="5">*Students will:*</td></tr>
<tr><td colspan="5">*Describe a community as a composite of populations in which individuals contribute to a gene pool that can change over time.*</td></tr>
<tr><td>30-D1.1K   describe the Hardy–Weinberg principle and explain its significance in gene-pool stability and non-equilibrium values</td><td>2</td><td></td><td></td><td></td></tr>
<tr><td>30-D1.2K   describe the factors that cause the diversity in the gene pool to change; i.e., natural selection, genetic drift, gene flow, nonrandom mating, bottleneck effect, founder effect, migration, mutation</td><td>1, 5</td><td>4</td><td>45</td><td>33, 36, 38, 48</td></tr>
<tr><td>30-D1.3K   apply, quantitatively, the Hardy–Weinberg principle to observed and published data to determine allele and genotype frequencies, using $p + q = 1$ and $p^2 + q^2 = 1$</td><td>3, 4, NR1, NR2, NR3</td><td>1, NR1, NR2</td><td>NR8</td><td>47, NR8</td></tr>
<tr><td>30-D1.4K   describe the molecular basis of gene-pool change and the significance of these changes over time; i.e., mutations and natural selection</td><td>6</td><td>2, 3</td><td></td><td></td></tr>
<tr><td colspan="5">*Explain the interaction of individuals in a population with one another and with members of other populations.*</td></tr>
<tr><td>30-D2.1K   describe the basis of species interactions and symbiotic relationships and describe the influence of these interactions on population changes; i.e., predator—prey and producer—consumer relationships, commensalism, mutualism, parasitism, interspecific and intraspecific competition</td><td>7, 16</td><td>5, 8</td><td>43</td><td></td></tr>
<tr><td>30-D2.2K   explain the role of defence mechanisms in predation and competition</td><td>8</td><td>9</td><td></td><td>44</td></tr>
<tr><td>30-D2.3K   explain how mixtures of populations that define communities may change over time or remain as a climax community; i.e., primary succession, secondary succession</td><td>14</td><td>10</td><td>44, 46</td><td></td></tr>
</table>

Explain, in quantitative terms, the change in populations over time.				
30-D3.1K describe and explain, quantitatively, the factors that influence population growth; i.e., mortality, natality, emigration, immigration, change in population size	13, NR4	11, NR3	47	46
30-D3.2K describe the growth of populations in terms of the mathematical relationship among carrying capacity, biotic potential, environmental resistance and the number of individuals in the population; i.e., growth rate, per capita growth rate, and population density	15, 9	7, NR4	NR7	NR7
30-D3.3K explain the different population growth patterns; i.e., logistic growth pattern (S-shaped curve) and exponential growth pattern (J-shaped curve), open and closed populations	10, 11	6	48	
30-D3.4K describe the characteristics and reproductive strategies of r-selected and K-selected organisms	12	12		41, 45

POPULATION AND COMMUNITY DYNAMICS

30-D1.1K describe the Hardy–Weinberg principle and explain its significance in population gene-pool stability and non-equilibrium values

30-D1.2K describe the factors that cause the diversity in the gene-pool to change; i.e. natural selection, genetic drift, gene flow, non-random mating, bottleneck effect, founder effect, migration, mutation

30-D1.3K apply, quantitatively, the Hardy–Weinberg principle to observed and published data to determine allele and genotype frequencies, using the related equations

30-D1.4K describe the molecular basis of gene-pool change and the significance of these changes over time; i.e. mutations and natural selection

HARDY–WEINBERG PRINCIPLE

Early in the 1900s, Hardy and Weinberg determined that the frequency of an allele in a population's gene pool would not change from generation to generation. They referred to this as Hardy–Weinberg equilibrium. The following factors can cause a population to no longer be in Hardy–Weinberg equilibrium:

- Gene flow—migration of an allele into or out of the population by immigration or emigration

- Non-random mating—certain genotypes are more likely to leave offspring

- Very small population—a limited population can result in a gene disappearing or increasing in frequency by chance (genetic drift)

- Mutation—a new mutation or a change in the mutation rate occurs

- Natural selection—certain genes are favoured for survival

When the frequency of the alleles in a population's gene pool changes over time, the population is evolving (microevolution).

The bottleneck and founder effect are two important examples of genetic drift. A bottleneck effect occurs when an extreme event rapidly reduces a population in size. If the genetic make-up of the survivor population is not typical of the original population then genetic drift has occurred. A founder effect occurs when a small group of non-typical individuals form a colony that leaves the original group. Because the colony is genetically different than the original group, genetic drift has occurred.

The problem of drug resistance demonstrates how natural selection changes gene pools and promotes evolution. Widespread and improper use of herbicides that kill weeds, and antibiotics that fight bacteria, have selected for resistant alleles. Because the frequency of resistant alleles is increasing, these populations of weeds and bacteria are evolving.

Hardy and Weinberg provided two equations that are used to calculate the frequency of alleles and genotypes within a population.

- $p + q = 1.0$, where p is the proportion of dominant alleles in the gene pool, q is the proportion of recessive alleles in the gene pool, and 1.0 represents all the alleles for this trait in the gene pool (Each individual contributes two alleles to the gene pool).

- $p^2 + 2pq + q^2 = 1.0$, where p^2 is the proportion of homozygous dominant individuals in the population (e.g., BB), $2pq$ is the proportion of heterozygote individuals (e.g., Bb), q^2 is the proportion of homozygous recessive individuals (e.g., bb), and 1.0 represents all of the individuals of the population.

Practice Questions: 1, 2, 3, 4, 5, 6, NR1, NR2, NR3

30-D2.1K describe the basis of species interactions and symbiotic relationships and describe the influence of these interactions on population changes; i.e., predator–prey relationships, mimicry, protective coloration, toxins, etc.

30-D2.2K explain the role of defence mechanisms in predation and competition

30-D2.3K explain how mixtures of populations that define communities may change over time or remain as a climax community; i.e., primary succession, secondary succession

30-D3.1K describe and explain, quantitatively, factors that influence population growth; i.e., mortality, natality, immigration, emigration, change in population size

30-D3.2K describe the growth of populations in terms of the mathematical relationship among carrying capacity, biotic potential, and the number of individuals in the population; i.e., growth rate, per capita growth rate, population density

30-D3.3K explain the different population growth patterns; i.e., logistic growth pattern (S-shaped curve) and exponential growth pattern (J-shaped curve), open and closed populations

30-D3.4K describe the characteristics and reproductive strategies of r-selected and K-selected organisms.

POPULATION GROWTH

Natality, mortality, immigration, and emigration are population determiners. The change in population size (ΔN) is positive if natality and immigration exceed mortality and emigration. The growth rate (*gr*) of a population is determined by $\dfrac{\Delta N}{\Delta t}$. Per capita growth rate is determined by dividing the change in population size by the original size of the population: $cgr = \dfrac{\Delta N}{N}$.

The density of a population is a better indicator of how much competition exists in a community: $Dp = \dfrac{N}{A}$ or $\dfrac{N}{V}$. Competition for scarce resources (such as food, territory, water, nesting sites, and shelter) increases with population size. Interspecific competition refers to the competition for resources between two different species (e.g., between moose and elk). Intraspecific competition involves competition for resources between members of the same species.

RELATIONSHIPS

Organisms have relationships with organisms of other species that co-exist in their communities. Mutualism is a relationship in which both organisms benefit. Commensalism is a relationship in which one organism benefits and the other is unaffected. Parasitism is a relationship in which one organism benefits and the other is harmed.

In predator-prey relationships, the sizes of both populations fluctuate together. When the number of prey animals increases, the number of predators also increases. The predators keep the prey population from getting too large, and they also keep the prey population healthy by feeding on the old, weak, and sick. The number of prey organisms always exceeds the number of predators. Adaptations that increase the competitiveness of both predators and prey are mimicry, protective colouration, and the ability to produce toxins.

REPRODUCTIVE STRATEGIES

The biotic potential (r) is the maximum rate at which a population can increase its size. All the limiting factors that keep a population from growing at its biotic potential are referred to as factors of environmental resistance. The carrying capacity (K) of a population is the maximum number of individuals that an environment can support. Limiting factors keep populations from reproducing at their biotic potentials and keep population numbers below the environment's carrying capacity. Limiting factors can also increase or decrease the carrying capacity of an environment. A limiting factor is density-dependent if the limiting factor has a greater impact when population density is greater. Density-dependent limiting factors tend to be biotic, and they include factors such as food supply, predators, or disease. Density-independent limiting factors have the same effect on population regardless of the density of the population. These factors tend to be abiotic, and they include factors such as climate or natural disasters.

Reproductive strategies are mechanisms by which species maximize their reproduction while using the minimum amount of energy. The two reproductive strategies are the r-selected strategy and the K-selected strategy.

An r-selected population relies on its high biotic potential to succeed. r-selected species are typically small, quick-growing organisms that produce a large number of offspring, provide little parental care, and have few offspring that survive to reach adulthood. The population size can increase rapidly but will fluctuate wildly and can crash as quickly as it rises. The size of an r-selected population tends to be controlled by density-independent factors, such as climate. If an r-selected population is released into a new area, the population size will increase rapidly, exceed the carrying capacity, and then crash. When plotted on a graph, the growth of an r-selected population shows a J-shaped curve. Populations of r-selected species tend to go through boom and bust cycles with exponential growth followed by rapid die-off.

A K-selected species relies on a high survival rate to maintain a population size that stays close to the environment's carrying capacity. These species are usually large, slow-growing organisms. They produce few offspring, but the parents nurture and educate their young, so there is high survival into adulthood. Their population numbers increase slowly but remain more stable. If a K-selected population is released into a new area, it will increase slowly to a population size known as the carrying capacity, (K) after which it levels off. When plotted on a graph, this situation shows an S-shaped or logistic growth curve. K-selected populations tend to be controlled by density-dependent factors such as food, water, territory, disease, and accumulation of wastes. Collectively, these density-dependent factors make up the environmental resistance that limits the population's size to carrying capacity.

SUCCESSION

The changes in the types of plant and animal species in a community over time is called succession. Each stage in the succession changes the environment slightly so it is less likely to survive and another stage is more likely to survive. For example, grass grows well on bare ground because it germinates well in hot, dry conditions. However, the growth of grass shades and cools the soil, so grass is less likely to germinate there; other species, such as thistles, are more likely to germinate in the cool soil.

If the succession begins from bare rock then it is a primary succession. The pioneer species in primary succession would be lichen and moss. Secondary succession begins from established soil. The pioneer species in secondary succession are usually grasses. Over time, the pioneer species will be replaced by other species, until a community of climax plant species for the region is finally reached. Plant successions are also accompanied by successions of animals that depend on the plants, which will form a part of the climax community.

Practice Questions: 7, 8, 9, 10, 11, 12, 13, 14, 15, NR4, 16

PRACTICE QUESTIONS—POPULATION AND COMMUNITY DYNAMICS

Use the following information to answer the next question.

The Amish are a group of people who rarely marry outside of their community. In one group of Amish in Ohio, the incidence of cystic fibrosis was 19 in 10 816 live births. A second group of Amish in Ohio had no affected individuals in 4 448 live births. No members of either group are closely related. These data illustrate what population geneticists refer to as the "founder effect."

from Klinger, 1983

CHALLENGER QUESTION   58.7

1. The "founder effect" seems to occur when

    A. a non-representative subpopulation forms the basis for an isolated population

    B. the environment favours one population over another population

    C. individuals from one population move into and become part of a second population

    D. two similar populations exist in the same community without being reduced in number

    Source: January 2000

Use the following information to answer the next question.

Polydactyly, the anatomical abnormality of having more than the normal number of digits (fingers or toes), is a common physical abnormality in cats. While normal cats have 5 toes on their front paws, polydactyl cats can have as many as 7 toes. This mutation is found on the dominant allele, which means that all cats that are heterozygous (Pp) as well as those that are homozygous for the dominant allele (PP) will exhibit polydactyly.

Numerical Response

1. If the dominant allele frequency is 0.02, what percentage of cats will be polydactyl?
___%
(Record your answer as the nearest whole number percentage.)

2. The Hardy–Weinberg principle allows population geneticists to quantify a population's

    A. genotype

    B. gene pool

    C. biotic potential

    D. carrying capacity

Use the following information to answer the next question.

Pendred syndrome is a genetically inherited, autosomal, recessive disease that causes deafness and decreases thyroid gland function. The syndrome is thought to affect 0.008% to 0.01% of the population and accounts for about 10% of all reported cases of deafness.

Numerical Response

2. If 0.008% of people have Pendred syndrome, what is the frequency of the abnormal allele that causes this syndrome?

_____

(Round and record your answer to **three decimal** places.)

Use the following information to answer the next question.

Cystic fibrosis is the most common fatal genetic disease in North America today. This disease is the result of an autosomal, recessive trait that is known to cause severe breathing difficulties. It is estimated that approximately 0.03% of children born in Canada have cystic fibrosis, while approximately 4% of the population are carriers.

3. What is the allele frequency of the abnormal allele that causes cystic fibrosis?
   A. 0.98
   B. 0.8
   C. 0.2
   D. 0.02

Use the following information to answer the next question.

Hitchhiker's thumb is a recessive trait that causes the thumb, when extended, to appear to bend backward toward the nail. Having this trait appears to have no effect on the function of the thumb. In Scotland, 14% of people surveyed appeared to have hitchhiker's thumb, while in Canada, 23% of people surveyed exhibited this trait.

4. What is the allele frequency of the abnormal (hitchhiker's) thumb allele in Scotland?
   A. 0.4
   B. 0.6
   C. 0.5
   D. 0.7

Use the following information to answer the next question.

Albinism is a genetic trait inherited through recessive alleles. Those who are homozygous for the albinism allele (*aa*) lack pigment in the eyes, skin, and hair. This condition is known to affect rodents, fish, reptiles, amphibians, and humans. In human populations, 1 in 17 000 people exhibit characteristics of albinism.

Numerical Response

3. What percentage of the population of humans are carriers for albinism?

_____

(Round and record your answer to **two decimal** places.)

Use the following information to answer the next question.

Tay-Sachs disease is a hereditary disease that kills 1 in 360 000 individuals in the general population, but 1 in 4 800 among the Ashkenazi (Eastern European) Jews. The disease disrupts or halts proper formation of lysosomes and increases fat deposition around the nerve sheath. Individuals that are homozygous for the defective allele have Tay-Sachs disease and die at an early age. Studies suggest that heterozygous individuals have a higher survival rate against tuberculosis than the rest of the population. Biochemical tests can be done to determine if parents are carriers.

– from Cummings, 1994

5. If tuberculosis regained its former role as one of the world's deadliest diseases, then the frequency of the Tay-Sachs allele over time would

A. decrease because of a decreased selective advantage

B. remain the same as a result of Hardy–Weinberg equilibrium

C. decrease because of an increased selective advantage

D. increase because of an increased selective advantage

Source: January 2001

Use the following information to answer the next question.

The Northern Elephant Seal is one of two species of elephant seal, both of which are characterized by a great elephant-like snout. In the 1700s, these seals were hunted for their blubber and their population was reduced to approximately 30 individuals by the 1890s. Since gaining protection by the Mexican government in the late 20th century, the population of the Northern Elephant Seal has grown, with current estimates of over 100 000 individuals.

6. In the Northern Elephant Seal population, genetic variation has likely

A. decreased as a result of random breeding

B. increased as a result of the founder effect

C. decreased as a result of the bottleneck effect

D. not changed as a result of the Hardy–Weinberg equilibrium

Use the following information to answer the next question.

	Initial population (N)	Births (n)	Deaths (m)	Immi-grants (i)	Emi-grants (e)
I	445	35	25	10	5
II	785	50	75	5	20
III	230	5	10	60	10
IV	500	30	15	20	35

Numerical Response

4. According to the information in the table, which population has experienced a decline, and by how much has its population declined?
Population ___, with a decline of – _____.
(Record your answer as a **three-digit** number.)

Use the following information to answer the next question.

The spermicide nonoxynol-9, which is applied to contraceptive devices such as diaphragms and condoms, has been linked to increased urinary tract infections in women. Although nonoxynol-9 is helpful in fighting the herpes virus and HIV, it also destroys beneficial bacteria (lactobacilli) that moderate the acidity of a woman's vagina. As a woman's vagina and external genitalia become more acidic, another bacterium, *Escherichia coli* (*E. coli*), increases in number and invades her urethra. This overpopulation of *E. coli* causes a bladder infection.

– from Vergano, 1996

7. Which of the following rows identifies the relationships described above between the human female, lactobacilli, and *E. coli*?

Row	Human female/ lactobacilli	Human female/ *E. coli*	Lactobacilli/ *E. coli*
A.	parasitic	mutualistic	interspecific competition
B.	mutualistic	mutualistic	interspecific competition
C.	mutualistic	parasitic	interspecific competition
D.	parasitic	parasitic	interspecific competition

Source: January 2000

Use the following information to answer the next question.

In areas where moose and caribou share habitat, they are both preyed upon by wolves. The population cycle of the moose is affected by the presence of a second prey species, the caribou.

– from Mech, 1996

8. A reasonable prediction based on these predator–prey relationships is that

   A. predator species would not show population changes caused by density-dependent factors

   B. an area would have the same carrying capacity for moose as it has for caribou, even though each species has different food preferences

   C. wolf and prey populations would decline as the same diseases spread through the three populations

   D. low numbers of caribou would cause wolf starvation if the moose population was also low

Source: January 2000

Use the following information to answer the next question.

Many elk live in and around an 80 km^2 area that includes the Jasper town site.

9. The elk population of this area at the beginning of a study year was 500. If there were 35 births and 5 deaths throughout the year, what was the per capita growth rate for the elk population during that year?

   A. 0.03

   B. 0.06

   C. 6

   D. 30

Source: January 2000

Use the following information to answer the next two questions.

A group of ecologists has studied the Jasper National Park animal populations and gathered data related to the growth of these populations.

J- and S-Shaped Growth Curves of Theoretical Populations

– from Levine and Miller, 1991

10. Ecological data gathered over a 20-year period indicate that the elk population fluctuates around the level marked **I** on the graph. The biotic factors that keep this population stabilized are

A. density dependent

B. density independent

C. independent of natality and mortality

D. independent of emigration and immigration

Source: January 2000

11. The level marked **I** on the graph represents the effect of factors such as climate, nutrients, soils, and water on the size of the elk population. A term to describe this section of the growth curve is

A. lag phase

B. biotic potential

C. climax community

D. carrying capacity

Source: January 2000

Use the following information to answer the next question.

The 42 000 wild horses and donkeys that live in the American West are reproducing at such a high rate that they could severely damage range lands in the future. In an effort to prevent overpopulation, some mares (females) are rounded up and injected with porcine zona pellucida (PZP), a long-lasting contraceptive. U.S. Food and Drug Administration guidelines prohibit the use of PZP until after a wild mare has had at least one successful pregnancy.

– from McInnis, 1996

12. Wild horses are considered to be a relatively *K*-selected species; however, one characteristic exhibited by these wild horses that is similar to an *r*-selected species is

A. their large size

B. their relatively long lifespan

C. their relatively high reproductive potential

D. the large amount of parental care devoted to their offspring

Source: June 2000

Use the following information to answer the next two questions.

The location of the Sonoran Desert results in unique climatic conditions. It has a warmer average temperature, less frequent frosts, and more rainfall than other deserts. This unique climate results in more diversity in the organisms that occupy this particular desert.

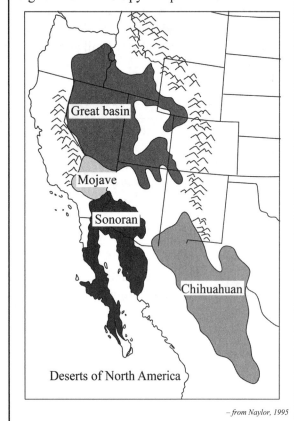

Great basin

Mojave

Sonoran

Chihuahuan

Deserts of North America

– from Naylor, 1995

13. The factors that contribute most to the relatively great diversity of organisms in the Sonoran Desert as compared with that in other deserts are

A. biotic factors that increase the biotic potential

B. abiotic factors that reduce reproductive isolation

C. abiotic factors that reduce environmental resistance

D. biotic factors that increase the carrying capacity of the area

Source: January 2001

14. In the Sonoran Desert, all the populations of all the organisms occupying that desert represent

A. a habitat

B. a community

C. a geographic range

D. an ecological niche

Source: January 2001

Use the following information to answer the next question.

In Canada, to manage the harvest of fish, government departments issue quotas based on population estimates. Problems in salmon and cod fisheries have drawn attention to problems in the calculation of the estimates. Quotas based on these estimates have led to overharvesting and have driven the cod fishery into disaster.

15. The Atlantic cod moratorium was a government-enforced period of no fishing. The original two-year moratorium was extended. Which of the following measures would be **most useful** when predicting the size of the cod population two years in the future?

A. Cod lifespan and natality rate

B. Cod biotic potential and future fishing quotas

C. Migration patterns and predator population size

D. Present population size and present population growth rate

Source: January 2001

Use the following information to answer the next question.

The red-winged blackbird's adaptability has allowed it to become one of the most abundant birds in North America.

A Study of a Red-Winged Blackbird Nesting Site

The initial population of red-winged blackbirds was 208.

	End of Year 1	End of Year 2
Births	22	43
Deaths	4	7
Birds entering area	0	2
Birds leaving area	2	5

---

16. Gause's principle states that when two different populations occupy the same ecological niche, one of the populations will be eliminated. Both the mallard duck and the red-winged blackbird occupy wetland areas. The mallard duck and the red-winged blackbird can live in the same habitat because there is

A. little intraspecific competition for food and breeding areas

B. little interspecific competition for food and breeding areas

C. significant intraspecific competition for food and breeding areas

D. significant interspecific competition for food and breeding areas

Source: January 2001

ANSWERS AND SOLUTIONS—PRACTICE QUESTIONS

1. A	3. D	6. C	9. B	13. C
NR1. 4	4. A	NR4. 240	10. A	14. B
2. B	NR3. 0.02	7. C	11. D	15. D
NR2. 0.009	5. B	8. D	12. C	16. B

1. A

The two populations of Amish are genetically different, since one population contains the cystic fibrosis gene and the other does not. As a result, at least one of the populations is non-representative of all Amish. It is an isolated population, since none of its members are closely related to the other population. The founder effect involves a small number of individuals beginning a new population. Their small gene pool may be different from the gene pool of the larger population that the founding individuals came from.

NR 1   4

Use the Hardy–Weinberg allele equation.
$p + q = 1$

If $p = 0.02$, then $q = 1 - 0.02 = 0.98$.

Now, use the Hardy–Weinberg genotype equation that deals with the frequency of individuals with different genotypes.
$p^2 + 2pq + q^2 = 1$

Homozygous dominant cats with polydactyly are symbolized as p^2. Heterozygous cats with polydactyly are symbolized as $2pq$. Therefore, the total frequency of polydactyl cats would be $p^2 + 2pq$.

$$p^2 = (0.02)^2$$
$$= 0.0004$$
$$2pq = 2(0.02)(0.98)$$
$$= 0.0392$$
$$p^2 + 2pq = 0.0004 + 0.0392$$
$$= 0.0396 \text{ or } 3.96\%$$

Therefore, approximately 4% of the cat population will be polydactyl.

2. B

The Hardy–Weinberg principle allows population geneticists to quantify a gene pool, which is the genetic information of an entire population. Using the Hardy–Weinberg equations, researchers can calculate allele or genotype frequencies.

NR 2   0.009

The information states that 0.008% of the population has Pendred syndrome. These people are homozygous recessive for Pendred (pp). The Hardy–Weinberg symbol that stands for the frequency of homozygous individuals in the population is q^2. Solve for the frequency of the recessive allele in the gene pool, which is symbolized as q.

$$f(pp) = q^2$$
$$= 0.008\% \text{ or } 0.000\ 08$$

Therefore, the frequency for a single abnormal allele (q) can be determined.

$$\sqrt{q^2} = \sqrt{0.000\ 08}$$
$$= 0.009$$

3. D

The information states that 0.03%, or 0.0003, of the population is homozygous recessive (cc) for cystic fibrosis. The frequency of individuals with the homozygous recessive genotype is symbolized as q^2. Solve for the frequency of the recessive allele in the gene pool, symbolized as q.

$$q^2 = 0.0003$$

Therefore, $q = \sqrt{q^2}$
$$= \sqrt{0.0003}$$
$$= 0.02$$

This means that of the alleles in the gene pool, only 2% are recessive.

4. A

In Scotland, 14% of the people surveyed were homozygous for the recessive gene (*hh*). Apply the Hardy–Weinberg genotype frequency equation $p^2 + 2pq + q^2 = 1$.

$f(hh) = q^2 = 14\%$ or 0.14

Therefore, the frequency for a single allele

$h = q$
$\quad = \sqrt{q^2}$
$\quad = \sqrt{0.14}$
$\quad = 0.4$

NR 3   0.02

The frequency of homozygous recessive genotype is $\dfrac{1}{17\ 000} = 0.00006$. The symbol for this is q^2.

Solve for the frequency of individuals that are heterozygous, or carriers, symbolized by $2pq$. Use the Hardy–Weinberg equations.

$p^2 + 2pq + q^2 = 1$
$\qquad\quad p + q = 1$

The frequency of homozygous recessive is $q^2 = f(aa) = 1 \div 17000 = 0.00006$.

Therefore, $q = \sqrt{0.00006} = 0.008$.

Now, using the allele frequency formula $p + q = 1$, determine the dominant allele frequency, where

$p = 1 - q$
$\quad = 1 - 0.008$
$\quad = 0.992$

Carriers of albinism are heterozygous (*Aa*); therefore, the genotype frequency is $2pq = 2(0.992)(0.008) = 0.02$. This means 2% of the population are carriers.

5. B

If tuberculosis regained its former role as a deadly disease, people would die from it. It appears from the reading that individuals that are heterozygous for Tay-Sachs are less likely to die from tuberculosis, so heterozygous individuals are more likely to survive tuberculosis and pass their genes on to the next generation. Therefore, the frequency of the Tay-Sachs allele, if it became advantageous, would be likely to increase.

6. C

When the Northern Elephant Seal was hunted to near extinction in the 19th century, the population was reduced to a small number of individuals, significantly decreasing the gene pool. A sudden population decrease that results in lower genetic variation is called the bottleneck effect.
The founder effect refers to a small group of individuals leaving one population to start another. Random breeding would not decrease genetic variation, and the conditions of Hardy–Weinberg equilibrium are not being met.

NR 4   240

Change in population is equal to natality and immigration minus mortality and emigration. When calculating change in population size, it is advisable to provide a positive or negative sign to indicate if the population is increasing or decreasing.

$\Delta N = [(n) + (i)] - [(m) + (e)]$

Therefore, population 1 has increased by 15 individuals, population 2 has decreased by 40 individuals, 3 has increased by 45 individuals, and 4 has maintained the same population size. The ΔN for population 2 is –40.

7. C

A mutualistic relationship is one in which both organisms are helped. The human female is protected from *E. coli*, and the lactobaccili are provided with the habitat they require. A parasitic relationship is one in which one organism benefits and the other is harmed. *E. coli* gains that habitat it needs, but the human female gets an infection. Interspecific competition involves competition between organisms of different species. In this case, both lactobaccili and *E. coli* are competing for the same habitat.

8. D

This is the most reasonable answer. If both the caribou population and the moose population were low, the wolves would probably face a shortage of food.

A is not correct because all populations change as a result of density-dependent factors.

B is not correct. Since moose and caribou do not share the same niche (that is, they have different specific requirements), the area's carrying capacity for the two animals would differ.

C is not correct because wolves, moose, and caribou are quite different animals and it is unlikely that there are many diseases that they all share.

9. B

Per capita growth rate is determined by dividing the change in number of organisms (+30) by the original number of organisms (500)

$$cgr = \frac{\Delta N}{N}$$
$$= \frac{30}{500}$$
$$= 0.06$$

10. A

Some of the biotic factors that keep the population stabilized are food supply, predators, diseases, competition between the elk, and competition between elk and other species. These are all density-dependent factors. That is, the larger the elk population is, the more these biotic factors limit the elk population.

11. D

Carrying capacity refers to the number of organisms that an area can support.

A. Lag phase refers to the time just prior to a rapid increase in population size.

B. Biotic potential means the maximum rate at which the population can increase if environmental conditions are perfect.

C. A climax community is a community in which successional changes are no longer occurring. This community is dominated by one species.

12. C

K-selected species tend to be large organisms, have a long life span, and devote a large amount of parental care for their few offspring. It is *r*-selected species that tend to have a high reproductive potential.

13. C

More diversity of organisms suggests that this is a favourable environment for many organisms. A very harsh environment such as Antarctica could be expected to have little diversity of organisms. Abiotic factors are non-living factors such as temperature, rainfall, sunlight, and wind speed. If abiotic factors are harsh, many species of organisms could not survive in the habitat. It seems that in the Sonoran Desert, abiotic factors are favourable. The environmental resistance is the sum of all the factors that restrict a population from thriving. The environmental resistance must be reduced in the Sonoran Desert if so many types of organisms can live there.

14. B

A population is all the organisms of one species that live and interact in one area. A community is defined as all the populations of organisms that live and interact in a particular area. An ecosystem is a community as well as its physical environment.

15. D

Natality (birth) rate and biotic potential (maximum reproductive rate) are important to population size but only when compared with mortality (death) rate, along with immigration and emigration. To predict the size of the population in the future, it is most useful to know the size of the population now and how fast the population is growing. Population growth rate is a sum of natality rate, mortality rate, immigration, and emigration.

16. B

Gause's principle states that two populations cannot both occupy the same niche and both survive there. The niche is more than just where the animals live. It includes what they eat, who their predators are, what kind of diseases affect them, and their nesting sites. It appears that although the blackbirds and mallards both live in wetlands, they do not occupy *exactly* the same niche. There is little competition between them for such things as food and breeding areas. Intraspecific competition means competition between members of the same species and interspecific competition is between members of different species, such as between blackbirds and mallards.

UNIT TEST—POPULATION AND COMMUNITY DYNAMICS

Use the following information to answer the next question.

Sickle cell anemia is caused by the sickle cell allele (Hb^S) of a gene that contributes to hemoglobin (Hb) production. The abnormal hemoglobin (hemoglobin-S) produced causes red blood cells to become deformed and block capillaries. Tissue damage results. Affected individuals homozygous for the sickle cell gene rarely survive to reproductive age. Heterozygous individuals produce both normal hemoglobin and a small percentage of hemoglobin-S. These individuals are more resistant to malaria than individuals who are homozygous for the allele for normal hemoglobin (Hb^A). Their red blood cells are prone to sickling when there is a deficiency of oxygen.

The malaria-causing microorganism *Plasmodium falciparum* is injected by mosquitoes into the bloodstream of humans. Historically, the frequency of the Hb^S allele in Africa relates directly to the presence of malaria-causing organisms. In western Africa, the frequency of the Hb^S allele in the gene pool is 0.15. In central Africa, the frequency is 0.10, and in southern Africa, the frequency is 0.05.

1. What is the frequency of the Hb^A allele in the human gene pool in western Africa?

   A. 0.72

   B. 0.85

   C. 0.90

   D. 0.95

Source: June 1999

Use the following information to answer the next question.

The fathead minnow is a small fish common in Alberta waters and is used as a food source by many different predators. When injured, some minnows secrete a chemical (called schreckstoff) that both attracts predators and causes other minnows to huddle in large groups. Approaching predators tend to be distracted by the mass of minnows and by each other. Often, the injured minnow can escape.

– from Gonick, 1996

CHALLENGER QUESTION　　　56.5

2. The frequency of the gene that controls the production of schreckstoff by minnows is likely

   A. to increase in the gene pool of the population

   B. to decrease in the gene pool of the population

   C. to stay the same in the gene pool of the population because natural selection is occurring

   D. to stay the same in the gene pool of the population because natural selection is not occurring

Source: January 2000

Use the following information to answer the next question.

Herbicide resistance in weeds has become an increasingly frustrating problem for weed management. A 2004 survey related to herbicide-resistant weeds across Alberta noted that 20% of fields had weeds that were resistant to herbicides.

3. If herbicides continue to be applied to these fields in the same quantity, what will happen to the frequency of the allele that codes for resistance to herbicides?

A. The allele frequency would increase as a result of the bottleneck effect created by the sudden death of the weeds after pesticides were applied.

B. The allele frequency would decrease as additional applications of herbicides finally eliminated plants bearing these alleles.

C. The allele frequency would not change because the population of herbicide-resistant plants would remain stable.

D. The allele frequency would increase because more plants with alleles providing resistance to herbicides would be naturally selected for.

CHALLENGER QUESTION   **41.3**

4. The flowers of the organ pipe cactus open during the night and close during the day to avoid dehydration during the heat of the day. This adaptation of the cacti to the desert climate **most likely** occurred as a result of

A. increased mutation rates in flowers stimulated by high temperatures

B. increased reproductive success of cacti with flowers that opened at night

C. the intense heat of the desert, which destroyed all flowers that opened during the day and caused the cacti to open its flowers at night

D. the reaction of the cacti to the extreme heat, which caused it to close its flowers during the day and to gradually develop the behaviour of opening its flowers at night

Source: January 2001

Use the following information to answer the next question.

A program to detect carriers of β-thalassemia (a mild blood disorder) found the incidence of the disease to be 4% in a particular population. A recessive allele found on an autosomal chromosome causes β-thalassemia.

CHALLENGER QUESTION   **44.4**

Numerical Response

1. What is the frequency of the recessive β-thalassemia allele in the gene pool of this population?

_____

(Record your answer as a **value from 0 to 1**, rounded to **one decimal place**.)

Source: June 1999

Use the following information to answer the next three questions.

From 1968 to 1990, the population of snow geese nesting near Churchill, Manitoba, increased from about 2 000 pairs (4 000 individuals) to about 22 500 pairs (45 000 individuals) with a nesting density of around 1 000 nests per square mile. Snow geese winter along the coasts of Texas and Louisiana. Prior to 1960, marshes along these coasts provided the main food sources (reeds, roots, and tubers) for the geese. Destruction of these marshes and increased crop production of rice, corn, and soybeans has occurred since that time. The stubble from these crops and spilled grains are easily obtained food sources for the snow geese. Reduction in hunting and greatly increased food supplies from cultivation near their wintering ground has cut mortality rates of snow geese in half over this period.

The high nesting density of the snow geese has left little foraging or nesting space for other species of birds, and a decline in several duck species and shore birds has been observed. Simultaneously, intensive foraging by the snow geese erodes and dries out patches of Arctic soil, reduces regrowth of grasses and sedges, and greatly increases soil salinity.

– from Brodie, 1997

CHALLENGER QUESTION   58.4

5. Given a further increase in the snow goose population in the Churchill, Manitoba, nesting area

   A. interspecific competition will increase because of decreased species diversity

   B. interspecific competition will increase and intraspecific competition will decrease

   C. intraspecific competition will decrease because fewer snow geese will be able to find nesting sites

   D. intraspecific competition will increase because available food supplies are decreasing

Source: January 1999

6. Prior to 1960, the winter food sources in the marshes controlled the growth of the snow goose population. The available supply of reeds, roots, and tubers in the marshes was

   A. an example of a community of climax species

   B. an example of a community of pioneer species

   C. a density-dependent limiting factor for snow geese

   D. a density-independent limiting factor for snow geese

Source: January 1999

CHALLENGER QUESTION   45.1

7. Based on the information provided, it would be reasonable to conclude that the snow goose population

   A. has increased its biotic potential

   B. has a higher mortality rate than natality rate

   C. is in a growth phase and environmental resistance is increasing

   D. has reached the carrying capacity of the ecosystem and environmental resistance is decreasing

Source: January 1999

Use the following information to answer the next question.

The gene for retinal disease, which causes blindness, is known to be a recessive allele. In Michigan, 9 people in a sample of 10 000 were found to have retinal disease. In Wisconsin, 2 500 people were surveyed.

Numerical Response

2. If allele frequencies are the same in Wisconsin as they are in Michigan, how many people would be expected to have retinal disease in Wisconsin?

_____

(Record your answer as a **whole** number.)

8. Which of the following relationships would be considered to be a mutualistic relationship?

A. The myxoma virus was introduced to control the rabbit population in Australia.

B. The abandoned burrows of woodpeckers often become nesting sites for bluebirds.

C. Blowfly eggs, laid on the skin of sheep, develop into larvae that feed on sheep tissues.

D. The stomachs of cattle contain large populations of bacteria that aid in the digestion of cellulose.

Source: June 1999

Use the following information to answer the next question.

The African Monarch, one of the best-known butterflies in Asia and Africa, is believed to be one of the first butterflies depicted in art. During their larval stage, they ingest chemicals called alkaloids that they can store in their adult bodies. These alkaloids make the Monarchs very unpalatable so that if consumed, they will make the predator vomit. The Indian Fritillary inhabits the same region and has very similar wing patterns to the African Monarch, but it does not store alkaloids in its body. Predators will nonetheless avoid eating the Indian Fritillary.

9. What is the primary defence mechanism of the Indian Fritillary?

A. Toxins

B. Mimicry

C. Cryptic coloration

D. Aversive behaviour

Use the following information to answer the next question.

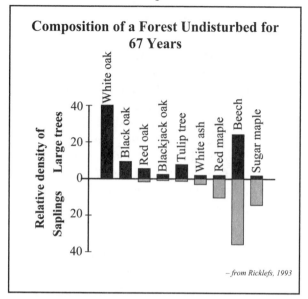

Composition of a Forest Undisturbed for 67 Years

– from Ricklefs, 1993

CHALLENGER QUESTION 58.0

10. In which of the following ways would you expect this forest to change in the next 50 years?

A. The relative density of all trees will increase.

B. There will be an emergence of coniferous trees such as spruce or pine.

C. There will be an increase in the relative density of beech and a decrease in the relative density of white oak.

D. The relative density of blackjack oak, white ash, red maple, and sugar maple will decrease as a result of competition from the larger trees.

Source: June 2000

Use the following information to answer the next question.

The black-footed ferret is considered one of the most endangered species in the American west. Captive breeding programs are trying to help re-establish a healthy population of these ferrets. Researchers have monitored the ferret populations at several sites of reintroduction.

Population data of black-footed ferrets at several reintroduction sites

Site	Initial Population (N)	Births (n)	Deaths (m)	Immigrants (i)	Emigrants (e)
1	17	9	5	4	2
2	32	15	3	2	6
3	24	11	7	2	1

Numerical Response

3. Overall, what is the total increase or decrease in population?

_____

(Record your answer as a **whole** number.)

Use the following information to answer the next question.

Lac la Biche Lake is one of the largest lakes in Alberta, covering an area of 234 km². Over the past century, intensive commercial and sport fishing practices have threatened the walleye fishery of the lake, and it is now being closely monitored and managed. Fish surveys conducted in the lake in 2003 estimated the adult walleye population at 2 800 individuals, far below the 50 000 adults needed to sustain a healthy population.

Numerical Response

4. What is the population density needed for a healthy population of walleye in Lac La Biche?
_____ adult walleye/km²
(Record your answer rounded to one decimal place.)

11. Which of the following statements about a closed population is **true**?

A. In a closed population, only natality occurs.

B. In a closed population, natality and mortality occur.

C. In a closed population, natality, mortality, and emigration occur.

D. In a closed population, natality, mortality, emigration, and immigration occur.

Use the following information to answer the next question.

At the global level, the human population growth rate has been changing at a rapid speed.

Estimates of World Population Growth Rates

1750	Population doubling every 100 years
1970	Population doubling every 40 years
1990	Population doubling every 34 years

– from Luttwak, 1996

12. The rapidly growing human population is endangering populations of *K*-strategists while favouring *r*-strategists. Examples of *K*-strategists and *r*-strategists are, respectively,

A. whales and houseflies

B. elephants and spruce trees

C. cockroaches and dandelions

D. mosquitoes and woodpeckers

Source: January 1999

ANSWERS AND SOLUTIONS—UNIT TEST

1. B	NR1. 0.2	NR2. 2	NR3. 19
2. A	5. D	8. D	NR4. 213.7
3. D	6. C	9. B	11. B
4. B	7. C	10. C	12. A

1. B

Use the Hardy–Weinberg equation, $p + q = 1$.
If the frequency of the abnormal recessive allele Hb^S is 0.15, then $q = 0.15$. The frequency of the normal dominant allele Hb^A is equal to p.

$$p + q = 1$$
$$p + (0.15) = 1$$
$$p = 1 - 0.15$$
$$p = 0.85$$

Therefore, the frequency of the HbA allele in western Africa must be 0.85.

2. A

Since only some of the minnows secrete schreckstoff and since schreckstoff appears to provide the minnow that secretes it a survival advantage, the frequency of the gene that codes for it is probably increasing in the gene pool. That is because minnows that have the gene are more likely to survive and have offspring. Individuals that do not have the gene are not as likely to survive.

3. D

Once the herbicides are applied to the fields, genes that make the weeds resistant to the chemicals become beneficial and weeds with these resistant genes become selected for, therefore increasing the gene frequency and, consequently, the allele frequency coding for resistance.

4. B

Perhaps at one time, the cactus flowers were open throughout the day and night. Water loss from the flowers during the day was a problem in the desert climate and reduced the survival rate of the cacti. Because there is variation in all organisms, there may have been some cacti that opened their flowers during the night and closed them during the day. Those cacti lost less water and therefore had a greater chance of survival to reproduce. They would have produced offspring that would also open their flowers only during the night. Since the cacti that opened their flowers only during the night had a higher survival rate, eventually all the cacti opened their flowers only at night.

NR 1   0.2

Use the Hardy–Weinberg equation
$p^2 + 2pq + q^2 = 1$ to calculate the frequency of the β-thalassemia allele.

Let q^2 be the frequency of the homozygous recessive genotype.

Determine the value of q.

$$q^2 = 0.04$$
$$q = \sqrt{0.04}$$
$$q = 0.2$$

Therefore, the frequency of the β-thalassemia allele in the gene pool is 0.2.

5. D

*Inter*specific competition refers to the competition between organism of different species.
For example, the competition between the snow geese and other shore birds and duck species.
*Intra*specific competition refers to the competition within the snow goose species. In the Churchill area, the increase in the snow goose population has already led to the decrease of other bird populations. A further increase in the snow goose population likely will lead to an increase in competition for nesting grounds and food among members of the snow goose population. That is, increasing numbers of snow geese will decrease the food supply until the snow geese compete among themselves (intraspecific competition) for the food. Statements **A** and **B** are incorrect because the interspecific competition can increase only if species diversity increases. In this example, the species diversity is decreasing.

6. C

Before 1960, reeds, roots, and tubers were the food supply for the snow geese in the wintering grounds. Recall that food supply is a density-dependent factor because a higher density of snow geese leads to a lower food supply. As a result of the limiting food supply when the population of geese was too high, the reeds, roots, and tubers acted as a factor that controlled the population size of the geese.

The definitions of climax and pioneer species are given below.

Community of climax species—final and relatively stable community of organisms developed following numerous stages of succession (rise and fall of different communities of various numbers and types of organisms).

Pioneer species—the first species to inhabit an area in the stages of succession.

7. C

The snow goose population is increasing, so it is reasonable to assume that the population is in a growth phase. As the population grows, nesting space and food supplies will become more limited. Both nesting space and food are environmental factors that will limit the growth of the goose population. Therefore, environmental resistance is increasing as the number of snow geese increases.

The biotic potential (defined as the maximum number of offspring that can be produced by a species under ideal environmental conditions) cannot be altered, so you could not conclude that it had increased. Since mortality is the death rate and natality is the birth rate, it would not be reasonable to conclude that the mortality right is higher than the natality rate. The snow goose population is still growing, so it cannot have reached the carrying capacity. Carrying capacity is the point at which the population size no longer increases because of the lack of resources.

NR 2   2

In Michigan, 9 in 10 000, or 0.09%, were blind, which is a homozygous recessive trait (*bb*). According to the Hardy-Weinberg genotype equation, the homozygous recessive genotype = $bb = q^2$ = 0.09%, or 0.0009. Therefore, the single allele frequency,

$$q = \sqrt{0.0009} = 0.03$$

Now, apply that allele frequency to the Wisconsin population. Since the allele frequency is the same, the genotype frequency for homozygous recessive genotype (*bb*) will also be the same as it was in Michigan, and therefore 0.09% of 2 500 people will have retinal disease: $0.0009 \times 2\,500 = 2.25$, or approximately 2 people of the group surveyed in Wisconsin will have retinal disease.

8. D

The stomachs of cattle contain large populations of bacteria that aid in the digestion of cellulose. Cattle depend on the bacteria to begin cellulose digestion. The bacteria depend on cattle to provide the ingested cellulose and to provide an environment in which to live. Cattle and gut bacteria are mutually dependent.

The myxoma virus is a parasite in rabbits. Woodpeckers do not benefit from bluebird activity. This is a one-way relationship called commensalism. Blowfly larvae are parasitic on sheep.

9. B

The Indian Fritillary has similar wing patterns to the African Monarch, which has toxins to defend it against potential predators. By imitating the toxic African Monarch, the Indian Fritillary is afforded the same protection against predation.

10. C

There are a lot of large white oak trees but no white oak saplings. Therefore, as the older white oak die, there are no young ones to take their place, so the density of white oak should decline. However, there are many beech saplings. As they get bigger, the density of beech should increase.

NR 3   19

Change in population $= [(n) + (i)] - [(m) + (e)]$

Site 1: change in population $= [9+4] - [5+2]$
$= 6$ more individuals

Site 2: change in population $= [15+2] - [3+6]$
$= 8$ more individuals

Site 3: change in population $= [11+2][7+1]$
$= 5$ more individuals

Therefore, the total for all three sites is
$6 + 8 + 5 = 19$.

The overall population has increased by **19** individuals.

NR 4   213.7

The population density is calculated by dividing population by the lake area.

Therefore,
$50000/234km^2 = 213.7$ adult walleye/km^2

11. B

A closed population experiences no form of migration (gene flow). Change in size and density is only determined by natality and mortality.

12. A

Recall the characteristics of both K-selected and r-selected populations.

K-selected	*r*-selected
• relatively stable environment	• fluctuating environmental conditions
• large size	• small size
• young are slow-growing; dependent on parents	• young are fast-growing; little or no dependence on parents
• long lifespan; e.g., bears, dolphins	• short lifespan; e.g., insects, bacteria

The best examples of K- and r-selected populations in the alternatives are given in **A**. Whales are large, few in number, have few offspring (1 or 2), and require parental help for growth and development.

Houseflies are a good example of an r-selected population because they produce many offspring, are small in size, and have young that develop independently of their parents. **C** and **D** are definitely incorrect. **B** is not the best alternative because although elephants are a good example of a K-selected population, spruce trees are not a good example of an r-selected population. Although trees have a large number of offspring that are independent of their parents, they grow slowly and have a long lifespan.

Written Response

WRITTEN RESPONSE QUESTIONS

Written response questions no longer appear on the Biology 30 Diploma Exam. However, these questions are helpful in preparing for written response questions on unit exams and in preparing for multiple choice questions.

Use the following information to answer the next question.

Sperm count is measured in millions of sperm per millilitre of semen. The normal amount of ejaculate is 3 mL, and 30 to 100 million sperm/mL is considered within the normal range. A generation ago, 100 million sperm/mL was considered normal. A male whose sperm concentration falls below 20 million sperm/mL is likely infertile.

While working at the National University Hospital in Copenhagen, Denmark, Niels Skakkebaek prepared a report that combined the results of 61 separate studies of sperm count and quality over the last 50 years. His report was based on data involving a total of 14 947 men from 21 countries, including the United States, Europe, Asia, and Africa. His results showed that the average sperm count had fallen from 113 million sperm/mL in 1940 to 66 million sperm/mL in 1990. French research also showed a decline, on average, from 89 million sperm/mL in 1973 to 60 million sperm/mL in 1992. A Scottish study of 600 men showed a 2% decrease in the average sperm count each year for the past two decades. Skakkebaek also reported that the lowest sperm counts are in younger men and that the proportion of their deformed sperm is steadily rising.

Research on conditions during pregnancy or immediately after birth that could reduce the number of certain cells within the testes, called Sertoli cells, may help explain the reported decline in sperm counts. The number of Sertoli cells that a male possesses establishes an upper limit on sperm production, as these cells nourish immature sperm.

The number of Sertoli cells is fixed in the fetal or newborn stage of human development, when the multiplication of these cells is catalysed by FSH. Dr. Richard Sharpe, of the Medical Research Council's Reproductive Biology Unit in Edinburgh, is investigating whether low sperm counts may be related to a reduction in the number of Sertoli cells in males. Estrogen-mimicking compounds found in the environment inhibit FSH production. People worldwide are exposed to thousands of chemicals, some of which mimic the effects of naturally produced estrogen. These chemicals include aromatic hydrocarbons produced by combustion, PCBs, and DDT.

– from Nichols, *1996*, Moomaw, *1996*, Stainsby, *1996*, Raloff, *1994*, Lambton, *1993*

1. **a)** Write a hypothesis that relates sperm count to estrogen-mimicking compounds in the environment.

(2 marks)

b) i) Draw and label a flow chart that illustrates the production of FSH and its effect on Sertoli cell development in male babies. Include all relevant organs and hormones.

(2 marks)

ii) On the flow chart you have drawn, indicate the proposed effect of estrogen-mimicking compounds on FSH production and Sertoli cell development.

(1 mark)

c) At low levels, estrogen-mimicking compounds in the environment appear to be harmful to fetuses but not to adults. Describe a possible reason for the greater sensitivity of fetuses to these compounds.

(1 mark)

d) i) Using the data from the French research, calculate the percentage decrease in sperm count from the original value in 1973 to the value in 1992. (Show all calculations.)

(1 mark)

ii) Predict a possible effect on French society or the French population if this trend continues.

(1 mark)

e) Given that only one sperm fertilizes an egg, describe two reasons why a man with a sperm count of less than 20 million sperm/mL is likely infertile.

(2 marks)

f) The effects of estrogen-mimicking compounds on sperm counts are not well established by scientists.

i) What is one possible question you would need answered before you could decide if there is a cause-and-effect relationship between environmental estrogen-mimicking compounds and lowered sperm counts?

(1 mark)

ii) How would an answer to this question help you evaluate whether this is a cause-and-effect relationship?

(1 mark)

Source: January 1999

Copyright Protected

Use the following information to answer the next question.

Ataxia telangiectasia (AT) is an autosomal recessive disorder occurring with an estimated frequency of 1 in 40 000 births. The first symptoms of the disease occur around two years of age and are progressive; they consist of a lack of balance and slurred speech. Soon after, tiny red (spider) veins appear in the corners of the eyes (telangiectasis). Older children with AT lose their ability to write, and reading becomes impossible as eye movements become difficult to control. Individuals are eventually confined to a wheelchair. Immune system disorders are common. Intelligence is normal in these individuals. Most individuals with AT die as children; however, some live up to 50 years.

Patients with AT develop blood system cancers 1 000 times more frequently than the general population. Treatment of cancer with conventional dosages of radiation can be fatal to AT patients because they are especially sensitive to radiation, which causes breakage of DNA. Even carriers have a higher incidence of cancer than does the general population.

The defect causing AT has been traced to a mutation on chromosome 11. The protein product of this gene is not expressed appropriately. The exact role of the gene remains a mystery. Normal cells respond to DNA damage by interrupting the cell cycle in interphase before DNA synthesis occurs. This allows for repair of the DNA. Scientists are investigating a link between the AT mutation and this cell repair process.

There is presently no cure for AT, but treatments to alleviate symptoms are currently being developed.

– from NCBI, 1997□A-T Children's Project,1997

2. Write a unified response addressing the following aspects of ataxia telangiectasia (AT).

Sketch a diagram of the human brain and label four parts. Identify the area of the brain most affected by AT. Identify the symptoms of AT that relate to degeneration of this area of the brain, and explain how these symptoms indicate that this area of the brain has degenerated.

Calculate the frequency of the AT allele and the percentage of the population that are carriers. (Show your work.) Identify and explain how two societal factors and/or technologies could decrease the incidence of the AT disorder in the population of future generations or alleviate the symptoms of AT in individuals.

Source: January 1999

152 Castle Rock Research

Use the following information to answer the next question.

On April 26, 1986, one of the worst technological, industrial, and environmental disasters known to humankind occurred. A nuclear reactor in Chernobyl exploded and showered radioactive debris over much of Eastern Europe. The extent of the environmental and health effects of the nuclear legacy of the Chernobyl disaster are still unknown.

Although the exact causes of many illnesses are not understood, there is little doubt that the enormous burst of radiation released from the reactor has had devastating effects on thousands of children. One of the most dangerous radioactive products released was iodine-131. It was inhaled by many children, exposing them to high levels of radiation. Iodine-131 was absorbed by the children's thyroid glands, causing inflammation of the gland and an increased incidence of thyroid cancer. Normally, iodine is absorbed from the blood by the thyroid gland in its synthesis of thyroxine.

The effects of this radiation over a long period of time were also studied. Researchers looked at DNA gene sequences five to 45 bases long from blood samples taken from parents and their children born in 1994 or later. They looked for any sequence in the child's DNA that did not occur in the blood cells of either parent. The children born near Chernobyl had twice as many of these mutations in their DNA as had the control group, which consisted of families in England whose children were also born in or after 1994.

– from Monmaney, *1996;* Shcherbak, *1996*

3. **a)** Explain one function of thyroxine.

(1 mark)

b) Draw a feedback loop that illustrates the regulation of the release of thyroxine. Include relevant glands and hormones.

(3 marks)

c) Thyroid cancer in infants can be treated by surgical removal of the thyroid gland. Identify two signs and/or symptoms that would indicate or would be caused by the absence of thyroxine in such an infant.

(2 marks)

d) The children exposed to radioactive iodine because of the nuclear accident were treated with high levels of non-radioactive iodine. Explain why this treatment was used.

(1 mark)

e) Describe and sketch one type of error at the molecular level of DNA that results in a mutation. (Create a hypothetical strand of DNA bases, then show the strand again, illustrating and clearly marking the change causing the error.)

(3 marks)

f) The evidence presented in the last paragraph of the reading suggests that mutations occurred in one of the parents' germ-line cells (precursor cells to oocytes or sperm cells). Describe how the germ-line cell mutations appeared in the children's white blood cells.

(2 marks)
Source: June 1999

Use the following information to answer the next question.

There is a worldwide shortage of organs for transplanting into humans. Some researchers are concentrating on xenotransplantation—using organs from other species—as a solution.

The pig is considered by researchers as the most suitable donor of transplant organs for humans, even though pigs are not as closely related genetically to humans as higher primates are. Pigs can be bred easily and up to three times a year. Sows have short pregnancies (about 115 days) and give birth to large litters. The offspring grow quickly to reach a large size.

Transplanted organs from ordinary pigs are quickly rejected by the human immune system. Researchers have isolated a human gene, called HDAF, that codes for a cell membrane protein known as RCA. The human HDAF gene can be inserted into pig DNA so the human RCA protein will be present on the surface of pig cells. Human RCA protein on cell membranes of pig cells is expected to inhibit the rejection of pig organs when they are transplanted into humans. A pig that has the human gene in all of its cells is referred to as a transgenic pig.

Fertilized eggs are harvested from a sow.

Injection of HDAF gene into the nuclei of the fertilized eggs.

Identification of heterozygote transgenic offspring (shaded grey) expressing RCA protein in their organs.

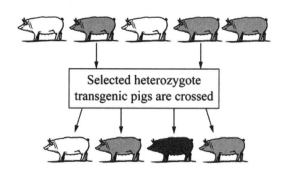

Identification of homozygote transgenic offspring (shaded dark grey) expressing RCA protein in their organs.

* Approximately 60% of these offspring were transgenic heterozygotes

*– from Lanza, Cooper and Chick, 1997;
Cozzi and White Hunter, 1996*

4. Write a unified response that addresses the following aspects of the use of pigs as a source of organs for transplantation.

Compare the biotic potential of pig populations with that of other mammals, such as primates or humans. Explain how two traits of pigs would have influenced researchers to choose pigs as the most suitable animals for xenotransplantation.

Describe one technology that researchers would have used to obtain the HDAF gene. Explain, in detail, what happens after the HDAF gene is injected into fertilized eggs to produce heterozygote transgenic offspring and normal offspring.

Explain why researchers performed crosses of heterozygote offspring and explain the observed outcome of these crosses using a Punnett Square to clarify your explanation.

Source: June 1999

Use the following information to answer the next question.

Scientists are working hard to learn about causes of cancers. It is known that in general terms cancer-causing agents produce mutations in a variety of genes that control cell reproduction.

Cancer can be caused by organisms. For example, when some viruses infect a human cell, the viral DNA may insert itself randomly into the DNA of human cells.

Of all the cancer-causing agents to which humans are commonly exposed, tobacco smoke appears to have caused the greatest harm. It is directly responsible for 30% of all cancer deaths in North America. Heavy smoking increases the likelihood of getting lung cancer by 2 000%. Passive (secondhand) smoke is less likely to cause cancer. It is about as harmful as all other forms of air pollution.

– from Trichopoulos, Li, and Hunter, 1996

5. **a)** A reasonable question for a researcher to ask would be "What percentage of smokers will die from cancer caused by tobacco smoke?" Assume that in a study to answer this question, you gather two groups of subjects and observe them over a long period of time.

   i) Identify the manipulated variable and the responding variable for your study.

   (2 marks)

ii) Identify two variables that you would be unable to control, and explain why these variables would influence the conclusions of your study.

   (3 marks)

b) Hypothesize how viral infection of human cells may lead to cancer.

   (2 marks)

Use the following additional information to answer the next part of the question.

Four percent of all cancer deaths can be linked to the reproductive history of a woman. Researchers have discovered that if a woman begins to menstruate at an early age and experiences late menopause, she is more likely to develop cancer in her reproductive organs. If a woman has several children and gave birth to them at a younger age, she is less likely to develop cancer of the ovary, breast, or endometrium.

– from Trichopoulos, Li, and Hunter, 1996

c) i) Identify a social or economic change in Canadian society over the past few decades that could have had an impact on the rate of cancer in women's reproductive systems.

(1 mark)

ii) Describe how this change could affect the frequency of cancer in the reproductive systems of women in the Canadian population.

(1 mark)

Use the following additional information to answer the next three parts of the question.

Scientists have been learning about a mechanism called the "cell cycle clock" that collects information from outside the cell. This information influences the activities of molecules within the cell that determine whether or not a cell will undergo mitosis. Some molecules take the form of "go" signals, stimulating a cell to go through mitosis. Other molecules take the form of "stop" signals to ensure that the cell does not start cell division. For example, some cyclins and CDKs are molecules that act as "go" signals. If these are present in appropriate amounts, DNA replication will occur.

– from Trichopoulos, Li, and Hunter, 1996

d) At which phase of the cell cycle do these cyclins and CDKs appear to operate?

(1 mark)

e) Drug companies are working on developing a drug that blocks the activities of these cyclins and CDKs. Predict how such a drug could act at the molecular level to prevent cancer.

(1 mark)

f) A mutation could disrupt the production or activation of molecules that act as "stop" or "go" signals. Describe how such a disruption could lead to cancer.

(1 mark)

Source: January 2000

Use the following information to answer the next question.

Adrenoleukodystrophy (ALD) is a rare disease of the central nervous system. ALD is characterized by the accumulation of very-long-chain fatty acids in the white matter of the brain and in the adrenal glands. These fatty acids cause the myelin sheath on nerve fibres within white matter of the central nervous system to degenerate. Symptoms of this degeneration become more severe as more and more fatty acids accumulate. Symptoms start with tantrums and other behavioural problems; then motor function, speech, and hearing are impaired; and finally blindness, mental deterioration, and death occur. ALD also affects the endocrine system by causing adrenal gland degeneration. ALD can be partially diagnosed by abnormally high ACTH levels in the blood.

Hereditary diseases have diverse causes. For example, the disease mutation may be dominant or recessive, or the mutated gene may be present on the X chromosome or on an autosome. In some cases, similar diseases are caused by mutations in two different genes. One such case is ALD, where one gene is autosomal and the other is X-linked. In both forms of inheritance, the disease mutation is recessive. Scientists continue to research the causes of ALD. The X-linked recessive form of ALD can be diagnosed prenatally.

ALD has not been treated successfully; however, bone marrow transplants and a diet restricted in very-long-chain fatty acids have shown promise. One dietary substance, oleic acid (Lorenzo's oil), has been successful in normalizing levels of very-long-chain fatty acids in blood plasma. However, the results of clinical trials on ALD patients showed little improvement in symptoms, particularly in brain degeneration. Lorenzo's oil did produce positive clinical results when the treatment of patients began before neurologic symptoms were present.

– from McKusick, et al, *1997*

6. Write a unified response that addresses the following aspects of adrenoleukodystrophy.

Explain how the degeneration of the myelin sheaths on cells in the white matter of the central nervous system could result in any of the impaired brain functions of ALD patients. Identify one hormone secreted by the adrenal gland, and describe how a decrease in secretion of this hormone would affect the body.

Describe one piece of evidence obtained from the analysis of a pedigree chart that could be used to determine whether the mode of inheritance of a human genetic disorder is X-linked or autosomal and one piece of evidence that could be used to determine whether it is recessive or dominant. Construct a pedigree of four generations that clearly illustrates one of the two types of inheritance of ALD. Clearly label where your pedigree shows evidence of X-linked recessive or autosomal recessive inheritance.

Describe one procedure that could be used to collect fetal cells for genetic screening. Describe a benefit and a risk to the individual and/or to society of early diagnosis of disorders like ALD.

Source: January 2000

Acquired immune deficiency syndrome (AIDS) research has centred on developing drug treatments and an AIDS vaccine. AIDS is caused by human immunodeficiency virus (HIV). The drug AZT can greatly reduce the chance of transmission of HIV from an infected woman to her unborn child. The current AZT treatment is very costly. To make the treatment more affordable, African researchers have conducted a number of studies in which one group of HIV infected women was given a shorter than normal course of AZT treatments and another group of HIV infected women received a placebo (pill without medication).

A vaccine made from only the outer coating of the HIV is attached to a harmless virus. The vaccine is being tested on healthy human volunteers to see whether they develop antibodies that would help them produce a natural defence against AIDS. This type of vaccine has not yet been sufficiently effective to induce the desired immunity. A similar AIDS vaccine tested in Canada did not work any better than a placebo.

Future treatments for AIDS may be based on newly acquired knowledge of how AIDS infection occurs and why some individuals are more resistant to infection. When body cells are damaged, they produce a protein (chemokine) to attract the body's immune cells (macrophages). The macrophages have receptors on their cell membranes that attach to the chemokine and rid the body of the damaged cells. The HIV attaches to one kind of chemokine receptor (CCR5) on the macrophage and enters the macrophage, but the HIV does not destroy it.

Ultimately, the virus also infects T-cells and takes over their DNA replicating mechanisms. The macrophage infection may be necessary to activate the replicating mechanisms of T-cells.

It has been discovered that some people have inherited a resistance to HIV because the gene that makes the CCR5 receptor is mutated (missing 32 nucleotides).

This CCR5 mutation results in a shorter receptor, thereby preventing the HIV from attaching to macrophages. Individuals in a study group who were homozygous for the mutant allele resisted infection despite many exposures to HIV. Individuals in the study group with one copy of the mutant allele had the onset of AIDS postponed for two to three years when compared with those in the study group that had no copies of the mutant allele. The mutated allele is most common in Caucasians.

– from Day, 1997; O'Brien and Dean, 1997

7. **a) i)** Using your knowledge of how experiments should be designed, explain why some African woman were given a placebo instead of the AZT drug.

(1 mark)

ii) Why could it be considered ethically wrong to give one group of African women a placebo in place of the real AZT treatments?

(1 mark)

b) Describe how it is physically possible for a pregnant woman with AIDS to pass the virus to her fetus.

(1 mark)

c) Describe briefly the cellular mechanisms of transcription, translation, and protein synthesis that are involved in the production of the CCR5 receptor molecule.

(3 marks)

Use the following additional information to answer the next three parts of the question.

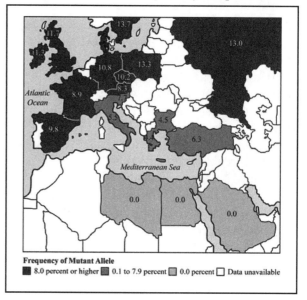

Frequency of Mutant Allele
■ 8.0 percent or higher ▨ 0.1 to 7.9 percent ▨ 0.0 percent □ Data unavailable

d) Hypothesize why the northern European population has a much higher frequency of the CCRS mutant allele than the African population.

(2 marks)

Use the following additional information to answer the next part of the question.

| Frequency of the Mutated CCR5 Allele in Various Populations ||
Population	Frequency of Mutant Allele
Caucasian-European	0.100
Caucasian-American	0.111
African-American	0.017
Native American, African, East Asian	0.000

e) What percentage of the Caucasian-American population would be heterozygous for the mutated CCR5 allele? Show all work and formulas.

(2 marks)

f) The discovery of how the mutant CCR5 allele works to make a person resistant to HIV infection has led scientists to work on new ways to treat or prevent AIDS. Describe a scientific technology that could be used to treat or prevent AIDS that utilizes this new knowledge.

(2 marks)
Source: June 2000

Use the following information to answer the next question.

Human growth hormone (HGH) stimulates the growth of bones and muscles and also has insulin-like properties that result in the deposition of fat in body tissues. Sometimes, for medical purposes, an individual is prescribed a supplement of HGH. Unfortunately, at high levels, HGH has some unpleasant side effects. At a high dosage, HGH can cause insensitivity to insulin. In extreme cases, permanent diabetes mellitus can result.

Dr. J.F. Mueller made an interesting discovery. He observed that mice infected with the plerocercoid larvae of the tapeworm *Spirometra mansonoides* showed accelerated growth. Careful analysis revealed that the larvae produced plerocercoid growth factor (PGF) that is remarkably similar to HGH in structure and function. Further study showed PGF to be molecularly similar to HGH, but it had no anti-insulin effect.

How is it that a tapeworm larva produces a substance so similar to HGH? Even closely related animals have quite different hormones, so it is not likely that this is a chance occurrence. One hypothesis that has been suggested involves viral transduction of the HGH gene. When a virus infects a host cell, the viral DNA becomes incorporated into the host DNA. Later, the host cell is tricked into assembling new viruses. The viral DNA is replicated and placed in the new viruses. Sometimes a section of host DNA is added along with the viral DNA. If the new virus infects a second host, the second host receives the DNA from the first host. This host-to-host transfer of DNA is called viral transduction.

The life cycle of the tapeworm allows it to easily infect not only humans but several other vertebrates. Almost all tapeworms are hermaphrodites (contain both male and female sex organs). Multiple testes and ovaries found in segments on a single tapeworm produce gametes that come together and result in the production of fertilized eggs (either by self-fertilization or cross-fertilization).

The fertilized eggs are released into the intestine of the final host and leave the host through the feces. The host's fecal matter enters the water system where the eggs hatch into ciliated coracidia (hair-covered circular organisms). The coracidia are eaten by small crustaceans called copepods. Copepods are ingested by fish, mice, cats, humans, and other organisms that drink the contaminated water.

Once inside the new host, each coracidium may develop into a pleurocercoid larva that forms a cyst in the muscle.

When this host is eaten by another animal, the pleuroceroid larva attaches to the small intestine wall and develops the reproductive segments of the adult tapeworm.

– from Barnard and Behnke, 1990; Phares, 1987

8. Write a unified response that addresses the discovery of the PGF protein in tapeworms and its potential use in science and medicine. Draw a diagram of the tapeworm life cycle, indicating the timing of important cell divisions such as mitosis and meiosis. Explain the value of these two types of cell divisions as they apply to the tapeworms.

Describe the series of steps that would have to occur in order for the gene for HGH to end up in tapeworm DNA as hypothesized.

Describe the disorder that results from not having enough HGH during childhood development. Treatment could involve the use of PGF instead of HGH. Identify specific effects that make it advantageous to use PGF instead of HGH.

Source: June 2000

Use the following information to answer the next question.

Insulin-dependent diabetes mellitus (IDDM), also known as Type I diabetes or juvenile diabetes is a disorder of glucose homeostasis in which the body's ability to produce insulin is impaired. People suffering from IDDM experience high blood sugar levels, increased thirst, frequent urination, extreme tiredness, and weight loss (despite an increased appetite). These symptoms can result in long-term complications that affect the eyes, kidneys, nerves, and blood vessels.

– from OMIM

9. **a)** Explain why people with untreated IDDM often suffer from extreme tiredness and why they experience weight loss even though their blood sugar levels are higher than normal.

(2 marks)

b) Diabetes insipidus is a disorder that results from underproduction of ADH. Both diabetes mellitus and diabetes insipidus result in a large increase of urine output. Explain how a urine sample produced by a patient with diabetes mellitus and a urine sample produced by a patient with diabetes insipidus are different.

(1 mark)

c) About one in seven IDDM diabetics also suffer from "polyglandular autoimmune syndrome." In addition to their diabetic symptoms, these individuals have thyroid disease and poorly functioning adrenal glands.

i) Identify a hormone that is produced in either the thyroid gland or the adrenal gland that affects blood sugar levels.

(1 mark)

ii) State the normal effect this hormone has on blood sugar levels when its secretion increases. Explain what causes the change in blood sugar levels.

(2 marks)

Use the following additional information to answer the next part of the question.

Of individuals with IDDM, 50% also suffer from diabetic neuropathy. Nerves are progressively destroyed, possibly due to blockage of the tiny blood vessels that supply blood to the nerves.

– from National Eye Institute

d) One patient with diabetic neuropathy walked on a broken ankle for two weeks without knowing it. Others, unknowingly, have foot ulcers (bleeding sores) on the soles of their feet. Based on this information, predict the type of neuron you suspect is damaged in these patients. Explain how the symptoms of diabetic neuropathy support your prediction.

(2 marks)

Use the following additional information to answer the next part of the question.

The most common eye disease in individuals with IDDM is "diabetic retinopathy."
This disease is characterized by changes in the blood vessels of the retina. In some people, the blood vessels may swell and leak fluid, and in other people, abnormal blood vessels grow on the surface of the retina.

– from National Eye Institute

e) Explain why diabetic retinopathy may result in some vision loss or blindness. In your answer, refer to the eye structure and the pathway of impulses to the brain.

(2 marks)

f) Insulin is a protein hormone. It has been hypothesized that a change in the 57th amino acid of this hormone from asparagine to another amino acid will result in an increased risk for developing IDDM.

i) Write a DNA triplet that codes for asparagine.

(1 mark)

ii) Show how a single base change in this DNA triplet would code for an amino acid other than asparagine. Identify the amino acid coded for by the mutated DNA triplet.

(1 mark)

Source: January 2001

Use the following information to answer the next question.

Larry and Danny Gomez, two boys known as "Wolf Boys," have made the circus their adoptive family. Both boys perform as trampoline acrobats, and Danny also does motorcycle stunts. The boys have a condition called congenital hypertrichosis (CH), which is a very rare X-linked dominant inherited condition. CH is characterized by the growth of dark hair over the body, particularly on the face and upper torso in males. The palms of the hands, soles of the feet, and mucus membranes are not affected by this condition.

A press release about the circus stated that Larry and Danny have travelled to many countries in search of a cure. When asked about the search for a cure in an interview by David Staples of *The Edmonton Journal* (May 14, 1997), Larry said, "I'd never take it off. I'm very proud to be who I am." Outside the circus, the boys enjoy activities typical of most boys their age. Danny likes to play video and board games, and Larry is interested in science and is taking astronomy by correspondence.

Researchers continue to investigate the process of hair growth and the causes of hair distribution at the molecular level. The relevant molecules are expected to act on hair follicles. Hair follicle distribution in humans is primarily a hormone-dependent secondary sex characteristic. In addition to searching for a cure for CH, research in this area may also have significant applications in the treatment of acquired or inherited baldness.

The incidence of CH is very rare: only about 50 affected individuals have been reported since the Middle Ages. The incidence of this condition is considerably higher in a small Mexican village than it is in the rest of the human population. In 1984, researcher Macias-Flores studied CH in a large, five-generation Mexican family and found 19 individuals with CH.

A partial pedigree showing the sampled individuals from the Macias-Flores study is shown below.

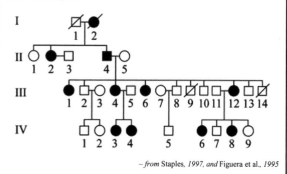

– *from* Staples, *1997, and* Figuera et al., *1995*

10. Write a unified response on the following aspects of CH.

Identify the hormone responsible for secondary sex characteristics in males or females, and describe the secondary sex characteristics, including hair follicle distribution patterns, resulting from this hormone's stimulation.

Identify the genotypes for individuals II-4, II-5, III-11, III-12, IV-6, IV-7, IV-8, and IV-9 in one of the lines of inheritance on the pedigree. (Provide a key for the allele symbols you use.) Construct a Punnett square to predict the probability of individuals III-11 and III-12's next child being a male with CH. Explain why more females than males inherited CH in generation III.

State a possible experimental problem that could be investigated to find out more about CH or hair follicle distribution. Evaluate whether conducting research would be useful for affected individuals or for society. (An evaluation includes at least one advantage and one disadvantage.)

Source: January 2001

Use the following information to answer the next question.

Although doctors were astonished, relatives were not surprised when Benjy Stacy was born with skin the colour of a bruised plum. Two days of medical tests to rule out possible heart and lung disease revealed no cause for the newborn's dark blue skin. Not until Benjy's grandmother asked the puzzled doctors if they had ever heard of the blue Fugates of Troublesome Creek was the mystery solved. When baby Benjy inherited his mother's red hair and his father's lankiness, he also received his great-great-great-grandfather Martin Fugate's blue skin.

In 1820, a French orphan named Martin Fugate settled on the banks of Troublesome Creek. He and his red-headed American bride Elizabeth had seven children, four of which were reported to be blue-skinned. Isolated in the hills of eastern Kentucky, the family multiplied. Intermarriages between "blue Fugates" were common. Over time, the inherited blue trait began to disappear as the arrival of railways and roads allowed family members to marry outside their communities. Six generations after Martin Fugate first settled in Troublesome Creek, baby Benjy was born.

Based on Benjy's grandmother's account and further testing, doctors concluded that the newborn carried one copy of a mutated gene for methemoglobinemia. Hereditary methemoglobinemia is a rare autosomal recessive blood disorder. Blue people have an absence of the enzyme diaphorase in their red blood cells. In a normal individual, hemoglobin, the blood's red, oxygen-carrying molecule, is slowly converted to a non-functional blue form called methemoglobin. Diaphorase then converts methemoglobin back to hemoglobin. The absence of diaphorase in affected individuals is caused by a mutation in the enzyme's structural gene. This causes the accumulation of blue methemoglobin, which replaces the red hemoglobin responsible for pink skin in most Caucasians.

– from Trost, 1982

11. **a)** Explain how a gene mutation could alter the diaphorase enzyme's amino acid sequence.

(2 marks)

Use the following additional information to answer the next three parts of the question.

In one account of the Fugate family's pedigree from 1750 to 1889, six of the 55 individuals expressed the blue phenotype as adults.

b) Determine the frequency of the recessive allele for the Fugate family during this time. Show your work.

(2 marks)

c) Predict the theoretical percentage of individuals in the Fugate family that were heterozygotes during this time. Show your work.

(2 marks)

d) Explain why the frequency of the blue skin phenotype was higher in the Fugate family than in the general American population.

(1 mark)

e) Identify two ways in which the population, which consisted of six generations of the Fugate family, did not meet the conditions for Hardy–Weinberg equilibrium.

(2 marks)

f) Although he was very blue at birth, within his first few weeks, Benjy's skin colour changed to normal with no treatment required. At the age of seven, other than purplish blue lips when he was cold or angry, Benjy's coloration was normal.

i) What is Benjy's genotype?

(1 mark)

ii) Give a possible explanation for the change in Benjy's phenotype over time.

(1 mark)

Use the following additional information to answer the next part of the question.

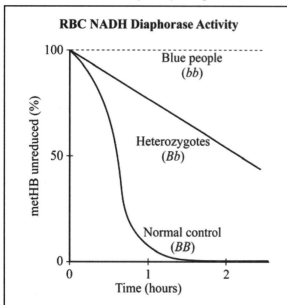

The data above were obtained by extracting red blood cells from three different groups of individuals. The red blood cells were then evaluated for their ability to convert methemoglobin to hemoglobin.

– from Huskey, 1996

iii) Individuals with hereditary methemoglobinemia can be treated easily with methylene blue pills. Methylene blue acts as an "electron donor" converting methemoglobin to hemoglobin, which results in pink skin colouration. Explain why treated blue people can still produce offspring with hereditary methemoglobinemia.

(1 mark)

Source: June 2001

Use the following information to answer the next question.

Development of a fetus in the uterus is of interest to both scientists and expectant parents. An embryo develops a neural tube (a fluid-filled structure that will later develop into a brain and a spinal cord) at five weeks and taste buds at 15 weeks. Fetuses have been known to show dream-like patterns through rapid eye movement (REM) at nine weeks. In the uterus, the fetus yawns and may experience taste and smell. The heart rate of a fetus decreases in response to its mother's voice. This suggests that the fetus somehow recognizes its mother's voice and is calmed by it. Even at birth, a baby already responds to and prefers its mother's voice. There is also evidence that stress in mothers increases cortisol levels and produces more active fetuses, and that more active fetuses are, in turn, more irritable infants. A baby's predisposition to certain tastes may be linked to what it was exposed to in the uterus. The amniotic fluid contains traces of chemicals from the foods the mother eats, and the fetus swallows amniotic fluids.

A study headed by pediatric neurologist Dr. Peter Hultenlocher has provided evidence that the majority of connections between neurons are made in the first three years of a child's life. The study indicates that a child's brain contains twice as many neurons and consumes twice as much energy as a normal adult brain. A study done at Baylor College of Medicine indicates that children who do not play or who are rarely touched by their mothers develop brains that are 20% to 30% smaller than normal for their age. Other studies show that in neural development from the fetal stage to ten years of age, connections between neurons develop as a result of the firing activity of neurons. Stimulation causes axons and dendrites to grow and produce synapses. If these connections are not reinforced by activity, they are eliminated from the brain's circuitry.

Studies of infants faced with emotional or physical trauma show that they also increase secretions of cortisol in response to stress. Cortisol has been shown to shrink regions of the brain involved in learning and memory. A newborn can also recognize and express emotion. Smiling mothers elicit a smiling, gurgling response in their babies. The infant's early response is linked to the social skill development needed for interpersonal relationships. The language spoken to a baby has been found to influence brain development. For example, babies spoken to in Japanese have different neural circuits than those spoken to in English.

Of the 100 000 human genes, 50 000 are dedicated to constructing and maintaining the nervous system. Some of these genes have been linked directly to learning. In fruit flies, a gene called CREB has been shown to increase its activity as a result of motor neuron stimulation. When this gene was inhibited in giant snails, their short-term memory developed but their long-term memory did not. The same gene is found in humans. Other genes may also be involved in learning.

– from Newberger, 1997 Nash, 1997 Hopson, 1998

12. Write a unified response addressing the following aspects of fetal development and development in early childhood.

- **Sketch** a diagram of the fetus and its environment at approximately three months development and **label** four structures that support the fetus in this environment. **Describe** how the environment in the uterus and structures associated with the fetus support the fetus during this stage of development.
- **Describe** the pathway for sensory interpretation in a fetus or newborn. Start from a **specific** stimulus to the part of the CNS that is stimulated in order for interpretation to occur.

- **Identify** and **describe** two technologies and/or government policies that might result in stimulation of appropriate neural development in children. **Explain** how each of these would affect neural development in early childhood.

Source: June 2001

Use the following information to answer the next question.

The Blood Reserve is Canada's largest First Nations reserve. Prior to 1700, the Blood Tribe migrated within the area surrounding what is now Red Deer. By 1750, their migration area had changed to include more of southern Alberta and part of what is now Montana. During the 1800s, two smallpox epidemics killed almost the entire Blood population. These epidemics may have influenced the decision of the Blood Tribe to sign a treaty that led to the creation of the Blood Reserve in southern Alberta. After settling on the reserve, an influenza epidemic in 1918 further reduced the population to about 1 100. The present population is about 7 000 people.

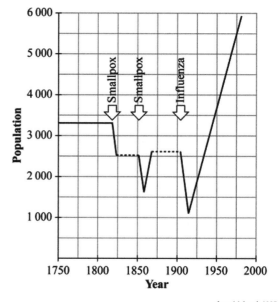

Population of the Blood Tribe

– from McLeod, 1987

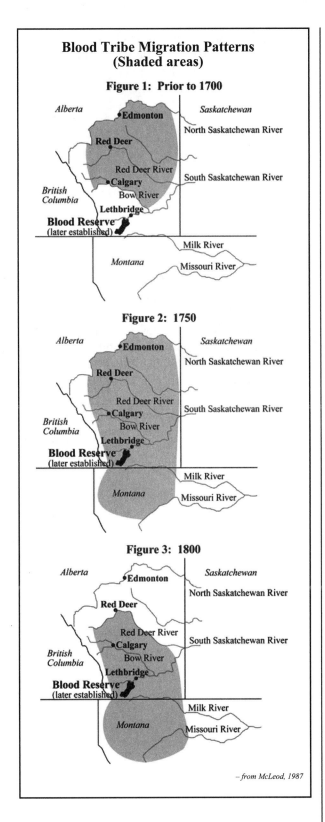

Blood Tribe Migration Patterns (Shaded areas)

Figure 1: Prior to 1700

Figure 2: 1750

Figure 3: 1800

– from McLeod, 1987

13. **a)** Examine the migration pattern maps for the Blood Tribe from prior to 1700 (Figure 1) and in 1750 (Figure 2). Describe a possible explanation for the change in migration pattern of the tribe over this period of time.

(1 mark)

b) The graph shows that from 1750 to 1817, the population of the Blood Tribe was stable. Describe two factors that might have contributed to this stability.

(2 marks)

c) Describe two possible explanations for the population change from 1920 to the present.

(2 marks)

Use the following additional information to answer the next three parts of the question.

Ornithine transcarbamylase (OTC) deficiency has been studied in a large Blood Tribe family that lived in an isolated area on the Blood Reserve. This X-linked recessive disorder has not been identified in any members of the Blackfoot and Peigan Tribes that, together with the Blood Tribe, make up the Blackfoot Nation.

The disorder is the result of an incorrectly formed or absent OTC enzyme. The normal OTC enzyme is part of a pathway that converts ammonia (from excess protein in the diet) into urea in liver cells. When the OTC enzyme is defective, ammonia accumulates in the blood. Ammonia is toxic to the central nervous system. Untreated OTC deficiency produces symptoms of lethargy, coma, and eventual death in early infancy.

The error in the OTC gene is usually a point mutation. Treatment is successful in prolonging life. However, in the Blood Tribe family studied, the mutation is a result of a large deletion of a portion of the gene. This results in more severe symptoms of the deficiency. Of males with this mutation, 100% die in early infancy.

Partial Pedigree of Ornithine Transcarbamylase Deficiency in a Blood Tribe Family

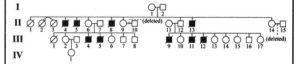

Note: Some of the pedigree was deleted for ease in interpretation. Some of the deceased males are assumed to be OTC deficient, although diagnosis did not occur before death.

– from McLeod, 1987 – Adapted from Emery and Rimoin's Principles and Practice of Medical Genetics 3/e, volume 1, edited by Alan E.H. Emery, David L. Rimoin, J Michael Connor, and Reed E. Pyeritz, pages 620–622, 1888, © 1997, by permission of the publisher Churchill Livingstone and by permission of Dr. David L. Rimoin.

d) Explain how it is possible that a male fetus with OTC deficiency could develop and the infant be born alive, yet become ill and die shortly after birth.

(2 marks)

e) Assume that individuals **III-2** and **III-3** are expecting another child. Construct two Punnett squares to illustrate the two possible crosses, based on the mother's **(III-2)** two possible genotypes. Calculate the probability of this child being a son with OTC deficiency. (Provide a legend to identify the symbols used for the two alleles.)

(4 marks)

Use the following additional information to answer the next part of the question.

A new therapy for OTC deficiency is being researched. In this therapy, viruses containing the normal OTC gene are injected into the bloodstream of an individual with OTC deficiency. These viruses travel to the liver and "infect" liver cells. Currently, this method has been successful in correcting OTC deficiency in mice. Approval is pending for human trials.

– Adapted from Emery and Rimoin's Principles and Practice of Medical Genetics 3/e, volume 1, edited by Alan E.H. Emery, David L. Rimoin, J. Michael Connor, and Reed E. Pyeritz, pages 620–622, 1888, © 1997, by permission of the publisher Churchill Livingstone and by permission of Dr. David L. Rimoin.

f) Explain how this viral therapy could be used to treat OTC deficiency in a patient.

(1 mark)

Source: January 2002

Use the following information to answer the next question.

Herbal medications have recently been gaining popularity in Canada and the rest of the western world. Most of these medications have been used for thousands of years in Native and Asian medicine. Many people assume that "natural" herbal medications are "safer" than western-style medicines produced in chemistry laboratories. However, like other medicines, herbal remedies contain chemicals that interact with other medications. As well, many natural plants such as hemlock (which was used by Socrates to commit suicide) and milkweed contain toxins that can cause serious damage to the body or be fatal.

The Canadian Health Regulatory Board classifies edible substances as either food or drugs. Most herbs have not been tested by pharmaceutical companies because companies cannot patent a naturally growing plant. For herbs to be classified as drugs and for companies to make health claims about them, they must go through tests similar to other drugs. Current herbal therapy regulations classify herbs as food supplements and, therefore, they are not controlled in terms of purity, concentration, or testing for drug interactions. For example, because Ginkgo biloba inhibits platelet action, it should not be used in conjunction with Aspirin.

Because herbal therapies are not classified as drugs, the cost to the consumer is not covered by most insurance companies or provincial health-care plans.

Consider the following sources.

Source 1: Wild Yam cream

In a report obtained from the Internet entitled "Everything your doctor hasn't shared with you about the causes of PMS and menopausal discomfort…and the revolutionary new natural solution," Beth Rosenthal describes her own personal experiences. She had very severe symptoms of premenstrual syndrome, which she attributed to supplements containing high levels of estrogen that her mother took during her pregnancy. (Symptoms of premenstrual syndrome include depression and premenstrual cramps.) Rosenthal began to use Wild Yam cream. She rubbed it into her skin three times a day for 21 of the 28 days of her menstrual cycle. She reported an increase in sex drive, a greater sense of well-being, and a dramatic decrease in the strength and pain of her menstrual cramps, all without side effects. She then began to advertise her story on the Internet so that she could sell the cream. She claims that the cream, which contains natural progesterone, overcomes "estrogen dominance," which is the cause of many women's menstrual cycle-related problems.

—from Rosenthal, 2000

Source 2: Ginkgo biloba

Ginkgo biloba has been used to treat nervous disorders such as mild Alzheimer's disease, short-term memory loss, lack of attention, and mild depression. Studies have shown that Ginkgo increases the flow of oxygenated blood to the brain. An abstract obtained from the Internet describes a year-long study conducted by Dr. Pierre LeBars to determine both the effectiveness and the safety of this herb. In the study, 202 people with mild-to-severe Alzheimer's disease were given three different tests of memory-related mental abilities, specifically designed to diagnose Alzheimer's disease. Subjects were assigned to two parallel groups and were either administered Ginkgo extracts in a pill form or a placebo pill (containing no active ingredient).

The study was a double-blind study conducted from several different medical centres. (In a double-blind study, neither the participants in the study nor the researchers know which group is receiving the placebo.) The cognitive tests were then readministered. The people who were given Ginkgo achieved significantly higher scores on all three tests after the year-long study than did those who were given the placebo. For example, 27% of those receiving the Ginkgo extract pills showed a four-point improvement on a cognitive scale called the ADAS-Cog (which tests memory function) compared with 14% of those taking the placebo pills. There was not a significant difference in either the number or the severity of side effects that were described by either group.

The researchers concluded that Ginkgo was safe and resulted in modest but significant improvements in cognitive function in people with Alzheimer's disease.

The Journal of the American Medical Association
– from Le Bars, Katz, Berman, Itil, Freedman, and Schatzberg, 1997

14. Write a unified response that addresses the following aspects of the use of herbal remedies in modern medicine.

- **Compare** the scientific validity of the two sources given.
- **Describe** the normal roles of estrogen and progesterone in the human female reproductive system. **Hypothesize** how Wild Yam cream would have to interact with a woman's hormones if it were to produce the benefits attributed to it by the source 1 article.
- **Describe** one advantage and one disadvantage of the current regulation of herbal therapies. **State** a revised regulation for herbal therapies, and **explain how** this revision would address the disadvantage(s) of the current regulations.

Source: January 2002

ANSWERS AND SOLUTIONS—WRITTEN RESPONSE

1. **a)**

- An increase in estrogen-mimicking compounds in the environment decreases sperm count.

  or

- Estrogen-mimicking compounds inhibit FSH production in male fetuses or newborns thereby decreasing multiplication of Sertoli cells and subsequently lowering sperm counts later in life.

  or

- If the level of estrogen-mimicking compounds is increased, then sperm count will decrease because estrogen-mimicking compounds inhibit FSH and thereby decrease Sertoli cell production.

b)

i)

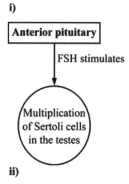

ii)

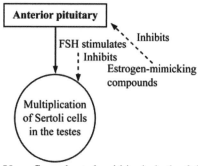

Your flow chart should include the following

- pituitary and indication of FSH production
- stimulatory effect of FSH on Sertoli cell numbers
- A broken line should be drawn that leads to the anterior pituitary or FSH

c)

- The number of Sertoli cells becomes fixed during the fetal or newborn stage of human development. As an adult, the number of Sertoli cells is established and therefore environmental levels of estrogen-mimicking compounds have little or no effect.

  or

- Fetal cells are rapidly dividing cells so environmental compounds can have a greater effect on them than on adult cells.

  or

- Estrogen-mimicking compounds activate or deactivate certain genes in the developing fetus with greater consequences than in the adult.

d) i) % decrease in sperm count

$$= \frac{89 - 60}{89} \times 100$$

$$= 33\% \ (\text{a decrease of } 33\%)$$

ii) Family size could be decreased on average.

  or

- The population structure could change, resulting in a decreased proportion of young individuals and an increased proportion of older individuals.

  or

- Total population size could start to decrease.

  or

- French couples could increase their use of sperm banks.

  or

- Adoption from other countries could increase in the society.

  or

- Any other reasonable answer.

e) Any two of the following for one mark each:

- Some sperm die as a result of the acidity of the female reproductive tract.

- Some sperm die as a result of the immune system of the female.

- Some sperm may miss the path to the fallopian tube.

- Some sperm may go up the fallopian tube that does not contain the oocyte.

- Many sperm are required for effective swimming or for protection.

- Some sperm are abnormal.

- Enzymes of approximately 500 sperm are required for a single sperm to penetrate the oocyte.

f) i) Any one of the following:

- Have there been changes in the amounts of estrogen-mimicking compounds in the environment, and do these changes correlate to changes in sperm count?

- Are the amounts of estrogen-mimicking compounds in the environment sufficient to inhibit FSH production in humans?

- Were the semen samples from the different time periods collected from men of the same age, health, etc.?

- Are there individual differences in exposure to estrogen-mimicking compounds, and do these differences correlate with lower sperm counts?

- Is there any evidence that the average number of Sertoli cells per male has declined since 1940?

- Does a reduction in the number of Sertoli cells decrease sperm count?

- Are there geographic regions in which estrogen-mimicking compounds are not present and, if so, is the average sperm count in these regions higher than elsewhere?

- Have other environmental chemicals increased since 1940 that might affect sperm count?

- Have other scientists provided evidence to support the hypothesis that reduced Sertoli cells produce a reduction in sperm count?

- Were the studies described in the article published in journals with high standards, were they conducted by credible researchers, and are the conclusions generally accepted in the research community?

- Or another question that deals with evidence, methods, cause-effect, or credibility.

ii) The student responses will vary with the answers given in part **f) i)**. The student should link his/her answer to his/her question to the decision he/she would make about the effect of these compounds on sperm counts.

2.

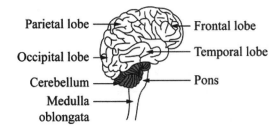

The sketch should include any four of the following labels: cerebrum, cerebellum, hypothalamus, pituitary gland, medulla oblongata, frontal lobe, parietal lobe, temporal lobe, occipital lobe, or any others.

Brain Area and Symptoms
The area of the brain affected by ataxia telangiectasia (AT) is the cerebellum or the motor cortex of the cerebrum (frontal lobe). This is shown by the decrease in motor coordination as the disease progresses. Related symptoms are lack of balance, slurred speech, loss of writing ability, difficulty controlling eye movements, and eventual use of a wheelchair (problems walking).

- **Environment Causes of DNA Damage/Repair Process**
  Possible causes of DNA damage are UV light, pesticides, X-rays, natural high-energy radiation, tobacco smoke, aromatic hydrocarbons (e.g. benzene), etc.

- **Cancer Link**
Disruption of the repair process could lead to cancer because mutations are not corrected. Mutations can lead to cancer if the mutation affects the control of cell division.

or

- The normal protein may be involved in arresting the cell cycle. The abnormal AT protein may therefore lead to increased cell division (cancer).

Calculation of AT Allele Frequency

The frequency of the homozygous recessive individuals in the population is q^2.

$$q^2 = \frac{1}{40\ 000}q$$
$$= 0.005$$

$\therefore$ The frequency of the AT allele is 0.005.

$$p = 1 - q$$
$$p = 0.995$$
$$2pq = 2(0.995)(0.005)$$
$$= 0.009\ 95$$

$\therefore$ this shows that approximately 1.0% or 0.995% of the population are carriers of the AT allele.

Two Societal Factors and/or Technologies
(Any two of the following)

Factors that could decrease the frequency of AT in the population

- Society could increase funding for genetic counselling. If this information were used to decrease the number of children produced by couples at risk, there would be a decrease in the frequency of the allele in the population.

or

- In vitro fertilization could be combined with pre-implantation screening to select embryos without the disorder for implantation. (In cases where there is a high risk of inheriting the AT disorder).

or

- A genetic screening test could be used to identify fetuses with AT. If this screening is followed by abortion, there would be a decrease in the frequency of the allele in the population.

Factors that could alleviate the symptoms of AT

- Gene therapy could be used to insert the normal gene from chromosome 11 into a bacterium. The bacterium could be cloned and then used to mass produce the protein coded for by the gene. This protein product could be used in treatment of AT to alleviate symptoms.

or

- Use an alternative treatment for cancer (e.g. chemotherapy) that does not use radiation for individuals with AT. This would prevent further chromosome damage.

or

- Electronic technology could be used to compensate for the lack of coordination displayed by individuals with AT (e.g., wheelchair).

or

- Laser surgery could be used to improve the appearance of the spider veins in the eye.
or
- Society could reduce the mutagens in the environment, which would reduce the incidence of cancer in AT patients.
or
- Physiotherapy could be used to improve the overall health and muscle coordination of the AT patient.
or
- Any other reasonable societal factor or technology.

3. **a)** Any one of the following:

- stimulates/regulates metabolic processes (metabolism)
- stimulates regulates cellular respiration (energy release, ATP production)
- stimulates/regulates heat production
- regulates body temperature

b)

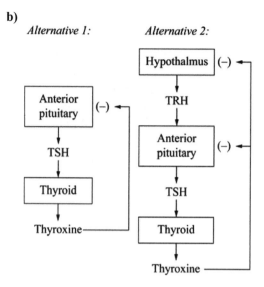

Alternative 1:   *Alternative 2:*

d) Any one of the following:

- High levels of non-radioactive iodine will be absorbed in greater amounts than the radioactive iodine, thereby reducing the effects of the radioactive iodine.

- The non-radioactive iodine will decrease the inflammation of the thyroid gland or decrease the incidence of thyroid cancer.

- Since part of the thyroid gland is destroyed, provision of non-radioactive iodine maximizes the production of thyroxine in the remaining functional portion of the thyroid gland.

c) Any two of the following:

- low energy (lethargy) (fatigue) (sleepiness)
- low metabolic rate (low BMR)
- blood test (low thyroxine, high TSH)
- stunted growth and development (failure to thrive)
- slowed mental development (cretinism)
- obesity
- low body temperature
- thick tongue, thick neck
- slowed heart rate
- constipation
- dry skin
- puffiness in the face
- increased blood cholesterol
- decreased breathing rate

Note: If more than two are given, mark the first two only.

e) Any one of these sketches of the mutation is acceptable.

	Deletion	Insertion	Substitution	Or Any Pairing Error
Was	T	T	T	
	G	G	G	
	C	C	C	A – T
	A	A	A	T – C
	T	T	T	T – A
	T	→T	T	
	↓	↓	↓	
Become	T	T	T	
	G	G	G	
	C	C	C	
	T	A	T	
	→T	T	T	
		A	T	
		T		

f) Germ cells (with mutations) combined in fertilization to form a zygote (fertilized egg).

The zygote divided by mitosis to form all the cells of the new individual; therefore all cells, including white blood cells, contain the mutation(s).

4. Biotic Potential Comparison

Pigs have a higher biotic potential than many other mammals of their size, e.g. humans or other primates because:

- pigs reach maturity at a younger age than primates and can therefore begin to produce offspring earlier

- pigs can be bred more than once per year (3 times), whereas primates can be bred only once a year

- pigs have many offspring per pregnancy as contrasted to primates, which usually have only one offspring per pregnancy

- pigs have shorter gestation periods (115 days) than primates, which allows pigs to have more litters per year

Researchers likely chose pigs for the following traits:

Any two of the following:

- the short pregnancy term, many offspring per litter, 3 litters per year possible, reach sexual maturity earlier than primates; yields many organs for transplants or further research

- organs of adequate size are produced

- pigs have a similar physiology to humans

- other animals, such as primates, have more complex social interactions and researchers may have felt that using these animals as donors would have been ethically unacceptable

- pigs are used as a source of food already, therefore more acceptable than using primate mammals

- relatively low cost because there is high output

- pigs are quite different genetically from humans and therefore the transmission of disease from pigs to humans is less likely than if primates were used

- or any other acceptable considerations

Technology

The student describes one of the following technologies that could have been used to obtain the HDAF gene.

- Restriction enzymes would have been used to cut out the HDAF gene from the human chromosome. These enzymes cut only specific sequences of DNA.

- Gel electrophoresis could be used to separate human DNA for analysis and help to locate the HDAF gene.

- Tissue sampling (such as blood sampling) would provide a source of human DNA from which to search for the gene or to detect expression of the RCA protein.

- Chromosome mapping (gene mapping) can be used to identify the position of genes on a chromosome. This can then be used to identify a candidate for the HDAF gene.

- Cloning of DNA would produce many copies of the desired gene to work with. Cloning can be achieved using recombinant bacteria or newer techniques such as PCR.

- Any other acceptable technology.

Outcome of HDAF Injection

After the HDAF gene is injected into a fertilized egg, the fertilized egg's DNA may recombine with the HDAF gene. If this occurs, every cell in the pig that arises from that fertilized egg will contain the HDAF gene. This produces the heterozygote transgenic offspring. Normal (non-transgenic) offspring arise when the fertilized egg's DNA does not recombine with the HDAF gene.

Crosses of Heterozygote Offspring

Crosses of heterozygote transgenic offspring were performed in order to produce offspring that were homozygous for the HDAF gene. The homozygous offspring could then be used for breeding stock to produce more homozygous transgenic pigs. These pigs would have organs that displayed more of the human RCA protein than the heterozygotes.

Researchers would want to use these organs in transplant trials since they would be less likely to be rejected by the recipient than the organs from heterozygote pigs or non-transgenic pigs.

Punnet Square

	HDAF⁺	*HDAF*⁻
HDAF⁺	HDAF⁺HDAF⁺	HDAF⁺HDAF⁻
HDAF⁻	HDAF⁺HDAF⁻	HDAF⁻HDAF⁻

The offspring of a cross between two heterozygous pigs would produce: homozygous transgenic pigs (HDAF⁺ HDAF⁺) expressing the RCA protein in their organs $\left(\frac{1}{4}\right)$, heterozygous transgenic pigs (HDAF⁺ HDAF⁻) $\left(\frac{1}{2}\right)$, homozygous non-transgenic pigs (HDAF⁻ HDAF⁻) $\left(\frac{1}{4}\right)$

5. **a)** **i)**

- mv—whether or not a subject smokes
- rv—death rate due to cancer

ii)

- not able to control diet, type of tobacco, exposure to radiation, environmental chemicals, and secondhand smoke, genetic predisposition to cancer, or other aspects of lifestyle
- other factors may influence the incidence of cancer, so conclusions about smoking may only be partly valid

b) If the viral DNA is inserted into a gene, it could lead to uncontrolled cell division (mitosis).

or

The virus attacks cells in the immune system and therefore the immune system is ineffective in destroying cancerous cells.

c) **i)** Any one of the following:

- women are living longer
- women are having fewer children
- women are having children later
- birth control pills are widely used
- nutrition has improved

- health care has improved
- environmental estrogens have increased

or

- any other acceptable social or economic changes

ii) Any one of the following linked to the corresponding change above.

- if women live longer, the chances are greater that they will develop cancer
- having fewer children is linked to a higher rate of cancer in reproductive organs
- having children later is linked to a higher rate of cancer in reproductive organs
- birth control pills allow women to reduce number of offspring and to have their children later, and they affect hormone levels. These could all lead to higher cancer rates in reproductive organs
- better nutrition has resulted in earlier sexual maturity which is linked to a higher rate of cancer in reproductive organs or better nutrition has reduced exposure to carcinogens, which leads to a lower rate of cancer in reproductive organs
- exposure to environmental estrogens are linked to a higher rate of cancer in reproductive organs
- better health care increases longevity, which leads to a higher rate of cancer in reproductive organs or better health care has decreased the rate of cancer in reproductive organs (e.g., Pap smears)

d) The phase in the cell cycle likely affected by cyclins and CDKs is interphase (G1, S-phase, G2).

e) If the drug blocked the CDKs or cyclin molecules then DNA replication would not occur and the cell would not divide.

or

The drug could block receptor sites within the cell (act as a competitive inhibitor) for CDKs or cyclins so that cell division is decreased (normal).

or

The drug could prevent the production of CDKs or cyclin molecules so that cell division is decreased (normal).

or

The drug could destroy the CDKs or cyclin molecules so that cell division is decreased (normal).

f) Too many "go" signals or not enough "stop" signals could lead to increased cell division and thus cancer.

6. Myelin Sheath Function

The myelin sheath surrounds the axons of neurons in the white matter of the central nervous system. It increases the speed of transmission of an action potential along the axon. Damage to the myelin sheath would slow down nervous response time or result in uneven nerve impulse transmission (if the myelin sheath were partially damaged). This would lead to the symptoms of motor function inhibition, impaired hearing, impaired speech, blindness, and mental deterioration.

Adrenal Gland Hormone

Damage to the adrenal cortex is indicated by high levels of ACTH in the blood.

Aldosterone is secreted by the adrenal cortex. It controls sodium ion concentration in the blood and helps regulate blood volume and pressure. With a decrease in aldosterone secretion, sodium ion concentration in the blood would decrease, blood volume would decrease, and blood pressure would decrease. Since sodium ions are not reabsorbed in the kidney nephrons, sodium ions in the urine and urine volume would both increase.

or

Cortisol is secreted by the adrenal cortex. It stimulates the liver to increase secretion of glucose into the blood. It does this by converting amino acids and glycerol into glucose. Cortisol also plays a role in stress control and in immune responses. It increases free amino acids in the blood. These can be used by cells for protein synthesis to repair damaged cells. A decrease in cortisol would lead to decreased use of amino acids and fats in metabolism. It would also decrease amino acids available to cells. This would cause fatigue and weakness.

It could also result in failure to cope with physical or mental stress.

or

Adrenal androgens are produced by the adrenal cortex. These have the same effects as male testosterone but are secreted in much smaller amounts. A decrease in secretion has little if any noticeable effects since other sex hormone secretions are responsible for primary and secondary sexual characteristics.

or

Adrenal medulla hormones, e.g., epinephrine, could be described although it is the adrenal cortex that is affected. Example: Epinephrine and norepinephrine are released in response to stress (real or imagined). It increases the conversion of fuels to glucose, increases heart rate and breathing rate, increases blood flow to skeletal muscles and to the heart and reduces blood flow to other areas of the body, and dilates the pupils. A decreased secretion of epinephrine would reduce the response to stress.

Determining Form of Inheritance

Evidence of X-linked Inheritance/Evidence of Autosomal Inheritance

- A greater number of males than females have the disorder/the number of males and females with the disorder is roughly equal.

- The disorder appears to be inherited from the maternal side of the family/the disorder appears to be inherited from either parent equally.

Evidence of Recessive Inheritance/Evidence of Dominant Inheritance

- Two parents without the disorder have a child with the disorder/two parents with the disorder have a child without the disorder.

- The disorder skips generations/the disorder is present in each generation or disappears completely from successive generations.

Sample Pedigree for an Autosomal Recessive Disorder

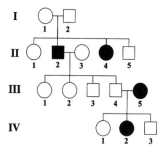

Labelling of this pedigree should indicate the following evidence:

This pedigree does not show any evidence that males or females inherit the disease more often, so there is no evidence that it is sex-linked. The first generation (parents) do not have the disorder, but two of their children have the disorder. This indicates that it is a recessive disorder that is not expressed in the parents, who are carriers of the disease allele.

Sample Pedigree for a Sex-linked Recessive Disorder

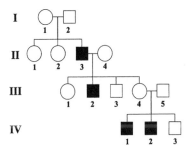

Labelling of the pedigree should indicate the following evidence:

This pedigree shows evidence that males inherit the disorder more often than females. This is consistent with a disease allele that is carried on the X chromosome. It is recessive: II-3 does not pass on the disease to any of his daughters, even though they would have a copy of his X chromosome with the disease allele.

Collection of Fetal Cells

Chorionic villus sampling (CVS) can be used to obtain fetal cells. In this procedure, a catheter is inserted through the cervix to the chorion and a sample of the chorionic villi is obtained. These cells are fetal cells.

or

Amniocentesis can be used to obtain fetal cells. In this procedure, a hollow needle is inserted through the abdominal wall into the amniotic cavity. Amniotic fluid and some sloughed off fetal cells are withdrawn.

Risks/Benefits of Early Diagnosis
(One risk and one benefit from the list below.)

Benefits
The individual who has a disorder like ALD diagnosed early can use any treatments or lifestyle modifications sooner to alleviate the disease symptoms or progression.

or

Early fetal diagnosis could lead to abortion of an affected fetus with a disorder. This would decrease the cost to the society of treating a medical disorder.

or

Any other reasonable benefit to society or the individual.

Risks
An individual who has a disorder like ALD diagnosed early will have to live with the knowledge of his/her inheritance of a progressively degenerative disease before the onset of any symptoms. This could cause increased stress.

or

Early diagnosis of disorders like ALD may be used inappropriately by outside sources if the diagnosis is not kept in confidence. This would harm society if it led to discrimination against these individuals, and therefore threatened the common good.

or

Any other reasonable risk to society or the individual.

Science

Score	Scoring Criteria
	The student…
5 **Excellent**	• clearly explains the effect of myelin degeneration on the CNS that results in ALD symptoms related to impaired brain function • identifies an adrenal hormone and clearly describes the symptoms resulting from a decreased secretion of this hormone • clearly describes two pieces of evidence used to determine the mode of inheritance illustrated by a pedigree • draws an accurate four-generation pedigree chart that clearly illustrates the mode of inheritance selected, and labels the evidence
4 **Proficient**	• explains the effect of myelin degeneration on the CNS • identifies an adrenal hormone and describes some of the symptoms resulting from a decreased secretion of this hormone • clearly describes one piece of evidence and suggests one piece of evidence used to determine the mode of inheritance illustrated by a pedigree • draws a four-generation pedigree chart that could illustrate the mode of inheritance selected
3 **Satisfactory**	• partially explains the effect of myelin degeneration • identifies an adrenal hormone and describes one of the symptoms resulting from a decreased secretion of this hormone • describes one piece of evidence used to determine the mode of inheritance illustrated by a pedigree **or** suggests two pieces of evidence • draws a partially correct pedigree chart that could illustrate either autosomal recessive or X-linked inheritance

Score	Scoring Criteria
2 **Limited**	• describes the function of the neuron or a part of the neuron • identifies an adrenal gland hormone **or** describes the function of this hormone **or** describes one symptom of decreased secretion of an adrenal hormone • partially describes one piece of evidence used to determine the mode of inheritance illustrated by a pedigree • draws a partial pedigree chart
1 **Poor**	• addresses only one of the four scoring bullets at 2, 3, or 4 level

INSUFFICIENT is a special category. It is not an indication of quality. It should be assigned to papers that do not contain a discernible attempt to address the questions presented in the assignment or that are too brief to assess in this or any other scoring category.

Technology and Society

Score	Scoring Criteria
	The student…
5 **Excellent**	• identifies either amniocentesis or CVS **and** clearly describes the technology • clearly describes a risk **and** a benefit of early diagnosis of ALD to an individual and/or to society
4 **Proficient**	• identifies either amniocentesis or CVS **and** partially describes the technology • clearly describes a risk or a benefit **and** partially describes another risk or benefit of early diagnosis of ALD
3 **Satisfactory**	• identifies either amniocentesis **or** CVS or partially describes one of the two technologies • clearly describes either a risk or a benefit of early diagnosis of ALD **or** partially describes both a risk and a benefit
2 **Limited**	• identifies **or** describes a technology that may have been used in genetic screening or ALD research • partially describes a risk or a benefit of early diagnosis of ALD **or** describes a risk or a benefit of the ALD disorder or of research into the ALD disorder

1 Poor	• addresses one of the two scoring bullets at a 2 level

INSUFFICIENT is a special category. It is not an indication of quality. It should be assigned to papers that do not contain a discernible attempt to address the questions presented in the assignment or that are too brief to assess in this or any other scoring category.

7. **a)** **i)** The women taking the placebo are the control group (used as a comparison with the women taking AZT).

or
A placebo is used to determine if the psychological effects of treatment (taking a pill) are causing any observed changes.

ii) Doctors should do everything in their power to help people with known diseases, especially if there is a chance of transmission to others.

b) Viruses are small enough to pass through the placental membranes from maternal blood to the fetal blood.

or
HIV can directly infect the baby at birth since there is a possibility of maternal/fetal blood contact.

c) The mutated DNA gene is transcribed into an mRNA molecule. The mRNA molecule leaves the nucleus and attaches to a ribosome in the cytoplasm. The mRNA is translated into a sequence of amino acids based on the three base codons of the mRNA molecule. Amino acids are brought to the ribosome by tRNA molecules, which have anti-codons to complement the mRNA codons. Amino acids join together to form the protein (CCR5 receptor molecule).

d) There may have been a epidemic of a infection similar to the HIV in northern Europe generations ago. Without treatment, many people would have died. People with a mutant CCRS allele would have a selective advantage over people without the allele, thereby increasing its frequency.

or
The mutated CCRS allele occurred in an European individual originally. The geographic isolation or reproductive isolation of the European people maintained the allele in Europe until recent times. (Founder effect and bottleneck effect)

e) $p + q = 1$
$q = 0.111$
$p = 0.889$
$2pq = 0.197$
so 19.7% or 20%

f) Possible technologies are:

• Use genetic engineering to introduce the CCR5 mutant allele into the macrophages, thereby preventing the HIV from attaching to them.

• Drugs or chemicals that would plug the CCR5 receptors and prevent the HIV from binding onto these sites.

• A vaccine made of fragments of CCR5 receptors that could induce the recipient's immune system to produce its own CCR5 binding antibodies.

• Or, any other reasonable answer.

8. Meiosis in a tapeworm results in haploid sperm and egg cells. This is necessary before a sperm and egg can recombine to form a diploid cell. Meiosis makes fertilization, which recombines genetic information to produce variation in a population, possible. Variations allow individuals in the population to survive under varying conditions.

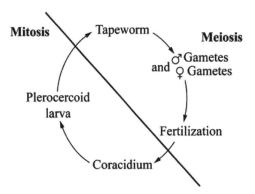

Life Cycle

Mitosis allows for growth of the tapeworm and repair of tissues in a tapeworm. It maintains all the instructions in the original cell since the cells produced are identical. The tapeworm also changes forms in various hosts to exploit various environments. Mitosis makes these changes possible.

Incorporation of HGH Gene Into Tapeworm
A virus entered a human body cell and its DNA became incorporated into the human DNA. By chance, the viral DNA became incorporated close to the human gene for HGH. When the human DNA began replicating viral DNA, the HGH was replicated as well and became a part of the viral genome.
The virus mutated in such a way as to allow it to enter the reproductive cells of a tapeworm gamete. Once inside a tapeworm cell, the viral genetic information became incorporated into the tapeworm DNA. The gene for HGH then became part of that tapeworm's DNA. Since it was a gamete, this altered gene would be passed on to subsequent generations of tapeworms.

Dwarfism and Treatment
Lack of HGH during childhood development results in the disorder known as dwarfism. Children with dwarfism develop at a greatly reduced rate, however body proportions are relatively normal. At puberty, children who lack HGH have long bones that are greatly reduced in length, and hence they are dwarfs as adults.

Advantages of using PGF instead of human HGH:

- produces growth in a similar way to HGH

- does not cause insensitivity to insulin

- no risk in leading to diabetes

- blood glucose would not elevate; other diabetic symptoms would not occur

- any other reasonable response

Science

Score	Scoring Criteria
	The student…
5 **Excellent**	• draws an accurate tapeworm life cycle diagram that includes most of the following: gametes, fertilized egg, coracidium, plerocercoid, and adult tapeworm. Mitosis and meiosis are clearly and correctly indicated on the diagram • clearly describes the value of mitosis and meiosis to a tapeworm • clearly describes the three necessary steps in the transfer of the human growth hormone gene to a tapeworm
4 **Proficient**	• draws a tapeworm life cycle diagram that is fairly complete and correctly indicates mitosis and meiosis on the diagram or draws an accurate tapeworm lifecycle with mitosis or meiosis indicated on the diagram • clearly describes the value of either mitosis or meiosis **and** partially describes the value of either mitosis or meiosis • clearly describes two of the three steps in the transfer of the HGH gene to a tapeworm or partially describes all three steps
3 **Satisfactory**	• draws a tapeworm life cycle diagram that is partially complete and correctly indicates mitosis or meiosis on it **or** clearly draws an accurate tapeworm life cycle diagram • clearly describes the value of either mitosis or meiosis **or** partially describes the value of both mitosis and meiosis • clearly describes one of the three steps in the transfer of the HGH gene to a tapeworm **or** partially describes two steps

2 Limited	• attempts a tapeworm life cycle diagram **or** describes when mitosis or meiosis occurs • partially describes the value of either mitosis or meiosis • partially describes one of the steps in the transfer of a human gene to another organism
1 Poor	• addresses only one of the three bullets at a 3 or 2 level

INSUFFICIENT is a special category. It is not an indication of quality. It should be assigned to papers that do not contain a discernible attempt to address the questions presented in the assignment or that are too brief to assess in this or any other scoring category.

Technology and Society

Score	Scoring Criteria
	The student…
5 Excellent	• clearly describes dwarfism **and** identifies two advantageous effects of using PGF in its treatment
4 Proficient	• describes dwarfism and identifies one advantageous effect of using PGF and suggests one advantageous effect **or** partially describes dwarfism and identifies two advantageous effects of using PGF in its treatment
3 Satisfactory	• partially describes dwarfism and identifies one advantageous effect of using PGF or identifies two advantageous effects of using PGF in treatment of low HGH **or** clearly describes dwarfism
2 Limited	• identifies or partially describes dwarfism and suggests one advantageous effect of using PGF in its treatment **or** identifies one advantageous effect of using PGF to treat low HGH
1 Poor	• identifies or partially describes dwarfism **or** suggests one advantageous effect of using PGF to treat low HGH

INSUFFICIENT is a special category. It is not an indication of quality. It should be assigned to papers that do not contain a discernible attempt to address the questions presented in the assignment or that are too brief to assess in this or any other scoring category.

9. a) Although there is a high level of glucose in the blood, in the absence of insulin, body cells are impermeable to glucose; therefore, glucose is not available as an energy source and fatigue results. Since glucose cannot be used as an energy source, fat or protein stores are metabolized which results in weight loss. Also, glucose is not stored, therefore weight gain is not possible.

b) Glucose would be found in the urine of the patient with diabetes mellitus.

or

The urine produced by a patient with diabetes insipidus would be insipid (tasteless). (The urine produced by a patient with diabetes mellitus would be sweet).

or

The urine of the patient with diabetes mellitus could also have ketones present and could be slightly acidic.

c) i) Thyroid gland → thyroxine
   Adrenal gland → cortisol, epinephrine

   ii) Thyroxine would decrease blood glucose levels by increasing cellular metabolism rates. Cortisol would increase blood sugar levels by converting amino acids (or fatty acids or glycerol or fats or proteins) to glucose. Epinephrine stimulates the conversion of glycogen to glucose by liver and muscle tissue, thereby increasing blood sugar levels.

d) Sensory neurons were damaged because the patients could not feel the pain caused by the broken ankle or lesions but could still move their limbs, (i.e., motor skill intact).

e) Damage to or irregular functioning of blood vessels of the retina may result in permanent damage to the cells making up the retina (i.e., lack of O_2/nutrients). If the rods or cones are damaged, then there will be reduced sensory reception and reduced impulses in neurons to the occipital lobe. This would result in some vision loss or even blindness.

or

If the optic nerve is damaged by decreased blood flow, the sensory information is not passed to the occipital lobe of the brain. This would result in vision loss or blindness.

or

The increase in blood vessels may obstruct the light reception by retina cells, resulting in vision loss or blindness. Reduced sensory stimulation would occur, so the neurons would send reduced impulses to the occipital lobe of the cerebrum.

f) i) DNA: TTA   or   DNA: TTG

   ii) Must show a point mutation (e.g., TTC codes for a.a. lysine).

10. **Male secondary sex characteristics**
Hormone: Testosterone

- Growth of facial, axillary, and pubic hair
- Receding hairline
- Growth of the larynx, which causes lowering of the voice
- Strengthening of the muscles
- Increased secretion of body oils (acne)
- Thickening of the skin
- Increased red blood cell count
- Growth of long bones (and final fusing of epiphyses)
- Increased basal metabolic rate

or
Female secondary sex characteristics
Hormone: Estrogen

- Growth of axillary and pubic hair
- Maintains low blood cholesterol levels
- Growth of the breasts
- Increased deposits of subcutaneous fat, especially in hips and breasts (female fat distribution)
- Widening (and lightening) of the pelvis
- Increased basal metabolic rate
- Facilitates calcium uptake
- Increased water content of skin

- Growth of long bones (and final fusing of epiphyses)
- Increased secretion of body oils (acne)
- Alleles: X^C – CH; X^c – normal

Genotypes:

II-4: $X^C Y$	IV-6: $X^C X^c$
II-5: $X^c X^c$	IV-7: $X^c Y$
III-11: $X^c Y$	IV-8: $X^C X^c$
III-12: $X^C X^c$	IV-9: $X^c X^c$

	X^C	X^c
X^c	$X^C X^c$	$X^c X^c$
Y	$X^C Y$	$X^c Y$

- Probability of III-11 and III-12's child being male with CH

$$X^C Y = \frac{1}{4} \text{ or } 25\%$$

- More females than males inherit CH in generation III because individual II-4, a male, has CH, and because CH is X-linked dominant, the father's will be passed on to all his female children in generation III (but not to his sons, who received the father's Y chromosome).

State a possible experimental problem

- What effect does increasing (or decreasing) testosterone (or estrogen) have on hair follicle distribution?
- What gene(s) on the X chromosome code(s) for hair follicle distribution?
- What effect would increasing (decreasing) testosterone (estrogen) levels have on CH individuals?
- What protein molecule is produced in CH individuals that differs from individuals with normal hair follicle distribution?
- Or any other reasonable experimental problem that could be investigated.

Evaluate whether conducting research would be useful for affected individuals

Possible Advantages

- An advantage of CH research for individuals is that the research might ultimately lead to a cure for CH.
- An advantage of CH research for individuals is that the research might lead to treatment for

individuals with acquired or inherited baldness.

- An advantage of CH research for individuals is that the information gained about the nature of CH could be used in counselling individuals who have CH and are planning on having children.

- An advantage of CH research to society is that it may lead to a better understanding of the actions of testosterone and estrogen. This increased knowledge could benefit society as a whole, potentially leading to health benefits for society.

- An advantage of CH research to society is that it may provide a better understanding of other X-linked traits. This increased knowledge could benefit society as a whole, potentially leading to health benefits for society.

- Other responses may be appropriate.

Possible Disadvantages

- A disadvantage to society of research to find a cure for CH is that it is very costly and may not be warranted for such a small population of affected individuals.

- A disadvantage to society of research to find a cure for CH is that it sends the message to society that if an individual does not appear normal, a cure must be found to rid society of a particular phenotype. Finding a cure does not promote the notion that society is at its best when made up of a mosaic of individuals.

- Other responses may be appropriate.

Science

Score	Scoring Criteria
	The student…
5 Excellent	• identifies testosterone or estrogen and describes three secondary sex characteristics (one of which is hair follicle distribution) resulting from stimulation by the identified hormone • correctly identifies all the individuals' genotypes, using sex-linked notation, and provides a clear legend for the symbols • communicates, using a Punnett square, the probability of a CH male clearly explains why more females than males inherit CH in generation III
4 Proficient	• identifies testosterone or estrogen and describes 2 secondary sex characteristics resulting from stimulation by the identified hormone **or** describes 3 secondary sex characteristics • correctly identifies most of the individuals' genotypes, using sex-linked notation • communicates, using a Punnett square, the probability of a CH male, and partially explains why more females than males inherit CH in generation III, **or** partially communicates the probability of a CH male and explains why more females than males inherit CH in generation III
3 Satisfactory	• identifies testosterone or estrogen and describes 1 secondary sex characteristic resulting from stimulation by the identified hormone **or** describes 2 secondary sex characteristics • correctly identifies some of the individuals' genotypes, using sex-linked notation • communicates, using a Punnett square, the probability of a CH male **or** explains why more females than males inherit CH in generation III **or** partially communicates the probability of a CH male and partially explains why more females than males inherit CH in generation III

2 **Limited**	• identifies testosterone or estrogen or describes one secondary sex characteristic resulting from stimulation by the identified hormone • identifies some of the individuals' genotypes as if autosomal dominant inheritance, autosomal recessive inheritance, or sex-linked recessive inheritance occurred • constructs a Punnett square, **or** communicates the probability of a CH male, **or** partially explains why more females than males inherit CH in generation III
1 **Poor**	• One of the bullets is addressed at a 2 or 3 level

INSUFFICIENT is a special category. It is not an indication of quality. It should be assigned to papers that do not contain a discernible attempt to address the questions presented in the assignment or that are too brief to assess in this or any other scoring category.

Technology and Society

Score	Scoring Criteria
	The student…
5 **Excellent**	• clearly states a possible experimental problem that could be investigated to find out more about CH or hair follicle distribution • evaluates whether conducting this research would be useful by describing one advantage and one disadvantage of CH research to the individual and/or society
4 **Proficient**	• states a possible experimental problem that could be investigated to find out more about CH or hair follicle distribution, but either the manipulated variable or responding variable is not clearly identified in the problem statement • evaluates whether conducting this research would be useful by describing one advantage and partially describing one disadvantage **or** by partially describing an advantage and describing one disadvantage of CH research to the individual and/or society

3 **Satisfactory**	• suggests an experimental problem, or identifies an area of research that could be investigated to find out more about CH or hair follicle distribution • evaluates whether conducting this research would be useful by describing one advantage or one disadvantage **or** partially describing one advantage and partially describing one disadvantage of CH research to the individual and/or society
2 **Limited**	• suggests one area of research that could be investigated to find out more about CH or hair follicle distribution • evaluates whether conducting this research would be useful by partially describing one advantage **or** one disadvantage of CH research
1 **Poor**	• One of the bullets is addressed at a 2 level

INSUFFICIENT is a special category. It is not an indication of quality. It should he assigned to papers that do not contain a discernible attempt to address the questions presented in the assignment or that are too brief to assess in this or any other scoring category.

11. **a)** A gene mutation alters the nitrogen-base sequence of the gene's DNA.

This change in the sequence results in an altered mRNA nitrogen-base sequence that, in turn, can alter the amino acids in the diaphorase enzyme.

b) $q^2 = \dfrac{6}{55}$
$ = 0.11$
$q = 0.33$
The frequency of the recessive allele is 0.33.

c) $p + q = 1$
$1 - 0.33 = p$
$p = 0.67$
$2pq = 2(0.33)(0.67)$
$ = 0.44$
Theoretically, 44% of the individuals were heterozygous for the allele.

d) The mutation first occurred in an individual in the Fugate family; therefore, more members of this family have the allele than do the general population.

or

Intermarriage within the Fugate family increased the probability of two carriers mating and producing blue offspring.

or

Because the Fugate family lived in an isolated area, the likelihood of carriers mating and producing blue offspring increased.

e) Any two of the following:

- The population was small, and a large population is required to meet the conditions for Hardy–Weinberg equilibrium.

- There was non-random mating rather than the random mating required for Hardy–Weinberg equilibrium.

- Mutation occurred to produce the defective diaphorase, and Hardy–Weinberg equilibrium requires no mutation.

- Emigration or immigration from the population occurred, and migration does not occur in populations that satisfy Hardy–Weinberg equilibrium.

f) i) *Bb* (heterozygous)

ii) Benjy produced some normal diaphorase and, over time, was able to convert enough methemoglobin into hemoglobin to express a normal skin colour.

or

Fetal hemoglobin is different than adult hemoglobin. Therefore, the expression of Benjy's phenotype may have changed shortly after birth.

or

Any other reasonable explanation.

iii) Treatment does not change the alleles present in the germ cells of the individuals; therefore, they can still be passed on to future generations.

12.

Three-Month-Old Fetus and Associated Structures

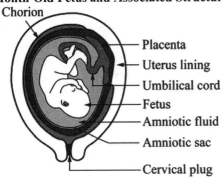

The amniotic fluid surrounding the fetus functions to protect the fetus from physical trauma. The amniotic sac that holds the amniotic fluid provides a protective barrier for the fetus, thereby preventing the entrance into the amniotic fluid of harmful bacteria, viruses, and other harmful pathogens and chemicals that would eventually affect the fetus. It also helps to regulate temperature for the fetus. The placenta acts as a barrier between the fetal blood supply and the maternal blood supply. It is the site of nutrient, gas, and waste exchange between the fetal circulation and maternal circulation. Nutrients and oxygen diffuse into the fetal blood while carbon dioxide and wastes diffuse into maternal blood. The placenta also produces hormones. HCC stimulates the corpus luteum to produce estrogen and progesterone in order to maintain pregnancy in the first trimester. The placenta also acts as a barrier to some pathogens that may be in the mother's body. The umbilical cord contains blood vessels that transport blood between the placenta and the fetus.

A mother's voice produces sound waves. Sound waves are converted to fluid waves in the ears of her fetus within her uterus. These fluid waves stimulate hair cells in the organ of Corti located within the cochlea. This creates action potentials in sensory neurons in the auditory nerve. The sensory neurons synapse with interneurons. Eventually, stimulation of interneurons occurs in the temporal lobe of the brain where auditory information is interpreted.

or

Any other specific stimuli pathway to the CNS could be described.

One technology that could stimulate appropriate neural development in infants is the use of colourful mobiles and learning centres. These would cause sensory receptors to be stimulated and eventually stimulate neurons in the brain. The stimulation of neurons creates appropriate synapses and helps neurons to develop.

A government policy that would also have a positive influence on fetal development would be the formation of a childhood development specialist team made up of early childhood educators, public health nurses, social workers, child psychologists, and early childhood movement specialists. This specialist team would be available to assess individual home situations, provide information seminars in prenatal classes and to parent groups, and offer assistance in setting up an environment that provides an optimal amount of stimulation for the infant. Appropriate stimulation will develop neuron connections, increase the size of the brain, and help develop appropriate social responses.

Other technologies or government polices that could be described are:

- any technology that stimulates the senses and therefore increases neural stimulation

- any government policy that would help increase appropriate stimulation of a child or appropriate interaction of a child with a significant adult

- technologies to investigate genetic causes of abnormal brain development and/or to correct these

- government policies or technologies that would protect the fetal environment from conditions that might affect neural development

Science

Score	Scoring Criteria
	The student
5 **Excellent**	• sketches the fetal environment accurately and correctly labels four parts • clearly describes in detail how the fetal environment supports the fetus at three months of development • clearly describes the pathway for sensory interpretation in a fetus or newborn from a specific stimulus
4 **Proficient**	• sketches the fetal environment accurately and correctly labels three parts • describes how the fetal environment supports the fetus • describes the pathway for sensory interpretation from a specific stimulus
3 **Satisfactory**	• sketches the fetal environment and correctly labels two parts • partially describes how the fetal environment supports the fetus • partially describes a pathway for sensory interpretation
2 **Limited**	• attempts a sketch of the fetal environment and correctly labels one part **or** an accurate sketch is drawn • describes at least one supporting structure in the fetal environment • identifies one step in a pathway for sensory interpretation
1 **Poor**	• only one of the bullets is addressed at a 2 or 3 level

INSUFFICIENT is a special category. It is not an indication of quality. It should be assigned to papers that do not contain a discernible attempt to address the questions presented in the assignment or that are too brief to assess in this or any other scoring category.

Technology and Society

Score	Scoring Criteria
	The student
5 **Excellent**	• identifies and describes two relevant technologies or government polices that would stimulate neural development • clearly explains how each technology or government policy would affect neural development
4 **Proficient**	• identifies two relevant technologies or government polices and describes one **or** identifies and partially describes two relevant technologies or government policies • explains how one technology or government policy would affect neural development and partially explains the other
3 **Satisfactory**	• identifies one relevant technology or government policy and partially describes the other **or** identifies or partially describes two. • explains how one technology or government policy would affect neural development **or** partially explains both
2 **Limited**	• identifies one relevant technology or government policy or partially describes one • partially explains how one technology or government policy would affect neural development
1 **Poor**	• addresses one of the two scoring bullets at a 2 level

INSUFFICIENT is a special category. It is not an indication of quality. It should he assigned to papers that do not contain a discernible attempt to address the questions presented in the assignment or that are too brief to assess in this or any other scoring category.

13. **a)** Population pressures may have resulted in a search for new food sources or living space and stimulated the change to a greater migration area in 1750 from the pattern prior to 1700.

or
Lack of food due to climatic changes (or overhunting, death of buffalo, etc) may have caused the tribe to migrate farther south in 1750 to seek new food sources.

or
Any reasonable answer related to an increased migration area or a more southern migration area.

b) The graph shows that from 1750 to 1817, the population of the Blood Tribe was stable. Describe two factors that might have contributed to this stability.

Any two of the following:

• food supply was constant and supported that number of individuals

• no new diseases changed mortality

• survival rate of offspring (or birth rate) was constant

• environmental conditions such as weather were relatively constant so the population could move freely since it was not restricted to a reserve

• any other reasonable answer

c) Describe two possible explanations for the population change from 1920 to the present.

Any two of the following:

• better health care resulted in lower mortality

• increased food supply from new agricultural practices resulted in higher natality and/or lower mortality

• lower mortality from disease occurred as the resistant individuals increased in the population (less death from smallpox)

• less warfare occurred after signing the treaty, therefore, mortality was lower

• improved shelter reduced winter mortality

• any other reasonable answer

d) Explain how it is possible that a male fetus with OTC deficiency could develop and the infant be born alive, yet become ill and die shortly after birth.

(2 marks)

Wastes (including ammonia) produced by the fetus diffuse across the placenta and the mother's liver (OTC enzymes) processes the wastes.

After birth, the child's own liver (OTC enzymes) needs to function or ammonia will accumulate and the infant will die.

e) Assume that individuals **III-2** and **III-3** are expecting another child. Construct two Punnett squares to illustrate the two possible crosses, based on the mother's (**III-2**) two possible genotypes. Calculate the probability of this child being a son with OTC deficiency if the mother is heterozygous. (Provide a legend to identify the symbols used for the two alleles.)

Mother Heterozygous (III-2)

	X^N	X^n
X^N	$X^N X^N$	$X^N X^n$
Y	$X^N Y$	$X^n Y$

Mother Homozygous Dominant (III-2)

	X^N	X^N
X^N	$X^N X^N$	$X^N X^N$
Y	$X^N Y$	$X^N Y$

The probability of a son with OTC if the mother is heterozygous is 0.25.

f) Explain how this viral therapy could be used to treat OTC deficiency in a patient.

The DNA in the virus for the OTC gene would be incorporated into liver cells. A correct OTC protein would be manufactured. This would convert ammonia to urea for the individual.

14. Write a unified response that addresses the following aspects of the use of herbal remedies in modem medicine.

Sample Answers

- **Compare** the scientific validity of the two sources given.

    Source 1: Wild Yam Cream
    The conclusions drawn are not valid because they are based on personal accounts of the effects of Wild Yam Cream over a very short period of time: one menstrual cycle. Beth Rosenthal did not set up a scientific investigation, complete with fused variables. There was no control group that received a placebo cream, and there were not enough participants in the study to produce accurate statistics necessary to draw accurate conclusions. There was no corroboration of her results by other independent researchers. The article is written by a person who is selling the product and may have a conflict of interest.

    Source 2: Ginkgo biloba
    The conclusions drawn from the Ginkgo biloba study are more valid than the conclusions drawn from the Wild Yam Cream study. Some of the reasons for this are as follows. A placebo pill was given to one of the groups to act as a comparison for the experimental group who received the Ginkgo biloba. A pre-test of all three tests of memory-related mental abilities was administered to act as a comparison for test results after the administration of Ginkgo biloba. All patients in both the control group and the experimental group were Alzheimer patients. The study was double-blind, which means that the researchers did not know which group was the experimental group and which group was the control group. A high number of participants were involved, which provides statistics that can be used to draw conclusions. A number of controls were used in the study so the effects of the Ginkgo biloba could more accurately be attributed to Ginkgo rather than to uncontrolled influences. The study took place over a long period of time (one year), which would act to control daily, weekly, or even monthly fluctuations in memory ability associated with uncontrolled influences.

The results (27% improvement for Ginkgo group versus 14% improvement for control group) are significantly different. The study was published in a scientific journal, indicating that peer review of the results had taken place.

- Describe the normal roles of estrogen and progesterone in the human female reproductive system. Hypothesize how Wild Yam cream would have to interact with a woman's hormones if it were to produce the benefits attributed to it by the source I article.

Roles of Estrogen:
In the female reproductive system, estrogen stimulates growth and maturation of all reproductive structures such as the ovaries, uterus, and breasts. Estrogen produces secondary sexual characteristics in adolescence and adulthood including female-type hair distribution, widened hips, and lengthening of the long bones. Estrogen stimulates the thickening of the endometrium during days 6 to 26 in the menstrual cycle. Estrogen stimulates growth of the uterus and mammary glands during pregnancy.

Roles of Progesterone:
In the female reproductive system, progesterone (along with estrogen) causes thickening of the endometrium from day 1 to day 26 of the menstrual cycle. Progesterone is also responsible for maintenance of the endometrium and prepares the endometrium for implantation of the embryo by increasing glandular development and blood vessel development. Progesterone prevents the contraction of uterine muscles during pregnancy.

Possible Hypotheses:

- Wild Yam cream would have to increase the level of progesterone in the body thereby playing a role in causing increased thickening of the endometrium (or preventing the contraction of the uterus), which would decrease menstrual cramping.

or

- Wild Yam cream would have to increase the level of progesterone in the body, which may interact with areas of the brain causing an increased sense of well-being or an increased sex drive.

or

- Any other appropriate hypothesis.

- Describe one advantage and one disadvantage of the current regulation of herbal therapies.

Possible advantages:

- Consumers can obtain herbs without a prescription from a doctor. This saves both time and money for the consumer and for the medical profession.

- Consumers can attempt to test the benefits of herbal remedies on their own without a doctor's consultation.

- Many people come from cultural backgrounds in which herbs are incorporated into cultural and religious ceremonies. The people can obtain the herbs without the interference or consultation of the medical profession.

Possible Disadvantages:

- The active chemicals in herbs are not explicitly stated on packaging, even though they may cause serious side effects or perhaps interact negatively with other medications.

- The drug companies may know that a certain herb is useful for treatment of a specific illness but do not release this information because it is not financially advantageous for them to do so.

- Because it is not financially advantageous for drug companies to research herbs, the action of certain herbs remains unknown even though some herbs may provide cures or remedies for specific illnesses or diseases.

- Herbs sold in health food stores may be contaminated and cause illness because the sale of herbs is not tightly controlled in terms of purity and/or concentration.

- Consumers may not try herbal remedies because the cost of obtaining the herbs is not covered by health plans. The herbal remedy route may have fewer side effects than prescribed drugs, but because prescribed drugs are covered by provincial health plans, consumers may choose prescribed drugs over herbal remedies.

- Companies may make unproven claims about the effectiveness of herbal remedies without proper scientific testing.

- State a revised regulation for herbal therapies, and explain how this revision would address the disadvantage(s) of the current regulations.

  - All herbs should be reclassified as drugs. This would result in testing of the herbs to determine their effects (purity, concentration, side effects, health effects, etc.) and protect consumers.

    or

  - Companies should be allowed to patent herbal remedies produced from plants. This would result in increased research into the possible benefits of herbal remedies because of possible increased profits for the company.

    or

  - Herbal remedies should be covered by provincial health-care plans. This would encourage the use of alternative health remedies by consumers.

    or

  - Any other revision to the regulations.

Science

Score	Scoring Criteria
	The student…
5 **Excellent**	• clearly compares the scientific validity of both sources • fully describes the roles of estrogen and progesterone in the human female • writes a clear hypotheses of how Wild Yam cream would interact with a woman's hormones and links it to the effects of the herbal remedy
4 **Proficient**	• compares the scientific validity of both sources • describes the roles of estrogen and progesterone in the human female • writes a hypothesis of how Wild Yam cream would interact with a woman's hormones and suggests a link to the effects of the herb remedy
3 **Satisfactory**	• describes one factor relating to the scientific validity of each source and suggests a comparison • partially describes the roles of both estrogen or progesterone • writes a partial hypothesis of how Wild Yam cream would affect a woman's hormones or describes an effect of the remedy that is linked to a physiological function
2 **Limited**	• identifies one factor relating to scientific validity of one of the sources or makes a comparison statement • identifies a role of estrogen or progesterone • identifies a benefit of the herbal remedy
1 **Poor**	• addresses only one of the bullets at a 2 or 3 level

INSUFFICIENT is a special category. It is not an indication of quality. It should be assigned to papers that do not contain a discernible attempt to address the questions presented in the assignment or that are too brief to assess in this or any other scoring category.

Technology and Society

Score	Scoring Criteria
	The student...
5 **Excellent**	• clearly describes one advantage and one disadvantage of the current regulation of herbal remedies • clearly states a revision to existing herbal remedy regulations and clearly explains how this will address disadvantages of the current regulations
4 **Proficient**	• describes one advantage and one disadvantage of the current regulation of herbal remedies • states a revision to existing herbal remedy regulations and explains how this will address disadvantages of the current regulations
3 **Satisfactory**	• describes one advantage or one disadvantage of the current regulation of herbal remedies **and** partially describes one advantage or one disadvantage **or** describes an advantage and disadvantage of herbal remedies • states a revision to existing herbal regulations **or** explains how disadvantages of the current regulations could be addressed
2 **Limited**	• describes one advantage or one disadvantage of the current regulation of herbal remedies or describes one advantage or one disadvantage of herbal remedies • states an existing herbal remedy regulation or partially explains how disadvantages of the current regulations could be addressed
1 **Poor**	• addresses one of the two scoring bullets at a 2 level

INSUFFICIENT is a special category. It is not an indication of quality. It should be assigned to papers that do not contain a discernible attempt to address the questions presented in the assignment or that are too brief to assess in this or any other scoring category.

NOTES

KEY Strategies for Success on Tests

KEY STRATEGIES FOR SUCCESS ON TESTS

AN OVERVIEW OF THE TEST

This section is all about the skills and strategies you need to be successful on the Alberta Biology 30 Grade 12 Diploma Examination. It is designed for you to use together with your classroom learning and assignments.

Finding Out About the Test

Here are some questions you may wish to discuss with your teacher to help you prepare for the Alberta Biology 30 Diploma Examination.

1.	What will this test assess, or cover?	The test assesses the expectations from the four units of study: Nervous and Endocrine Systems; Reproduction and Development; Cell Division, Genetics and Molecular Biology; and Population and Community Dynamics.
2.	What materials do I need to bring to write the test?	You need a pencil, an eraser, and a calculator.
3.	Can I use a calculator during the test?	Yes, you are allowed to use an approved calculator.
4.	Are there any materials provided for the test?	Data pages containing references such as the hormone abbreviations, pedigree symbols, amino acid chart, Hardy-Weinberg Law, etc. will be provided with the exam.
5.	What kinds of questions are on the test?	The test consists of 48 multiple choice and 12 numerical-response questions, for a total of 60 questions.
6.	How much time do I have to write the test?	You will have two hours, plus 60 minutes of additional time to complete the examination.
7.	How important is this test to my final grade?	This exam is worth 50% of your final grade.
8.	How many questions will be on each content strand?	The breakdown of questions will be approximately: 22% Nervous and Endocrine Systems, 8% Differentiation and Development, 27% Cell Division and Mendelian Genetics, 12% Molecular Biology, and 18% Population and Community Dynamics.

Having an understanding of effective test-taking skills can help your performance on the test. Being familiar with the question formats may help you to prepare for quizzes, unit tests, and year-end assessments.

TEST PREPARATION AND TEST-TAKING SKILLS

THINGS TO CONSIDER WHEN TAKING A TEST

- It is normal to feel anxious before you write a test. You can manage this anxiety by:
  - Thinking positive thoughts. Imagine yourself doing well on the test.
  - Making a conscious effort to relax by taking several slow, deep, controlled breaths. Concentrate on the air going in and out of your body.
- Before you begin the test, ask questions if you are unsure of anything.
- Jot down key words or phrases from any instructions your teacher gives you.
- Look over the entire test to find out the number and kinds of questions on the test.
- Read each question closely and reread if necessary.
- Pay close attention to key vocabulary words. Sometimes these are **bolded** or *italicized*, and they are usually important words in the question.
- If you are putting your answers on an answer sheet, mark your answers carefully. Always print clearly. If you wish to change an answer, erase the mark completely and then ensure your final answer is darker than the one you have erased.
- Use highlighting to note directions, key words, and vocabulary that you find confusing or that are important to answering the question.
- Double-check to make sure you have answered everything before handing in your test.

When taking tests, students often overlook the easy words. Failure to pay close attention to these words can result in an incorrect answer. One way to avoid this is to be aware of these words and to underline, circle, or highlight them while you are taking the test.

Even though some words are easy to understand, they can change the meaning of the entire question, so it is important that you pay attention to them. Here are some examples:

all	always	most likely	probably	best	not
difference	usually	except	most	unlikely	likely

1. Which of the following equations is **not** considered abiotic?

    A. wind

    B. bacteria

    C. sunlight

    D. precipitation

HELPFUL STRATEGIES FOR ANSWERING MULTIPLE-CHOICE QUESTIONS

A multiple-choice question gives you some information, and then asks you to select an answer from four choices. Each question has one correct answer. The other answers are distractors, which are incorrect. Below are some strategies to help you when answering multiple-choice questions.

- Quickly skim through the entire test. Find out how many questions there are and plan your time accordingly.

- Read and reread questions carefully. Underline key words and try to think of an answer before looking at the choices.

- If there is a graphic, look at the graphic, read the question, and go back to the graphic. Then, you may want to underline the important information from the question.

- Carefully read the choices. Read the question first and then each answer that goes with it.

- When choosing an answer, try to eliminate those choices that are clearly wrong or do not make sense.

- Some questions may ask you to select the best answer. These questions will always include words like *best*, *most appropriate*, or *most likely*. All of the answers will be correct to some degree, but one of the choices will be better than the others in some way. Carefully read all four choices before choosing the answer you think is the best.

- If you do not know the answer, or if the question does not make sense to you, it is better to guess than to leave it blank.

- Do not spend too much time on any one question. Make a mark (*) beside a difficult question and come back to it later. If you are leaving a question to come back to later, make sure you also leave the space on the answer sheet, if you are using one.

- Remember to go back to the difficult questions at the end of the test; sometimes clues are given throughout the test that will provide you with answers.

- Note any negative words like *no* or *not* and be sure your choice fits the question.

- Before changing an answer, be sure you have a very good reason to do so.

- Do not look for patterns on your answer sheet, if you are using one.

HELPFUL STRATEGIES FOR ANSWERING OPEN-RESPONSE QUESTIONS

A written response requires you to respond to a question or directive such as **explain**, **predict**, **list**, **describe**, **show your work**, **solve**, or **calculate**. In preparing for open-response tasks you may wish to:

- Read and reread the question carefully.

- Recognize and pay close attention to directing words such as *explain*, *show your work*, and *describe*.

- Underline key words and phrases that indicate what is required in your answer, such as *explain*, *estimate*, *answer*, *calculate*, or *show your work*.

- Write down rough, point-form notes regarding the information you want to include in your answer.

- Think about what you want to say and organize information and ideas in a coherent and concise manner within the time limit you have for the question.

- Be sure to answer every part of the question that is asked.

- Include as much information as you can when you are asked to explain your thinking.

- Include a picture or diagram if it will help to explain your thinking.

- Try to put your final answer to a problem in a complete sentence to be sure it is reasonable.

- Reread your response to ensure you have answered the question.

- Think: Does your answer make sense?

- Listen: Does it sound right?

- Use appropriate subject vocabulary and terms in your response.

ABOUT SCIENCE TESTS

What You Need to Know about Science Tests

To do well on a science test, you need to understand and apply your knowledge of scientific concepts. Reading skills can also make a difference in how well you perform. Reading skills can help you follow instructions and find key words, as well as read graphs, diagrams, and tables.

Science tests usually have two types of questions: knowledge questions and skill questions. Knowledge questions test for your understanding of science ideas. Skill questions test how you would use your science knowledge.

How You Can Prepare for Science Tests

Below are some strategies that are particular to preparing for and writing science tests.

- Note-taking is a good way to review and study important information from your class notes and textbook.

- Sketch a picture of the process or idea being described in a question. Drawing is helpful for learning and remembering concepts.

- Check your answer to practice questions the require formulas by working backward to the beginning. You can find the beginning by going step-by-step in reverse order.

- When answering questions with graphics (pictures, diagrams, tables, or graphs), read the test question carefully.

  – Read the title of the graphic and any key words.

  – Read the test question carefully to figure out what information you need to find in the graphic.

  – Go back to the graphic to find the information you need.

- Always pay close attention when pressing the keys on your calculator. Repeat the procedure a second time to be sure you pressed the correct keys.

TEST PREPARATION COUNTDOWN

If you develop a plan for studying and test preparation, you will perform well on tests.

Here is a general plan to follow seven days before you write a test.

Countdown: 7 Days before the Test

1. Use "Finding Out About the Test" to help you make your own personal test preparation plan.

2. Review the following information:
   – Areas to be included on the test
   – Types of test items
   – General and specific test tips

3. Start preparing for the test at least 7 days before the test. Develop your test preparation plan and set time aside to prepare and study.

Countdown: 6, 5, 4, 3, 2 Days before the Test

1. Review old homework assignments, quizzes, and tests.

2. Rework problems on quizzes and tests to make sure you still know how to solve them.

3. Correct any errors made on quizzes and tests.

4. Review key concepts, processes, formulas, and vocabulary.

5. Create practice test questions for yourself and then answer them. Work out many sample problems.

Countdown: The Night before the Test

1. The night before the test is for final preparation, which includes reviewing and gathering material needed for the test before going to bed.

2. Most important is getting a good night's rest and knowing you have done everything possible to do well on the test.

Test Day

1. Eat a healthy and nutritious breakfast.

2. Ensure you have all the necessary materials.

3. Think positive thoughts: "I can do this." "I am ready." "I know I can do well."

4. Arrive at your school early so you are not rushing, which can cause you anxiety and stress.

SUMMARY OF HOW TO BE SUCCESSFUL DURING A TEST

You may find some of the following strategies useful for writing a test.

- Take two or three deep breaths to help you relax.

- Read the directions carefully and underline, circle, or highlight any important words.

- Look over the entire test to understand what you will need to do.

- Budget your time.

- Begin with an easy question, or a question you know you can answer correctly, rather than following the numerical question order of the test.

- If you cannot remember how to answer a question, try repeating the deep breathing and physical relaxation activities first. Then, move on to visualization and positive self-talk to get yourself going.

- When answering a question with graphics (pictures, diagrams, tables, or graphs), look at the question carefully.

  - Read the title of the graphic and any key words.

  - Read the test question carefully to figure out what information you need to find in the graphic.

  - Go back to the graphic to find the information you need.

- Write down anything you remember about the subject on the reverse side of your test paper. This activity sometimes helps to remind you that you do know something and you are capable of writing the test.

- Look over your test when you have finished and double-check your answers to be sure you did not forget anything.

DIPLOMA EXAMINATION SAMPLE 1

Use the following information to answer the next two questions.

Between seven and 12 months of age, infants begin to display a marked fear of strangers. Infants also begin to socially reference their responses during the same period.
Some research indicates that extremely fearful children often have very anxious parents.

1. The division of the nervous system that is directly responsible for physiological responses to fear is the

    A. sensory nervous system

    B. somatic nervous system

    C. sympathetic nervous system

    D. parasympathetic nervous system

    Source: June 2001

Use the following additional information to answer the next question.

Biofeedback consists of conscious efforts to control body responses that are normally involuntary. This technique can be used to control abnormal fear.

2. Conscious efforts to control body responses through biofeedback originate in the

    A. medulla

    B. cerebrum

    C. cerebellum

    D. hypothalamus

    Source: June 2001

Use the following information to answer the next three questions.

Parkinson's disease is a degenerative brain disorder. Symptoms of the disease include tremors, rigid muscles, and problems with coordinated movements such as walking and talking. Researchers have discovered that in people with Parkinson's disease, the neurons that produce dopamine, a neurotransmitter in the brain, have died. Based on this research, a number of potential treatments for the disease are being tested. Three of these treatments are explained as follows.

1. In one treatment, fetal pig brain cells that produce dopamine were used. After cloning these cells, the cloned cells were injected into 11 people with Parkinson's disease. Most of the people showed some improvement in their symptoms during the following year.

2. Levadopa is a drug that replaces missing dopamine. Unfortunately, in large doses, it has severe side effects, including nausea and heart problems.

3. A new drug called seligiline acts as an inhibitor of the enzyme monoamine oxidase B, which breaks down dopamine.

—from Henahan, 1998

3. During the cloning of a fetal pig's brain cells, the cells underwent the process of __*i*__, which increased their numbers, and after injection into people with Parkinson's disease, the cells produced dopamine when the __*ii*__ code for it was translated.

The row that completes the statement above is row

Row	*i*	*ii*
A.	meiosis	DNA
B.	meiosis	mRNA
C.	mitosis	DNA
D.	mitosis	mRNA

Source: June 2001

Use the following additional information to answer the next question.

Schematic Diagram of the Actions of Levadopa, Dopamine, Seligiline, and Monoamine Oxidase B in a Neural Synapse

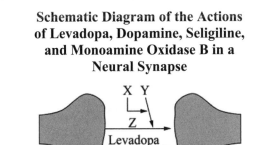

4. Which of the following rows correctly identifies the substances that correspond to X, Y, and Z in the diagram above?

Row	Dopamine	Seligiline	Monoamine Oxidase B
A.	X	Y	Z
B.	Z	Y	X
C.	Z	X	Y
D.	X	Z	Y

Source: June 2001

Use the following additional information to answer the next question.

People affected by Parkinson's disease have unusually low levels of the neurotransmitter dopamine. Studies have shown that the risk of developing Parkinson's disease is about double for non-smokers than for smokers. Brain scans of smokers and non-smokers reveal that levels of the enzyme monoamine oxidase B (MAOB) are about 40% lower in smokers than in non-smokers. MAOB is one of the enzymes involved in breaking down dopamine.

5. A possible reason for the link between smoking and a reduced risk of developing Parkinson's disease is that smoking

A. reduces the level of dopamine and of MAOB

B. increases the level of dopamine and of MAOB

C. reduces the level of dopamine by increasing the level of MAOB

D. increases the level of dopamine by decreasing the level of MAOB

Source: June 2001

Use the following information to answer the next question.

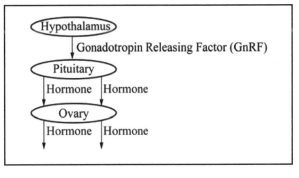

6. In humans, high levels of GnRF cause the pituitary to release

A. LH and FSH

B. LH and estrogen

C. progesterone and FSH

D. estrogen and progesterone

Source: January 2000

Use the following information to answer the next question.

Individuals know that touching a hot stove can be painful. When an individual accidentally touches a hot stove, a reflex arc is initiated, which causes the person to withdraw his or her hand before he or she senses the pain.

7. Which of the following lists identifies the neural pathway in a reflex arc?

A. Receptor, sensory neuron, effector, motor neuron

B. Motor neuron, interneuron, sensory neuron, effector

C. Sensory neuron, receptor, interneuron, motor neuron

D. Receptor, sensory neuron, interneuron, motor neuron

Source: June 2001

Use the following information to answer the next question.

Alternative medicine, such as aromatherapy, is becoming increasingly popular in western society. Aromatherapy uses natural oils and plant extracts. The scents of the oils and extracts are inhaled, or the fragrant oils are massaged into the skin. Proponents of aromatherapy hypothesize that odours affect the brain and its release of neurochemicals. These neurochemicals may then relieve pain.

Hypothesized Steps in Aromatherapy Action

1. Olfactory neurons depolarize.

2. Olfactory receptors are stimulated.

3. Neurochemicals affect pain interpretation.

4. Neurochemicals are released from axon terminals.

Numerical Response

1. If it is assumed that the hypothesis is correct, the order in which the steps above would occur to result in pain relief in a person having just inhaled the scent from an aromatherapy oil or extract is ____, ____, ____, and ____.
(Record your answer as a **four-digit** number.)

Source: June 2001

Use the following information to answer the next three questions.

Erectile dysfunction is defined as the inability to maintain an erection adequate enough to achieve a satisfactory sexual experience. When erectile dysfunction is related to inadequate blood flow to the penis, the medication Viagra can be prescribed.

A side effect of Viagra is that it sometimes results in temporary difficulties in distinguishing between the colours of blue and green. For this reason, pilots have been banned from using the drug within six hours of a flight.

The Human Eye

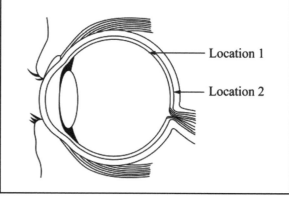

8. The cells in the eye that are affected by Viagra and the primary location of these cells, as labelled above, are, respectively,

A. rod cells and location 1

B. rod cells and location 2

C. cone cells and location 1

D. cone cells and location 2

Source: June 2001

Use the following additional information to answer the next two questions.

Erectile dysfunction can result in the inability of a couple to conceive. However, infertility is more commonly associated with insufficient sperm production. The feedback loop below illustrates the hormonal control of sperm production.

Hormonal Regulation of Sperm Production

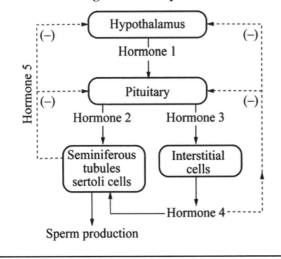

9. In the diagram above, the hormones FSH, LH, and testosterone are labelled, respectively,

   A. 2, 3, 4

   B. 2, 3, 5

   C. 3, 2, 4

   D. 3, 2, 5

   Source: June 2001

10. If infertility were due to decreased production of hormone 1 by the hypothalamus, then fewer sperm would be produced because there would be

   A. low levels of hormone 2

   B. high levels of hormone 3

   C. high levels of hormone 4

   D. low levels of hormone 5

   Source: June 2001

11. Diabetes insipidus can be caused by the failure of the posterior pituitary to secrete enough ADH, a condition that can be indicated by the

   A. appearance of glucose in the urine

   B. production of high volumes of urine

   C. production of highly concentrated urine

   D. appearance of sodium in the urine

Use the following information to answer the next two questions.

The spermicide nonoxynol-9, which is applied to contraceptive devices such as diaphragms and condoms, has been linked to increased urinary tract infections in women. Although nonoxynol-9 is helpful in fighting the herpes virus and HIV, it also destroys beneficial bacteria (lactobacilli) that moderate the acidity of a woman's vagina. As a woman's vagina and external genitalia become more acidic, another bacterium, *Escherichia coli* (*E. coli*), increases in number and invades her urethra. This overpopulation of *E. coli* causes a bladder infection.

– from Vergano, 1996

12. Another contraceptive, the birth control pill, causes negative feedback on the pituitary, which prevents the release of eggs. Typically, the hormones in the birth control pill are similar to

   A. FSH and LH

   B. oxytocin and prolactin

   C. estrogen and progesterone

   D. relaxin and gonadotropins

   Source: January 2000

13. Which of the following rows gives the site of sperm production and the gland that produces an alkaline secretion that neutralizes the acidity of the vagina?

Row	Site of Sperm Production	Gland that Produces an Alkaline Secretion
A.	seminiferous tubules	testis
B.	seminiferous tubules	prostate gland
C.	seminal vesicles	testis
D.	seminal vesicles	prostate gland

Source: January 2000

Use the following information to answer the next question.

Sex-based differences in mental ability are controversial subjects of research. An article by Doreen Kimura in *Scientific American* summarized some of the studies conducted in this area. One study was carried out to compare males' and females' performance on a variety of mental tasks. The males and females in the study had either relatively low testosterone or relatively high testosterone levels. (Females produce small amounts of testosterone in the adrenal cortex.) Results for the spatial skills component of the study are provided below.

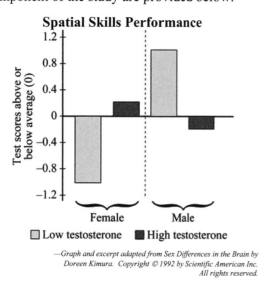

Spatial Skills Performance

☐ Low testosterone ■ High testosterone

—Graph and excerpt adapted from Sex Differences in the Brain by Doreen Kimura. Copyright © 1992 by Scientific American Inc. All rights reserved.

14. The cells that produce testosterone in females and in males are given in row

Row	Females	Males
A.	follicle cells	interstitial cells
B.	adrenal cortex cells	interstitial cells
C.	follicle cells	seminiferous tubule cells
D.	adrenal cortex cells	seminiferous tubule cells

Source: June 2001

Use the following information to answer the next question.

Yaws, bejel, and syphilis are three diseases known to be caused by strains of bacteria in the genus *Treponema*. Syphilis is a sexually transmitted disease, whereas yaws and bejel are not sexually transmitted. Studies of 800-year-old to 16 000-year-old skeletons from Florida, Ecuador, and New Mexico show that these people suffered from syphilis. Studies on 6 000-year-old skeletons from Illinois, Virginia, and Ohio show that these people suffered from yaws.

– from Zabludoff, 1996

15. Which of the following conclusions can be made about these related diseases?

A. A person can easily contract syphilis in warm climates.

B. The syphilis strain of *Treponema* may have mutated from the yaws strain.

C. Non-sexually transmitted diseases have developed from sexually transmitted diseases.

D. Older people tend to suffer from yaws, and younger victims develop syphilis when exposed to *Treponema*.

Source: January 2000

Use the following information to answer the next question.

Biologists using light microscopes to study mitosis noticed that the nuclear membrane of a cell disappeared and then re-formed during the process. They could not explain this disappearance until they used electron microscopes to view mitotic cells.
These observations revealed a large number of vesicles (small bubble-shaped structures bound by membranes) that appeared in the cytoplasm during mitosis and then disappeared when mitosis was nearly complete. During mitosis, the nuclear membrane appeared to disintegrate and form these tiny vesicles.
The vesicles disappeared when new nuclear membranes formed.

CHALLENGER QUESTION   **59.9**

16. The vesicles observed with the aid of an electron microscope appeared and disappeared, **respectively**, during

    A. prophase and anaphase

    B. interphase and anaphase

    C. prophase and telophase

    D. interphase and telophase

Source: January 1999

Use the following information to answer the next question.

Premature infants born at 24-weeks gestation face a wide spectrum of physiological problems.

17. These problems arise because prior to the third trimester of pregnancy, fetuses

    A. have organs that are underdeveloped

    B. have not yet begun cell specialization

    C. depend upon amniotic fluid for oxygen

    D. depend upon amniotic fluid for nutrients

Source: January 2001

Use the following information to answer the next question.

Alpha reductase type II is an enzyme that converts the hormone testosterone into dihydroxytestosterone (DHT). A variation in the allele that codes for the enzyme results in a single amino acid change: a valine replaces a leucine. The enzyme that contains valine instead of leucine is more efficient and results in the production of more DHT. DHT may increase the susceptibility of prostate cells to cancer.

—from Travis, 1996

18. Possible DNA triplets for valine and leucine are identified in row

Row	Valine	Leucine
A.	CAT	GTG
B.	CAA	GAA
C.	GTT	CTT
D.	GUU	CUC

Source: June 2001

Use the following information to answer the next two questions.

One cause of reduced fertility in males may be related to azoospermia. Males with this condition are not completely sterile but produce low numbers of sperm, which results in reduced fertility. The gene *DAZ* located on the Y chromosome may be vital to spermatogenesis. Deletion of this gene by mutation may lead to infertility, even if the rest of the Y chromosome is intact. In a particular study, tissue samples from a male with azoospermia revealed the lack of the *DAZ* gene in blood cells and in sperm.

—from Travis, 1996

19. Which of the following pieces of evidence would indicate that the male examined in this study did not experience a genetic mutation in his gonadal cells but more likely inherited the condition?

   A. Azoospermia is found in 3% to 4% of males.

   B. The *DAZ* gene once deleted can never be regained.

   C. Deletion of the *DAZ* gene occurs more commonly during meiosis.

   D. Both blood cells and sperm of the subject were lacking the *DAZ* gene.

   Source: June 2001

20. If a male with azoospermia were to father sons through *in vitro* fertilization, what percentage of his sons would be expected to have azoospermia?

   A. 0%

   B. 25%

   C. 50%

   D. 100%

   Source: June 2001

Use the following information to answer the next question.

Ideas concerning the nature of inheritance have very early origins, but the conceptual breakthrough that established modern genetics as a science was made less than 150 years ago by an Austrian monk, Gregor Mendel.

21. An organism is heterozygous for two pairs of genes. The number of different combinations of alleles that can form for these two genes in the organism's gametes is

   A. 1

   B. 2

   C. 4

   D. 8

   Source: June 2001

Use the following information to answer the next question.

A five-month-old human female fetus produces approximately seven million developing ova (eggs) in her ovaries. Approximately 400 000 of these developing ova survive to puberty. Of these, approximately 400 will complete development and be released during a woman's lifetime.

22. This process is similar to spermatogenesis in males in that

   A. eggs and sperm are both diploid

   B. eggs and sperm are both haploid

   C. eggs and sperm are both produced before puberty

   D. an equal number of both eggs and sperm reach maturity

   Source: June 2000

Use the following information to answer the next two questions.

Meiosis is a process that results in the reduction of the chromosome number from diploid to haploid. Sometimes chromosomes fail to separate, which results in an abnormal number of sex chromosomes.

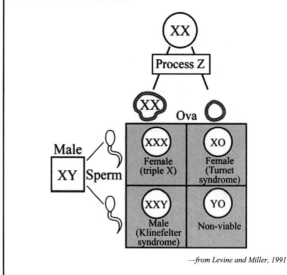

—from Levine and Miller, 1991

23. In the diagram above, process Z represents

    A. fertilization

    B. crossing-over

    C. nondisjunction

    D. spermatogenesis

Source: January 2001

Use the following additional information to answer the next question.

Partial Human Karyotype

XX XX XX XXX XX Xx

CHALLENGER QUESTION	53.6

24. This partial human karyotype represents the **last** six chromosome pairs, in numerical order. The karyotype presented is that of a

    A. male with trisomy 21

    B. female with trisomy 21

    C. male with Turner syndrome

    D. female with Turner syndrome

Source: January 2001

Use the following information to answer the next question.

Deaf-mutism is an autosomal recessive trait that is caused by two genes. Individuals who are homozygous recessive for either gene will have deaf-mutism. The two genes are designated as *D* and *E* in the diagram below.

Partial Pedigree for Deaf-Mutism

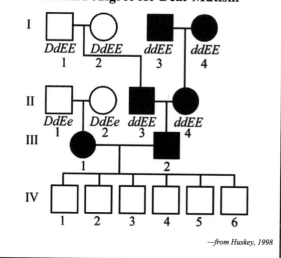

—from Huskey, 1998

Numerical Response

2. What is the probability of a couple that are heterozygous for both genes having a child with deaf-mutism?

Answer: _____

(Record your answer as a value from 0 to 1, rounded to two decimal places.)

Source: June 2001

Use the following information to answer the next question.

Chromosome Content of Human Cells During a Series of Events

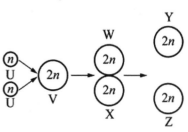

Numerical Response

3. Identify the stages in the conifer life cycle, as numbered above, that correspond with the letters that represent these stages on the diagram.

Stages: ___ ___ ___ ___
Diagram: **A**   **B**   **C**   **D**

Source: January 2001

25. In humans, cells **Y** and **Z** represent individual cells that

A. are two eggs

B. will no longer divide

C. will become a $4n$ cell

D. could develop into identical twins

Source: January 2000

Use the following information to answer the next two questions.

In the hypothetical pedigree below, shaded individuals have sickle cell anemia and are homozygous for the defective allele Hb^S. The normal allele is Hb^A. Carriers of the Hb^S allele are not identified in the pedigree.

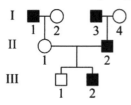

Use the following information to answer the next question.

Conifer Life Cycle

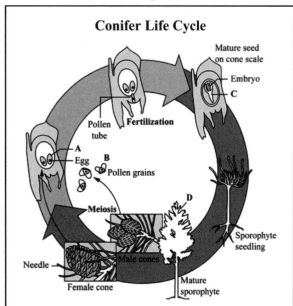

Major Stages in the Conifer Life Cycle

1. Haploid stage

2. Diploid stage

– from Levine and Miller, 1991

26. If individual II-1 has blood type A and individual II-2 has blood type B, which of the following genotypes would be possible for their third child, if they had one?

A. $I^A i\ Hb^A Hb^S$

B. $I^A I^A\ Hb^S Hb^S$

C. $I^B I^B\ Hb^A Hb^S$

D. $I^A I^A\ Hb^A Hb^A$

Source: June 2001

27. Which of the following rows indicates the relationship between the I^A and I^B alleles and the relationship between the I^A and i alleles for the blood type gene?

Row	Relationship between I^A and I^B	Relationship between I^A and i
A.	codominant	codominant
B.	codominant	dominant-recessive
C.	dominant-recessive	codominant
D.	dominant-recessive	dominant-recessive

Source: June 2001

Use the following information to answer the next question.

Erwin Chargaff found that the relative amount of each of the base pairs that make up DNA varies from species to species. He analyzed a sample of DNA from *Escherichia coli* (a bacterium) and found that 23.6% of the nitrogen base molecules present in this sample were thymine.

– from Curtis, 1983

28. In this sample of *Escherichia coli* DNA, the percentage of the nitrogen base molecules that would be adenine is

A. 76.4%

B. 38.2%

C. 23.6%

D. 11.8%

Source: January 2000

Use the following information to answer the next two questions.

A dominant allele, X^E, carried on the X chromosome causes the formation of faulty tooth enamel and causes either very thin or very hard enamel.

Hypothetical Pedigree Showing the Incidence of Faulty Tooth Enamel

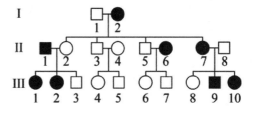

29. The genotypes of individuals II-6 and III-7 are identified in row

Row	II-6	III-7
A.	$X^E X^e$	$X^e Y$
B.	$X^E X^E$	$X^E Y$
C.	$X^e X^e$	$X^E Y$
D.	$X^E X^E$	$X^e Y$

Source: June 2001

Numerical Response

4. A woman heterozygous for faulty tooth enamel marries a man with normal tooth enamel. What is the probability that their first child will be a boy with normal tooth enamel?

Answer: _____

(Record your answer as a value from 0 to 1, rounded to **two decimal** places.)

Source: June 2001

Four Theoretical Models of DNA Replication

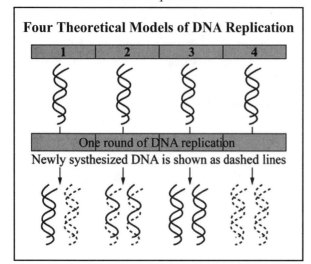

One round of DNA replication

Newly systesized DNA is shown as dashed lines

30. Which number in the diagram represents the model of DNA replication that occurs in human cells?

A. 1

B. 2

C. 3

D. 4

Source: June 1999

31. A woman with AB– blood type and a man with A+ blood type whose father was O– are planning to have children. What proportion of the offspring from this couple would likely have the mother's phenotype?

A. 0

B. $\dfrac{1}{8}$

C. $\dfrac{1}{4}$

D. $\dfrac{3}{8}$

Cross-over Frequencies of Some Genes on Human Chromosome 6

Genes	Approximate Cross-over Frequencies
Diabetes mellitus (1) and ovarian cancer (2)	21%
Diabetes mellitus (1) and Rhesus blood group (3)	12%
Ragweed sensitivity (4) and Rhesus blood group (3)	10.5%
Rhesus blood group (3) and ovarian cancer (2)	9%
Ragweed sensitivity (4) and ovarian cancer (2)	19.5%

Numerical Response

5. On human chromosome 6, the order of the genes numbered above is

____, ____, ____, and ____.
(Record your answer as a **four-digit** number.)

Source: June 2001

Use the following information to answer the next question.

Researchers have found a gene known as *p*53. It codes for a protein that binds to specific areas of DNA and activates them. This causes the production of a set of proteins that halts cell division or, in some cells, activates the cell's suicide program (apoptosis). The *p*53 gene is activated when a cell is damaged and/or undergoes a DNA mutation.

– from Seachrist, 1996

32. The normal function of the *p*53 gene is likely to

A. encourage a cell to undergo mitosis

B. encourage a cell to undergo meiosis

C. prevent an abnormal cell from reproducing

D. prevent the transcription of a cell suicide gene

Source: January 2001

Use the following information to answer the next three questions.

Desert-grassland whiptail lizards are all female, so they must reproduce by parthenogenesis. This is a type of reproduction in which females produce offspring from unfertilized eggs that have undergone chromosome doubling after meiosis. Although all whiptail lizards are females, they undergo courtship patterns similar to other types of lizards that have both sexes.

Sexual Behaviour in Parthenogenetic Lizards

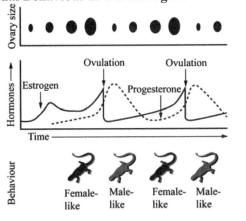

33. A correlation that can be made based on the data above is that

A. male-like behaviour is correlated with relatively large ovaries

B. female-like behaviour is correlated with relatively small ovaries

C. male-like behaviour is correlated with high blood levels of estrogen

D. female-like behaviour is correlated with high blood levels of estrogen

Source: June 2001

34. A similarity between lizard reproductive hormones and human reproductive hormones is that

A. after ovulation, ovaries decrease in size

B. before ovulation, ovaries increase in size

C. before ovulation, estrogen is secreted in decreasing amounts

D. after ovulation, progesterone is secreted in increasing amounts

Source: June 2001

35. According to the information on parthenogenetic lizards, the somatic cells of offspring produced from the whiptail lizard's unfertilized eggs would have a chromosome number of

A. n

B. $2n$

C. $4n$

D. $n + 2$

Source: June 2001

Use the following information to answer the next question.

Elephants communicate mainly by means of infrasonic sound. This means that the sound is below the frequency of sound that a human can hear. Elephants also emit a few higher-frequency trumpeting sounds that are audible to humans.

The infrasonic calls of elephants travel great distances. Researchers are now beginning to understand elephant behaviour based on this communication method. Certain calls are crucial in reproductive behaviour. The females use a distinctive infrasonic call when they are sexually receptive, which occurs for only four days every four years.

—*from The Edmonton Journal, 1997*

36. In the human ear, audible trumpeting sounds would be translated into nerve impulses in the

A. ossicles

B. oval window

C. organ of Corti

D. semicircular canals

Source: June 2001

Use the following information to answer the next question.

Fertilization occurs when a sperm fuses with an egg to form a zygote. In this diagram of a zygote, the sperm and egg nuclei are just fusing. (One polar body is also visible.)

Fertilization

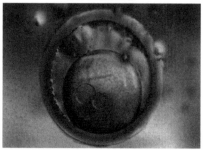

37. The event depicted in the image normally occurs in the

A. ovary

B. uterus

C. vagina

D. Fallopian tube

Source: June 2001

Use the following information to answer the next question.

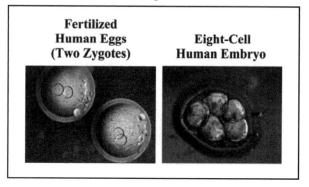

38. Which of the following statements **best** describes one of the diagrams above?

A. The two zygotes will form identical twins.

B. The two zygotes are about to undergo meiosis.

C. The cells of the eight-cell human embryo have differentiated.

D. The cells of the eight-cell human embryo contain identical DNA.

Source: June 2001

Use the following information to answer the next question.

The flowering plant *Mirabilis jalapa* (*M. jalapa*) may have branches with all white leaves, all green leaves, and all variegated leaves (leaves with green and white patches) on the same plant. Leaf colour is dependent on the colour of plastids present in cytoplasm. As in the case of other plants, pollen (containing sperm nuclei) contributes chromosomes but almost no cytoplasm to the zygote. The ovule contributes both chromosomes and cytoplasm to the zygote. The following data of offspring phenotypes were collected from crosses between flowers from various branches.

Source of pollen (male)	Source of ovule (female)	
	White branch	Green branch
White branch	White offspring	Green offspring
Green branch	White offspring	Green offspring
Variegated branch	White offspring	Green offspring

CHALLENGER QUESTION   **50.8**

39. These data indicate that, regardless of its branch source, pollen has no effect on the leaf colour of resulting offspring. A reasonable explanation for this observation is that

A. leaf colour is a codominant trait

B. leaf colour is a dominant-recessive trait

C. cell organelles or cytoplasm are active only in pollen

D. cell organelles or cytoplasm contain genetic information

Source: January 2000

Use the following information to answer the next two questions.

Sam Wasser, a biologist, trains drug-sniffing dogs to locate feces of owls, wolves, and bears. The feces contain DNA that can be extracted and analyzed.

Researchers have used feces located by the dogs to obtain evidence to evaluate a wildlife management strategy that was being used by timber companies. The timber companies were feeding bears to discourage them from tearing bark off trees. Genetic analysis of their fecal matter indicated that the male bears were eating the food supplied and the female bears were eating bark from the trees.

—*from Simon, 1997*

40. One piece of evidence that the researchers used to determine that the timber companies' strategy was not working for all bears was that some of the feces contained

A. bark chips and cells with two X chromosomes

B. bark chips and cells with one Y chromosome

C. food particles consistent with the food provided and cells with two X chromosomes

D. food particles consistent with the food provided and cells with one Y chromosome

Source: June 2001

Use the following additional information to answer the next question.

Biologists have been able to map the large territory inhabited by the bear population by locating their feces. In order to use DNA found in feces to track bears, it is necessary to identify individual bears by the DNA found in their feces. One technique that is used to do this is DNA fingerprinting.

41. In DNA fingerprinting, gel electrophoresis is used to

A. cut DNA into fragments

B. match a gene with its function

C. separate fragments of DNA

D. pair homologous chromosomes

Source: June 2001

Use the following information to answer the next two questions.

Researchers analyzing spotted owl pellets found high levels of stress hormones in owls whose nests are within a quarter mile of logging areas. This information could be used to determine how large of a buffer zone is needed between the birds and the logging areas.

Animal Stress Response Flowchart

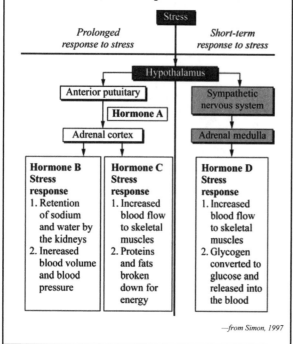

—from Simon, 1997

Hormones Involved in an Owl's Stress Response That Could be Measured by Scientists

1. Cortisol

2. Aldosterone

3. ACTH

4. Epinephrine

Numerical Response

6. Match the hormones, as numbered above, to the letters **A**, **B**, **C**, and **D** in the flowchart above.
Hormone Number: ___ ___ ___ ___
Flowchart Letter: **A**   **B**   **C**   **D**
(Record your answer as a **four-digit** number.)

Source: June 2001

42. In the owls, short-term response to stress occurs faster than prolonged response to stress because the

A. blood from the adrenal medulla travels faster than does the blood from the adrenal cortex

B. adrenal medulla responds to nervous stimulation, which is faster than hormonal stimulation

C. adrenal medulla is controlled by the hypothalamus whereas the adrenal cortex is controlled by the pituitary

D. hormone from the adrenal medulla acts on cells more quickly than the hormones from the adrenal cortex

Source: June 2001

Use the following information to answer the the next two questions.

The burrowing owl is an endangered species in Canada's western provinces. Research data collected in Saskatchewan's Burrowing Owl Recovery Project indicate that the population has declined by 20% per year over the past five years. In 1996, a population estimate showed that the number of burrowing owls had declined to 800 breeding pairs.

To obtain this population data, researchers reached into the burrows to collect and count baby owls. When they did this, the researchers heard a hiss like a rattlesnake coming from the baby owls in the burrow. The owls were attempting to scare off the intruders.

—from The Globe and Mail, 1997

Numerical Response

7. If the decline of the burrowing owl population continued at the same rate, how many breeding pairs would there have been in 1998?

Answer: _____ breeding pairs
(Record your answer as a **whole** number.)

Source: June 2001

Use the following additional information to answer the next question.

The burrowing owl habitat is open prairie grass. The owls live in ground squirrel holes that have been enlarged by badgers. The young owls are cared for by both parents who feed them a diet consisting of mice, moles, and insects.
Other prairie predators such as the rattlesnake and kestrel (sparrow hawk) also rely upon these same food sources.

43. The relationship between the kestrel and the burrowing owl and the relationship between the burrowing owl and badger are given in row

Row	Kestrel/ Burrowing Owl	Burrowing Owl/Badger
A.	predator–prey	mutualism
B.	predator–prey	commensalism
C.	interspecific competition	mutualism
D.	interspecific competition	commensalism

Source: June 2001

44. Scientists around the world have noted an alarming global decline in genetic diversity in plants and animals. This decline in diversity is due, in part, to

A. captive animal and plant-breeding programs

B. the introduction of non-native plants and animals

C. the establishment of natural reserves and parks

D. restrictions on the import and export of live goods between countries

Use the following information to answer the next question.

A community of Pima Indians in the American Southwest has a very high rate of diabetes in their adult population. Of the population of adults over the age of 35, 42% to 66% develop diabetes. The recessive trait that causes diabetes in this population is a distinct disadvantage to individuals whose diets are rich in carbohydrates.

– from Cummings, 1993

CHALLENGER QUESTION	35.5

Numerical Response

8. If 42% of the population has diabetes, then the percentage of the population who are carriers is calculated to be
_____ %
(Record your answer as a **whole** number.)

Source: January 2000

Use the following information to answer the next question.

A high percentage of purebred dogs have genetic defects. Some examples of these defects follow.

1. Hip dysplasia, a defect in the hip joints that can cripple a dog, occurs in 60% of golden retrievers.

2. Hereditary deafness, due to a recessive autosomal disorder, occurs in 30% of Dalmatians.

3. Retinal disease, which may cause blindness, occurs in 70% of collies.

4. Hemophilia, an X-linked recessive disorder, is common in Labrador retrievers. Dwarfism is also common in this breed of dog.

– from Lemonick, 1994

45. The breeding of purebred dogs for certain characteristics related to appearance is blamed for the disturbing number of genetic defects in these animals. These defects are **most likely** the result of

A. natural selection

B. non-random mating

C. geographic isolation

D. high rates of mutation

Source: January 2001

Use the following information to answer the next question.

In heavily populated regions of Canada, the landscape is now dominated by what scientists call "invasive" non-native species. Horticultural expert Bill Granger has described the Norway maple as a "tree on steroids" because of its dense rooting system. This tree reaches sexual maturity quickly and spreads many seeds over a wide area. Another invasive species, pampas grass, is described by Dr. Spencer Barrett as an "excellent opportunist." Pampas grass relies on allies such as humans to cut out vegetative competition before it proceeds to dominate the landscape.

– from Cundiff, 1996

46. By maintaining a stronghold on the environment and preventing further environmental changes, the Norway maple could be described as

A. a climax species

B. a pioneer species

C. a seral stage species

D. an intermediate species

Source: January 2002

Use the following information to answer the next question.

Pacific herring play a key role in the marine food web of Canada's West Coast. They are prey fish and comprise 30% to 70% of the summer diets of Chinook salmon, Pacific cod, lingcod, and harbour seals in the coastal waters of southern British Columbia. The eggs of Pacific herring are important to the diets of migrating sea birds, gray whales, and some invertebrates. Pacific herring are not mature enough to spawn until age three. Spawning takes place in coastal areas where algae beds are abundant and the water is uncontaminated.

CHALLENGER QUESTION	34.5

47. Salmon fishing is an important industry on the West Coast of Canada. If the salmon population were to decrease because of overfishing, the Pacific herring population would probably remain relatively stable if other predators showed which of the following changes?

A. Increased mortality and decreased emigration

B. Decreased mortality and increased emigration

C. Increased mortality and decreased immigration

D. Decreased mortality and increased immigration

Source: June 2000

48. Which of the following statements about exponential growth and logistic growth is **true**?

A. Exponential growth occurs in *K*-selected organisms.

B. Logistic growth rates fall as environmental resistance increases.

C. Exponential growth is controlled by density-dependent factors.

D. Logistic growth is characterized by a J-shaped growth curve.

ANSWERS AND SOLUTIONS—DIPLOMA EXAMINATION
SAMPLE 1

1. C	12. C	24. A	32. C	NR7. 512
2. B	13. B	NR2. 0.44	33. D	43. D
3. D	14. B	25. D	34. D	44. B
4. C	15. A	NR3. 1122	35. B	NR8. 46
5. D	16. C	26. A	36. C	45. B
6. A	17. A	27. B	37. D	46. A
7. D	18. B	28. C	38. D	47. D
NR1. 2143	19. D	29. A	39. D	48. B
8. D	20. D	NR4. 0.25	40. A	
9. A	21. C	30. B	41. C	
10. A	22. B	31. B	NR6. 3214	
11. B	23. C	NR5. 1432 or 2341	42. B	

1. C

The sympathetic system is one of the two divisions of the autonomic nervous system, which has involuntary control over breathing rate, heart rate, and other vital functions. The sympathetic division is active when the brain perceives a physical or emotional threat such as fear. Sympathetic responses include the diversion of blood from the skin and internal organs to skeletal muscles, the heart, the lungs, and the brain. Pupils dilate to allow more light into the eyes and bronchioles dilate to allow more air into the lungs. The heart speeds up and more glucose is added to the blood. The parasympathetic division of the autonomic nervous system calms the body after a threat has passed. There is no sensory nervous system. The peripheral nervous system is divided into the autonomic nervous system and the somatic nervous system. The somatic nervous system is made of the sensory and motor neurons that account for voluntary motion and conscious sensation. The responses of the sympathetic system are due to the neurotransmitter norepinephrine.

2. B

The cerebrum is the only part of the brain listed that operates consciously. All other distractors operate unconsciously and involuntarily. The medulla oblongata is responsible for such unconscious activities as swallowing, breathing, and altering heart rate. The cerebellum coordinates fine motor skills. The hypothalamus is the part of the brain that controls the body's endocrine system.

3. D

The term cloning means making exact copies. Mitosis is the type of cell division in which daughter cells are formed that are exact copies of the mother cell. Translation is the second part of protein synthesis. A messenger RNA molecule is read or translated by a ribosome, and the desired protein is assembled.

4. C

Dopamine (Z) is a neurotransmitter that is released from the synaptic knob and diffuses across a synapse to stimulate the postsynaptic membrane of a dendrite. Monoamine oxidase B is an enzyme that acts on dopamine, breaking it down. In the diagram, Y is shown as acting on Z. Seligiline is an inhibitor of monoamine oxidase B. X is shown as acting on Y.

5. D

Levels of monoamine oxidase B (MAOB) are lower in smokers than in non-smokers. MAOB breaks down dopamine, and a low level of dopamine is linked to Parkinson's disease. Smoking in some way reduces the level of MAOB so that the level of dopamine is increased.

6. A

A releasing factor or releasing hormone is a hormone from the hypothalamus that stimulates the pituitary to release another hormone.
A gonadotropin is a hormone that stimulates release of a hormone in a gonad (testes or ovaries). GnRF (also known as GnRH) causes the pituitary to release LH (leutenizing hormone), which causes ovulation and progesterone secretion from the ovary and the release of testosterone from the testes. GnRF also causes the pituitary to release FSH, which in turn acts on the ovaries to stimulate follicles to develop ova, and acts on the testes to develop sperm.

7. D

A reflex is a response that does not involve the brain, is involuntary, and is inborn. All processing occurs in the spinal cord. During a reflex, a receptor (in this case, a pain receptor) stimulates a sensory neuron. The sensory neuron carries an impulse to the spinal cord. An interneuron within the spinal cord formulates a response.
The response (in this case, the withdrawing of the hand) is directed to the muscles through a motor neuron. Note that the brain will experience pain well after the hand has been removed, indicating that the brain is informed of the situation only after the reflex is complete.

NR 1   2143

1 Olfactory neurons depolarize.
2 Olfactory receptors are stimulated.
3 Neurochemicals affect pain interpretation.
4 Neurochemicals are released from axon terminals.

Olfactory (smell) receptors are stimulated by the molecules of the aroma. Olfactory neurons are sensory neurons that carry the depolarization towards the brain. When the depolarization reaches the axon terminal of the sensory neuron it releases neurochemicals from the synaptic knobs of the axon terminals. The result is that the interpretation of pain is affected and perception is altered.

8. D

When Viagra interferes with the perception of colours, it is affecting the cones. The rods are receptors that perceive light only in black and white. They are responsible for vision in low light conditions. Location 2, straight back from the lens, is the fovea, a spot densely packed with cones, where humans see with greatest detail. Location 1, off to the periphery, has fewer receptors, most of which are rods. At location 2, images are not seen with great clarity.

9. A

FSH is 2, a hormone that is released from the anterior pituitary gland and that stimulates the Sertoli cells of the testes to produce sperm in the seminiferous tubules. LH is 3, a hormone that is released from the anterior pituitary gland and that stimulates the interstitial cells of the testes to produce testosterone. Testosterone is 4. It is produced by the testes, and as its level rises in the blood, it has a negative feedback effect on the hypothalamus and pituitary, causing a reduction in LH production. (In females, FSH causes egg and estrogen production in the ovary, and LH causes ovulation, formation of the corpus luteum, and production of progesterone and estrogen).

10. A

If there is a low level of hormone 2 (FSH), there will be fewer sperm produced in the seminiferous tubules of the testes. A high level of 3 (LH) or 4 (testosterone) will stimulate the seminiferous tubules to create more sperm. A low level of 5 will result in no negative feedback effect on the hypothalamus and pituitary and, therefore, no restriction in sperm production.

11. B

Antidiuretic hormone (ADH) causes the kidneys to reabsorb more water from the urine into the bloodstream, increasing the concentration of waste urea in urine and producing a lower volume of urine. Since the failure of ADH production causes diabetes insipidus, a symptom of the condition is a higher volume of urine that is very dilute. ADH has no effect on glucose or sodium

12. C

When estrogen and progesterone blood levels are high, negative feedback occurs, preventing GnRH secretion from the hypothalamus and FSH and LH secretion from the anterior pituitary. The result is that follicles in the ovary do not develop, and ovulation does not occur. Therefore, the birth control pill contains hormones similar to estrogen and progesterone.

13. B

Sperm production occurs inside seminiferous tubules, which are inside the testes. The testes also produce testosterone. The prostate gland produces an alkaline secretion that is added to the semen. The seminal vesicles add fructose sugar to the semen.

14. B

The information given indicates that in females, testosterone is produced in the cells of the adrenal cortex. In males, testosterone is produced by the interstitial cells, which are squeezed in between the seminiferous tubules of the testes. Note that males also secrete small amounts of testosterone from the adrenal cortex. In a female, follicle cells stimulate egg development and produce estrogen. In a male, the seminiferous tubules produce sperm.

15. A

Syphilis may have mutated from yaws, but it is not possible to tell that from the given information. It appears that yaws and bejel existed before syphilis, and they are similar disease organisms, all being members of the same genus. Even though people in Florida had syphilis 800 to 1 600 years ago, that does not mean it was easy to contract it in a warm climate. Since syphilis (sexually transmitted) appears later, it is not logical to suggest that the earlier forms, yaws and bejel (non-sexually transmitted), came from the sexually transmitted disease. The age of the sufferers is not given in the information.

16. C

Recall the cell cycle.

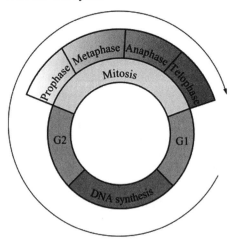

Note that interphase, which consists of G1, DNA synthesis and G2, is the phase between cell divisions. Therefore interphase is not part of mitosis and distractors **B** and **D** can be rejected. The vesicles must appear in prophase. Telophase is the last phase of mitosis so vesicles must disappear at this time.

17. A

Prior to the third trimester organs are not fully developed. Cell specialization begins embryonically at the gastrula stage. The amniotic fluid at no time provides nutrients or oxygen. These are the functions of the placenta.

18. B

To answer this question use the data table "Messenger RNA Codons and Their Corresponding Amino Acids," which will provide mRNA codons that stand for each amino acid. Note that the question is asking for DNA triplets not mRNA codons. Convert the correct mRNA codon to DNA remembering that DNA bases are complementary to RNA and that thymine in DNA is replaced by uracil in RNA.

Amino acid	Possible mRNA codons	Possible DNA triplets
Valine	GUU	CAA
	GUC	CAG
	GUA	CAT
	GUG	CAC
Leucine	UUA	AAT
	UUG	AAC
	CUU	GAA
	CUC	GAG
	CUA	GAT
	CUG	GAC

Note that the mRNA codons that code for valine all start with G, so the DNA triplets for valine must start with C. This eliminates distrators **C** and **D**. Note also that choice **D** has a uracil (U) in it which is not found in DNA molecules. Note that mRNA codons for leucine always have U as the second base, therefore the DNA triplet for leucine must have A as the second base. Only distractor **B** works.

19. D

Gonadal cells are cells that will become sperm. If the mutation occurred in gonadal cells no cells other than sperm would be affected. The question indicates that both blood cells and sperm cells were affected. Therefore the mutation did not occur in gonadal cells.

20. D

The *DAZ* gene is on the Y chromosome. All sons receive a Y chromosome from the father. Therefore, all sons of a man with azoospermia will have the condition.

21. C

An example of a genotype that is heterozygous for two genes is *TtRr*. During gamete formation, the homologous pair of chromosomes with *Tt* segregate, as does the homologous pair with *Rr*. The chromosomes assort independently of each other; therefore *T* could end up in the same gamete as *R* or *r*. The same is true of *t*. Therefore 4 possible combinations of sperm could occur: *TR, Tr, tR*, and *tr*.

22. B

Eggs and sperm are each haploid, or *n*. They contain 23 unpaired chromosomes and are both produced by meiosis after puberty. Many more sperm are produced than eggs because spermatogenesis is continuous after puberty and oogenesis only occurs once monthly. Because of unequal cytokinesis, only one egg is produced from meiosis of one primary oocyte while four sperm are produced from the meiosis of one primary spermatocyte.

23. C

The diagram indicates that instead of the normal segregation of XX into separate gametes during meiosis, both Xs have entered one gamete. The other gamete has no sex chromosome. The non-separation of a chromosome pair during meiosis is referred to as nondisjunction.

24. A

The last pair of chromosomes (23rd pair) are the sex chromosomes. In this karyotype the sex chromosomes are not the same size indicating one is an X and one is a Y. That makes the individual a male, so the answer must be **A** or **C**. The third-last pair (21st pair) is actually three chromosomes indicating a trisomy due to a nondisjunction of the sex chromosomes. Trisomy 21 is the chromosomal abnormality that causes Down syndrome. Turner's syndrome is also due to a nondisjunction and results from a monosomy X.

NR 2　0.44

If a couple is heterozygous for both genes, they both have the genotype *DdEe*. The following Punnett square shows the cross of *DdEe × DdEe*.

	DE	*De*	*dE*	*de*
DE	*DDEE*	*DDEe*	*DdEE*	*DdEe*
De	*DDEe*	*DDee*	*DdEe*	*Ddee*
dE	*DdEE*	*DdEe*	*ddEE*	*ddEe*
de	*DdEe*	*Ddee*	*ddEe*	*ddee*

As the Punnett square shows, $\frac{7}{16}$ of the children, or 0.44, will be homozygous recessive for one of the two genes and will be deaf-mute. These genotypes are shaded on the Punnett square.

25.　D

The diagram shows haploid egg and sperm (**U**) fusing in the process of fertilization to form a diploid zygote (**V**). The zygote divided in the process of mitosis to form two diploid cells (**W** and **X**). For some reason the two cells have separated from each other. Because they are the products of mitosis, the two cells are identical and each could therefore go on to become a complete organism genetically identical to the other, as in identical twins.

NR 3　1122

The term haploid refers to cells that are *n*. In *n* cells, only one chromosome of each homologous pair is present. Haploid cells result from meiosis of a diploid or *2n* cell. Gametes (sperm and egg) are haploid. When gametes fuse in fertilization, a diploid zygote is formed.
A zygote divides by mitosis, producing many cells, but the chromosome number of each cell remains the same. The diagram shows two cells (egg and pollen) fusing together in fertilization, therefore **A** and **B** must be haploid cells. When haploid cells fuse they form a diploid cell, so **C** must be diploid. Because meiosis has not occurred between **C** and **D**, there is no reason to assume the chromosome number is any different in **D**.

26.　A

Individual II-1 has blood type A, so her genotype could be $I^A I^A$ or $I^A i$. She does not have sickle cell anemia, but she had a child who does have the disease, so her genotype for that $Hb^A Hb^S$. Individual II-2 has blood type B, so his blood genotype could be $I^B I^B$ or $I^B i$. Since he has sickle cell anemia, his genotype for this gene is $Hb^S Hb^S$. Their child could have the genotype $I^A i\ Hb^A Hb^S$.

27.　B

The alleles I^A and I^B are codominant because when an individual has the heterozygous genotype, $I^A I^B$, both alleles are expressed in the phenotype. Neither dominates over the other. However, if an individual is $I^A i$, the *i* allele is not expressed, so I^A is dominant over *i*.

28.　C

There must be the same amount of adenine in DNA as thymine because adenine and thymine are complementary base pairs. Wherever there is thymine on one side of a DNA strand, there must be adenine on the other side. Therefore, the amount of adenine and thymine are always equal.

29.　A

II-6 is a woman with faulty tooth enamel. Since this is an X-linked dominant trait, she has a genotype of $X^E X^E$ or $X^E X^e$. However, since she had a son with normal tooth enamel, ($X^e Y$) she must be able to provide the normal allele (X^e), so it is logical to conclude that she is $X^E X^e$.
Individual III-7 is a male with normal tooth enamel. His genotype must be $X^e Y$.

NR 4　0.25

The cross between a woman heterozygous for faulty tooth enamel ($X^E X^e$) and a man with normal tooth enamel ($X^e Y$) is shown below.

	X^E	X^e
X^e	$X^E X^e$	$X^e X^e$
Y	$X^E Y$	$X^e Y$

The boy with normal tooth enamel is shaded.

Of the children, $\frac{1}{4}$, or 0.25, will be boys with normal tooth enamel.

30. B

Model 2 shows a parent DNA strand replicating into two daughter strands. Each daughter strand contains one of the parental strands and a new strand. This is semi-conservation replication. Alternative **A** can be rejected as both parent strands have stayed intact. Alternative **C** can be rejected because there is no new DNA present. Alternative **D** can be rejected as there is no old or parental DNA remaining.

31. B

The cross involves two genes: ABO blood type and the Rhesus antigen. In the blood type gene, the *A* and *B* alleles are codominant, but both are dominant to the *i* allele. In the Rhesus gene, the *Rh+* allele is dominant over the *Rh–* allele. The female has the genotype *AB Rh–Rh–*. She can therefore produce two types of eggs. The male's genotype is *Ai Rh+Rh–*. He can produce four types of sperm. The following punnet square shows the possible offspring from this couple:

	A+	*A–*	*i+*	*i–*
A –	*AA + –*	*AA – –*	*Ai + –*	*Ai – –*
B –	*AB + –*	*AB – –*	*Bi + –*	*Bi – –*

One out of eight offspring will have the same phenotype (AB–) as the mother. Therefore, the proportion of children with the mother's phenotype is $\frac{1}{8}$.

NR 5   1432 OR 2341

Determining the order of the genes on a chromosome is called gene mapping. The cross-over or recombination frequency can be used as a map distance between two genes. Cross-over frequency is the percentage of the time that two genes linked on the same chromosome become separated on different chromosomes because of crossing over (synapsis). The farther apart two genes are on a chromosome, the higher the cross-over frequency and the greater the map distance between the two genes. The following is a gene map for these genes:

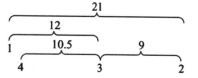

Thus, the order of the genes is 1432 or 2341.

32. C

The information explains that *p53* is activated when a cell is damaged or mutated. The *p53* gene then causes the cell to halt cell division or undergo suicide. As a result, *p53* ensures that a damaged or mutant cell does not reproduce. If *p53* works properly, cancer should never occur, which suggests that whenever a person gets cancer, the *p53* gene is one part of the DNA that is damaged.

33. D

The diagram and graph show that when estrogen level and ovary size increase, the behaviour is female-like. Ovulation brings a drop in estrogen levels, a reduction in ovary size, and a conversion to male-like behaviour. Therefore, the statement that "female-like behaviour is correlated with high blood levels of estrogen" correctly links female-like behaviour with a high level of estrogen.

34. D

The graph shows that the lizards' progesterone levels increase following ovulation. Levels of progesterone also increase in humans following ovulation, when the remains of the follicle re-form into the corpus luteum and produce progesterone. In humans, the ovaries do not change in size during the monthly cycle. The graph shows estrogen levels increasing prior to ovulation. That is true in humans as well. Therefore, estrogen secretion does not decrease prior to ovulation.

35. B

The information states that the offspring form from unfertilized eggs that have undergone chromosome doubling after meiosis. The unfertilized eggs are n, but after chromosome doubling, the eggs would become $2n$. This would provide the same chromosome number as if the egg had been fertilized by a sperm.

36. C

The organ of Corti is the actual hearing organ in mammals. It is the site where pressure waves moving through the fluid of the cochlea deflect hair cells. The deflection is converted into an action potential carried in the auditory nerve to the brain. The ossicles are the bones of the middle ear. The oval window is the membrane on the surface of the cochlea that the ossicles press on to create the pressure waves in the fluid. The semicircular canals are parts of the inner ear that monitor balance, not hearing.

37. D

Fertilization refers to the fusion of a sperm with an egg. Ovulation occurs halfway through a woman's monthly cycle. Normally, the egg is drawn into the fallopian tube (oviduct) where it can survive unfertilized for 24 hours. If sperm are in the fallopian tube at this time, they can fertilize the egg there. An unfertilized egg would be unlikely to reach the uterus alive.

38. D

During interphase between mitotic divisions the DNA replicates so that the two cells formed through mitosis are genetically identical. Each of the eight cells that make up the embryo in the diagram contains identical DNA because they formed through mitosis. Distractor **A** is not true because two different zygotes have been formed from two different eggs and two different sperm cells. The individuals that result from these two zygotes are not necessarily even related. If the two zygotes were formed in the same mother because of the unusual ovulation of two eggs at the same time, then these two zygotes would become fraternal (non-identical twins). Differentiation does not occur until the embryonic stage called the gastrula. Zygotes undergo mitosis, not meiosis.

39. D

The female gamete (ovule) contributes all the cytoplasm, including the plastids, to the zygote. It would appear that the colour of the plastid is not dependent on genes from the pollen or ovule nucleus. From this, it is reasonable to conclude that the plastids (cell organelles of the cytoplasm) contain their own genetic information.

40. A

The researchers found food particles consistent with the food provided in male bears' feces, but that would indicate that the strategy was working. They found bark in the feces of female bears. They would have identified the feces as coming from female bears because it would have contained cells with two X chromosomes. It was this evidence—the bark in the feces of bears that also had cells with two X chromosomes—that showed that the timber company's strategy was not working, at least with female bears.

41. C

DNA fingerprinting is a technique used to match DNA samples from different or the same individuals. Gel electrophoresis is a process in which particles can be separated by their size and their electrical charge. In DNA fingerprinting a sample of DNA is subjected to restriction enzymes that cut the DNA sample at given base sequences, producing DNA fragments. The fragments are loaded into a well, and a current applied. Because all DNA fragments have a negative charge, the electrical charge separates the fragments, moving them through the gel. Those fragments with the smallest mass (longer fragments) will move the furthest. Those that are heavier will not move as far. Once the fragments are distributed in a line through the gel, they are stained, showing each fragment as a dark band at a certain position relative to each other. This image forms the DNA fingerprint. If the procedure was repeated with a sample of DNA from the same person, the fingerprint would be the same. The more related two individuals are the more similar the DNA fingerprints are. The fingerprint of a parent would show half the bands at the same positions as the fingerprint of their child.

NR 6   3214

Hormone A, which is released from the anterior pituitary and which stimulates the adrenal cortex, is ACTH (**3**) or adrenocorticotrophic hormone. It stimulates the adrenal cortex to releases its hormones. Hormone B causes more sodium and thus more water to be drawn back into the blood, increasing blood volume and pressure. This is the hormone aldosterone (**2**). Hormone C causes an increase in blood glucose (sugar) as proteins are converted for energy. This hormone is cortisol (**1**). The release of hormone D from the adrenal medulla is stimulated by the sympathetic nervous system. The result is a diversion of blood to the brain, heart, and skeletal muscles from the internal organs, and an increase in blood glucose, heart rate, and breathing rate. This hormone is epinephrine (**4**), which is sometimes referred to as adrenaline.

42. B

The adrenal gland has a core called the adrenal medulla and a superficial layer called the adrenal cortex. When an immediate perceived threat causes short-term stress, sympathetic nerve impulses from the medulla cause the adrenal medulla to secrete norepinephrine/epinephrine into the blood stream, resulting in immediate sympathetic fight-or-flight responses.
In prolonged or chronic stress, the reaction is hormonal and through the bloodstream, which is much slower. The hypothalamus releases ACTHRF, activating the pituitary to produce ACTH, which stimulates the adrenal cortex to release cortisol, aldosterone, and testosterone, which collectively fight the effects of chronic stress. Clearly, the reactions to long-term or chronic stress are much slower.

NR 7   512

If there were 800 breeding pairs in 1996, and they are declining in number by 20% per year:

20% of 800 is
$800 \times 0.2 = 160$
so $800 - 160 = 640$ breeding pairs in 1997

20% of 640 is
$640 \times 0.2 = 128$
so $640 - 128 = 512$ breeding pairs in 1998

43. D

Since the burrowing owl and the kestrel eat many of the same types of food, they are competitors. Competition between members of different species is interspecific competition. The badger enlarges the ground squirrel hole for its own purposes, but that provides a subsequent benefit to the burrowing owl. Since the badger gains no advantage from the burrowing owl, the relationship between owl and badger is commensalism. In a commensal relationship, one organism benefits and the other is unaffected.

44. B

Non-native plants and animals reduce genetic diversity by out-competing existing populations for resources as well as introducing new diseases into the communities where they were introduced, often eliminating local plants and animals, thus decreasing diversity. The establishment of natural parks, restrictions on movement of live goods, and breeding programs all attempt to preserve or increase genetic diversity.

NR 8   46

Because this is a recessive trait, carriers must be heterozygous. To calculate the percentage that is heterozygous, use the Hardy–Weinberg formula.

$$p^2 + 2pq + q^2 = 1.0$$

42% of the population has the recessive condition diabetes. Therefore, using the symbol f to refer to frequency:

$q^2 = 0.42$ (f of homozygous recessive genotype)
$q = 0.65$ (f of recessive allele)
$p = 1 - q = 1 - 0.65 = 0.35$ (f of dominant allele)
$2pq = 2 \times 0.35 \times 0.65 = 0.46$ (f of heterozygous genotype)

45. B

The breeding of dogs involves non-random mating. That is, the breeder selects dogs with certain desired characteristics to breed. This is a form of inbreeding that reduces genetic variety and increases the frequency of genetic defects. It is not natural selection because nature is not selecting which animals will reproduce, humans are. Geographic isolation refers to a population being separated from other populations of the same species by a physical barrier such as a mountain range or a river. Geographic isolation by itself will not affect the frequency of genetic defects. Mutations can happen spontaneously or can be caused by something in the environment.
There is no reason to assume that mutation rates will be higher in purebred dogs than in crosses or wild animals.

46. A

A climax species can be defined as one that is so dominant that it keeps other organisms at bay, and so, puts successional changes on hold. A pioneer species is one such as moss or lichen that begins a new community where there was not one before. Seral stage species and intermediate species refer to organisms such as poplar trees that invade an area, perhaps dominating for a while, but are eventually pushed out themselves.

47. D

Note that change in population size (ΔN) is due to the combined effects of four population determining factors: natality and immigration which increase ΔN, and mortality and emigration which decrease ΔN. The question intimates that if salmon populations fall, their prey species with which it competes (herring) should increase. To keep the herring population stable, there would need to be an increase in other predators which could be accomplished by either reduced mortality or increased immigration.

48. B

Exponential growth is found in r-selected species, such as mosquitoes and dandelions, and produces a J-shaped growth curve controlled by density-independent factors such as climate. Logistic growth is found in K-selected species, such as whales and wolves, and produces an S-shaped curve that begins the same as the J curve but then begins to flatten finally levelling off as resources become scarce and environmental resistance rises. Eventually, the population comes to a population size (N) called the carrying capacity (K) that can be supported by the environment. Therefore, the statement that logistic growth rates fall as environmental resistance increases is correct.

DIPLOMA EXAMINATION SAMPLE 2

*Use the following information to answer
the next three questions.*

The thyroid gland secretes the hormones
thyroxine and calcitonin. Embedded in the
thyroid gland are the four parathyroid glands.
The parathyroid glands secrete the parathyroid
hormone (PTH). Calcitonin and PTH work
antagonistically to maintain homeostasis of
calcium ion concentrations in the blood.
High levels of calcium ions stimulate the
secretion of calcitonin, which causes deposition
of calcium in the bones.

1. Low levels of calcium ions in the blood cause
   A. decreased secretion of PTH and increased
      deposition of calcium in the bones
   B. decreased secretion of calcitonin and
      increased deposition of calcium in
      the bones
   C. increased secretion of PTH and movement
      of calcium from the bones to the blood
   D. increased secretion of calcitonin and
      movement of calcium from the bones to
      the blood

Source: January 2002

2. The release of thyroxine from the thyroid is
   directly regulated by
   A. TSH
   B. TRH
   C. iodine
   D. thyroxine

Source: January 2002

3. A characteristic symptom of hyperthyroidism,
   a disorder of the thyroid gland, is
   A. lethargy
   B. weight loss
   C. intolerance to cold
   D. slowed mental processes

Source: January 2002

4. Which of the following hormones plays a role
   in returning the salt concentration in the blood
   to homeostatic levels following heavy
   exercise?
   A. Cortisol
   B. Thyroxine
   C. Aldosterone
   D. Epinephrine

Source: January 2002

*Use the following information to answer
the next question.*

Reabsorption of water in the kidney tubules
occurs passively as a result of the active
reabsorption of sodium in the tubule.
The reabsorption is influenced by aldosterone.

5. The release of aldosterone is stimulated by a
   drop in
   A. blood volume
   B. basal metabolic rate
   C. antidiuretic hormone
   D. water content of the blood

*Use the following information to answer
the next question.*

Parathyroid hormone increases blood calcium
concentration by increasing the absorption of
calcium from the intestines and the release of
calcium ions from bones.

6. In which of the following individuals might
   parathyroid hormone levels be relatively low?
   A. Pregnant women
   B. Growing children
   C. Elderly people with brittle bones
   D. Babies with poor tooth development

Use the following information to answer the next three questions.

Multiple sclerosis (MS), a disease of the nervous system, typically has symptoms of uncontrolled muscle responses, weakness, paralysis, and vision difficulties. Researchers believe that MS occurs as a result of the body's immune system destroying the myelin sheath that surrounds the axon of a nerve cell.
The result is a scarring of brain tissue or of spinal cord tissue.

7. Damage to the myelin sheath of an optic neuron affects the speed of neural transmission to the visual centre, which is found in which lobe of the cerebrum?

   A. Frontal lobe

   B. Parietal lobe

   C. Occipital lobe

   D. Temporal lobe

   Source: January 2002

Numerical Response

1. Another symptom of MS is an exaggerated pupillary light reflex. Some of the events that occur during this reflex are listed below.

   1 Motor neuron depolarizes
   2 Sensory neuron depolarizes
   3 Interneuron depolarizes
   4 Light receptors stimulated

   The order in which the events listed above occur during a pupillary light reflex is ____, ____, ____, and ____.
   (Record your answer as a **four-digit** number.)

   Source: January 2002

Use the following additional information to answer the next question.

Stimulation of a sensory neuron produces an action potential. An abnormal pattern in this action potential can be used to detect MS in its early stages. The graph below illustrates the membrane potential of a normal neuron after stimulation.

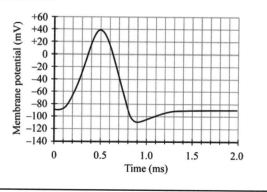

Numerical Response

2. What is the resting membrane potential for this neuron, expressed to two digits, **and** what is the maximum membrane potential during depolarization, expressed to two digits?

   $-$_____, $+$_____
   Membrane Resting   Maximum During
   Potential   Depolarization
   (Record your answer as a **four-digit** number.)

   Source: January 2002

Use the following information to answer the next four questions.

Monoamine oxidase (MAO) is an enzyme that breaks down the neurotransmitters dopamine, serotonin, and norepinephrine. Individuals who are involved in extreme sports, such as rock climbing, generally have low levels of MAO and, therefore, higher-than-normal levels of these neurotransmitters.

Dopamine and serotonin are linked to pleasurable feelings. Norepinephrine is released in the fight-or-flight response. One hypothesis for why individuals participate in extreme sports is that in order for individuals with high resting levels of these neurotransmitters to achieve a pleasurable sensation, they require a greater surge of these chemicals than do other people.

– from Zorpette, 1999

8. The site in the neural pathway where MAO is active is the

   A. axon

   B. synaptic cleft

   C. cell body

   D. Schwann cell

   Source: January 2002

9. The area of the brain that normally initiates the fight-or-flight response is the

   A. pons

   B. cerebrum

   C. cerebellum

   D. hypothalamus

   Source: January 2002

Use the following additional information to answer the next two questions.

Serotonin stimulates the release of endorphins, and endorphins eventually cause the release of more dopamine. Studies of individuals involved in extreme sports have found that these people have lower-than-normal numbers of two of the five types of dopamine receptors.

– from Zorpette, 1999

10. The endorphin met-enkephalin is comprised of the amino acids methionine, phenylalanine, glycine, glycine, and tyrosine. Possible mRNA codons for the production of met-enkephalin are

    A. ATG TTT GGT GGT TAT

    B. ATG TTG GGC GGC TAT

    C. AUG UUC GGT GGT UAC

    D. AUG UUU GGC GGC UAC

    Source: January 2002

11. When individuals participate in extreme sports, their neurons release more dopamine, which results in a pleasurable sensation because

    A. less serotonin is released from neurons

    B. more dopamine receptors are produced

    C. the fight-or-flight response is inhibited

    D. a neuron containing dopamine receptors reaches threshold depolarization

    Source: January 2002

New research has led to advances in the development of male contraceptives. One of the most promising contraceptive methods involves injecting androgens (testosterone or other male hormones) into a male's muscles.

The androgens produce a negative feedback effect on the hypothalamus and pituitary gland. In trials involving a combination of androgens, sperm counts were reduced to zero in test subjects, but this method was effective for only three weeks.

Events in a Negative Feedback Loop Controlling Sperm Production

1. Production of sperm is inhibited

2. Hormone levels in the blood return to normal

3. Production of FSH and LH is inhibited

4. High levels of the injected androgens circulate in the blood

– from Alexander, 1999

Numerical Response

3. The order in which the events listed above would occur following the injection of androgens into a male's muscle is ____, ____, ____, and ____.
(Record your answer as a **four-digit** number.)

Source: January 2002

Researchers developing male contraceptives have found other methods of interfering with various stages of sperm development and sperm release from the body. Some methods of contraception currently being investigated are given below.

1. Interfering with the process of meiosis by which sperm are produced

2. Blocking the release of hormones that stimulate the release of FSH and LH

3. Using removable polyurethane plugs to block the tubes that transport sperm

4. Administering a calcium-blocking drug that interferes with the final maturation of sperm

Numerical Response

4. Match each of the methods of contraception described above with the structure given below that is targeted by that method.

Structure:	Method of Contraception:
Seminiferous tubules	____
Epididymis	____
Vas deferens	____
Hypothalamus	____

(Record your answer as a **four-digit** number.)

Source: January 2002

Benign prostatic hyperplasia (BPH), an enlargement of the prostate gland, causes urination problems such as dribbling and pain. BPH is not a precursor to prostate cancer. Prostate cancer is linked to the absence of a protein coded for by the *p27* gene. The absence of this protein leads to uncontrolled cell growth in prostate tissue.

– from Seppa, 1998

Some Male Reproductive Structures

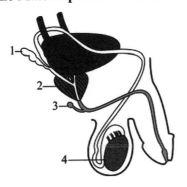

12. In the diagram above, the structure **most affected** by the absence of the protein coded for by the *p27* gene is numbered

A. 1   B. 2
C. 3   D. 4

Source: January 2002

13. In normally functioning cells, the protein coded for by the *p27* gene is produced continuously. The process by which the *p27* gene's code is read from the DNA and the name of the molecule formed in the process are identified in row

Row	Process	Molecule
A.	transcription	mRNA
B.	translation	mRNA
C.	transcription	tRNA
D.	translation	tRNA

Source: January 2002

Chordoma is a rare cancer that can occur anywhere along the spine and head. Chordomas occurring in the head are sometimes called brain tumours; however, they do not actually form from brain cells. Chordomas are thought to form from cellular remains of the notochord, which is derived from the mesoderm.

14. The organ or tissue that could be the site of chordoma development is the

A. bones

B. epidermis

C. endocrine tissue

D. lining of the digestive tract

15. Low maternal progesterone concentrations in the second and third trimester of pregnancy can lead to a miscarriage. Low progesterone concentrations at this time could indicate a problem with which of the following extra-embryonic membranes?

A. Amnion

B. Chorion

C. Placenta

D. Allantois

Use the following information to answer the next two questions.

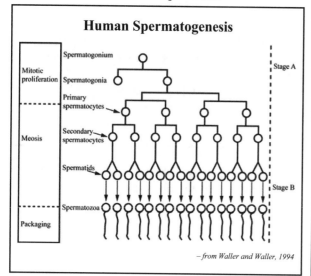

Human Spermatogenesis

– from Waller and Waller, 1994

Use the following information to answer the next question.

The birth of the Dionne Quintuplets on May 28, 1934, near Callander, Ontario, surprised the world. The quintuplets had a combined weight of 6 kg, and theirs was the first known case in which all members of a quintuplet set survived. The process by which the quintuplets were formed is thought to be as diagrammed below.

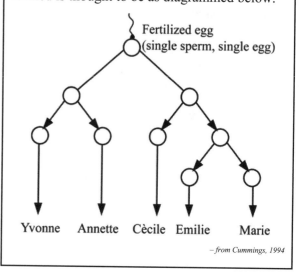

– from Cummings, 1994

16. The mitotic proliferation stage of spermatogenesis occurs in the

   A. epididymis

   B. vas deferens

   C. seminal vesicles

   D. seminiferous tubules

Source: January 2002

17. The chromosome number at stage **A** and the chromosome number at stage **B** are, respectively,

   A. 46 and 46

   B. 46 and 23

   C. 23 and 46

   D. 23 and 23

Source: January 2002

18. The development of the Dionne Quintuplets was **most likely** the result of

   A. pre-embryo splitting, which resulted in fraternal quintuplets

   B. pre-embryo splitting, which resulted in identical quintuplets

   C. fertility drugs, which resulted in multiple ovulation and produced fraternal quintuplets

   D. fertility drugs, which resulted in multiple ovulation and produced identical quintuplets

Source: January 2002

Use the following information to answer the next three questions.

Most autosomal trisomies are lethal.
The average survival age for infants with Patau syndrome (trisomy 13) is six months.
Infants with Edward syndrome (trisomy 18) survive, on average, only two to four months.
Individuals with Down syndrome (trisomy 21) can survive into adulthood. In order to identify autosomal trisomies, chorionic villus sampling (CVS) can be used to obtain cells that are then used to create a karyotype like the one shown below.

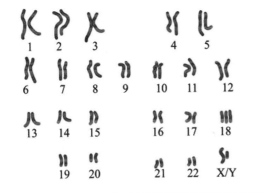

19. The sex and the condition of the individual whose karyotype is shown above are given in row

Row	Sex	Condition
A.	female	Patau syndrome
B.	female	Down syndrome
C.	male	Edward syndrome
D.	male	Normal

Source: January 2002

20. The villus region sampled using CVS develops from the

A. amnion

B. chorion

C. ectoderm

D. endoderm

Source: January 2002

Use the following additional information to answer the next question.

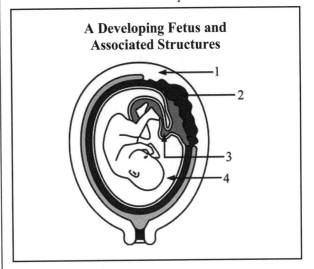

A Developing Fetus and Associated Structures

21. Progesterone and HCG, which are used to maintain the developing fetus, are both produced in the structure numbered

A. 1

B. 2

C. 3

D. 4

Source: January 2002

Use the following information to answer the next four questions.

Mutated mitochondrial DNA has been linked with many disorders. For example, mitochondrial DNA mutations are believed to cause approximately 1.5% of all cases of diabetes mellitus. Type I diabetes mellitus is characterized by low insulin levels. In addition to insulin, blood glucose can be affected by glucagon.

– from Wallace, 1997

22. Which of the following statements summarizes the effect of insulin and the effect of glucagon on blood glucose levels?

   A. Both insulin and glucagon tend to raise blood glucose levels.

   B. Both insulin and glucagon tend to lower blood glucose levels.

   C. Insulin tends to raise blood glucose levels; whereas, glucagon tends to lower blood glucose levels.

   D. Insulin tends to lower blood glucose levels; whereas, glucagon tends to raise blood glucose levels.

   Source: January 2002

Use the following additional information to answer the next three questions.

A deletion mutation in mitochondrial DNA causes Kearns–Sayre syndrome (KSS). A large sample of different types of somatic cells was removed from a male with KSS, tested, and found to contain the deletion. The only type of mitochondrial DNA that was found in somatic cells from the man's mother was mitochondrial DNA that did not have the KSS deletion.

23. A reasonable hypothesis to explain these results is that the mutation in the mitochondrial DNA that caused KSS in the man first occurred in the

   A. mother's oocytes

   B. man's somatic cells

   C. man's spermatocytes

   D. mother's somatic cells

   Source: January 2002

24. Both males and females can be affected by mitochondrial mutations, but only females can transmit genetic mutations to their offspring. For this inheritance pattern, which of the following rows gives the contributions to the zygote made by the sperm and by the egg?

Row	Sperm Contribution	Egg Contribution
A.	nuclear contents only	both nuclear and cytoplasmic contents
B.	both nuclear and cytoplasmic contents	nuclear contents only
C.	neither nuclear nor cytoplasmic contents	both nuclear and cytoplasmic contents
D.	both nuclear and cytoplasmic contents	neither nuclear nor cytoplasmic contents

Source: January 2002

25. Mitochondrial DNA and nuclear DNA both code for the formation of proteins. Which of the following statements about protein synthesis is **true**?

A. An mRNA anticodon binds with an amino acid codon, which results in the placement of a specific tRNA molecule in the polypeptide chain.

B. An mRNA anticodon binds with a tRNA codon, which results in the placement of a specific polypeptide molecule in the amino acid chain.

C. A tRNA anticodon binds with a polypeptide codon, which results in the placement of a specific mRNA molecule in the amino acid chain.

D. A tRNA anticodon binds with an mRNA codon, which results in the placement of a specific amino acid molecule in the polypeptide chain.

Source: January 2002

Use the following information to answer the next three questions.

Descriptions and Symbols Used to Represent One Type of Coat Colour in Horses

1	2	3	4
DNA sequence for coat color	*TT, Tt*	*T*	Tobiano (white spotting pattern)
	tt	*t*	Not tobiano (no white for coat spotting pattern)

Numerical Response

5. Using the numbers above, match these descriptions and symbols with the term below to which they apply.

Number: ____ ____ ____ ____
Term: gene allele phenotype genotype
(Record your answer as a **four-digit** number.)

Source: January 2002

26. What are the genotypes for coat colour of two horses that are predicted to produce offspring in a 1:1 genotypic ratio?

A. *Tt* and *tt*

B. *Tt* and *Tt*

C. Tobiano and tobiano

D. Tobiano and not tobiano

Source: January 2002

Numerical Response

6. Given that the diploid number for horses is 64, what is the number of chromosomes found in a horse's somatic cell and what is the number of chromosomes found in a horse's gamete cell?

Number of Chromosomes: _____, _____
Cell Type: somatic cell   gamete cell
(Record your answer as a **four-digit** number.)

Source: January 2002

Use the following information to answer the next five questions.

Cat coat colour results from the interaction of three different genes. A gene for black-based colours is located on an autosomal chromosome. A gene for red-based colours is located on the X chromosome. A different gene located on a separate autosomal chromosome determines pigment density in cat hair.

The black-based gene has three possible alleles: *B*–black, *b*–chocolate, and b^l–cinnamon. If pigmentation in cat hair is dense, the phenotypes listed below are possible.

Genotype	Phenotype
BB, Bb, Bb^l	black
bb, bb^l	chocolate
b^{l}b^l	cinnamon

27. According to the data above, the relationship among these alleles is such that the

A. black allele is codominant with the chocolate and cinnamon alleles

B. black allele is codominant with the chocolate allele, and the chocolate allele is codominant with the cinnamon allele

C. black allele is dominant over the chocolate and cinnamon alleles, and the chocolate allele is dominant over the cinnamon allele

D. black allele is dominant over the chocolate and cinnamon alleles, and the chocolate and cinnamon alleles are codominant

Source: January 2002

Use the following additional information to answer the next two questions.

There are two alleles for the pigment-density gene: dense pigment (D) and dilute pigment (d). The chart below shows the interaction of two autosomal genes affecting coat colour—the black-based gene and the density gene.

Black-based pigment gene	Density gene	
$B\_$	$D\_$	Dd
$B\_$	$B\_D\_$ black colour	B_dd blue colour
$bb; bb^l$	$bbD\_$; $bb^lD\_$ chocolate colour	$bbdd$; bb^ldd lilac colour
b^lb^l	b^lb^lD cinnamon colour	b^lb^ldd fawn colour

28. A blue-coloured female cat is bred with a cinnamon-coloured male cat. The offspring produced are black-coloured, blue-coloured, chocolate-coloured, and lilac-coloured. The genotypes of the parental cats are indicated in row

Row	Female Cat	Male Cat
A.	Bb^ldd	b^lb^lDd
B.	Bb^ldd	b^lb^lDD
C.	$Bbdd$	b^lb^lDd
D.	$Bbdd$	b^lb^lDD

Source: January 2002

29. A black-coloured female cat with the genotype $BbDd$ is bred with a fawn-coloured male cat. The percentage of their offspring predicted to be chocolate-coloured is

A. 13%

B. 19%

C. 25%

D. 50%

Source: January 2002

Use the following additional information to answer the next two questions.

In cats, red pigmentation is dominant to black pigmentation. The red pigment gene, which is located on the X chromosome, has two alleles: X^R and X^r. Cats with at least one X^R allele have some orange-coloured hair as a result of having the red-based pigment. Cats with only X^r alleles have no red-based pigment. Male cats with the X^R allele will be orange. However, female cats express the genes on only one X chromosome in each cell. This expression is random.
Therefore, an orange-and-black (tortoiseshell) female cat is possible if it is $X^R X^r$.
Some genotypes and their resulting phenotypes are shown below. In all cases, pigment density is high.

Genotype	Phenotype
$X^R YBb$	Orange male cat
$X^r YBb^l$	Black male cat
$X^R X^r Bb$	Orange-and-black female cat (tortoiseshell)

30. The phenotype of a female cat with genotype $X^r X^r Bb^l$ would be

   A. a black cat

   B. an orange cat

   C. an orange-and-black cat

   D. an orange, black, and cinnamon cat

Source: January 2002

31. A cinnamon-coloured male cat ($X^r Yb^l b^l$) is bred with an orange-coloured female cat ($X^R X^R BB$). What possible phenotypes could be produced in the offspring?

   A. Tortoiseshell-coloured female cats and orange-coloured male cats

   B. Cinnamon-coloured male cats, orange-coloured female cats, and tortoiseshell-coloured female cats

   C. Tortoiseshell-coloured female cats, black-coloured female cats, and black-coloured male cats

   D. Cinnamon-coloured male cats, black-coloured male cats, black-coloured female cats, orange-coloured female cats, and tortoiseshell-coloured female cats

Source: January 2002

Use the following information to answer the next seven questions.

Sickle cell anemia is an autosomal recessive genetic disorder. Because individuals affected by sickle cell anemia have defective hemoglobin proteins, their blood cannot transport oxygen properly. There appears to be a relationship between the incidence of malaria and sickle cell anemia. Individuals with sickle cell anemia and carriers of the sickle cell allele have some resistance to malaria. Malaria is caused by the parasite *Plasmodium* and is transmitted between humans by mosquitoes.

32. The probability of two carrier parents having a child with sickle cell anemia is

   A. 25%

   B. 50%

   C. 75%

   D. 100%

Source: January 2002

33. If scientists are successful in significantly reducing or eliminating malaria, the **best** prediction for what will happen to the allele for sickle cell anemia in the population is that it will

A. not be affected by the elimination of malaria

B. increase as its selective advantage is increased

C. be reduced as its selective advantage is decreased

D. quickly disappear as its selective advantage is increased

Source: January 2002

Use the following additional information to answer the next two questions.

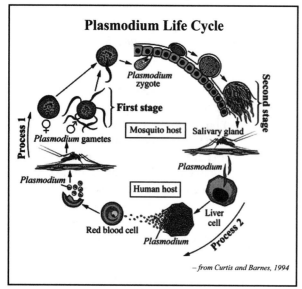

Plasmodium Life Cycle

– from Curtis and Barnes, 1994

34. The row below that identifies process **1** and process **2** is

Row	Process 1	Process 2
A.	mitosis	meiosis
B.	mitosis	mitosis
C.	meiosis	mitosis
D.	meiosis	meiosis

Source: January 2002

35. The row below that identifies the chromosome number at the first stage and the chromosome number at the second stage is

Row	First Stage	Second Stage
A.	diploid	haploid
B.	diploid	diploid
C.	haploid	diploid
D.	haploid	haploid

Source: January 2002

Use the following additional information to answer the next three questions.

Insecticides have been used to control mosquito populations in order to prevent the spread of malaria, but mosquitoes in malaria-infested areas are developing resistance to these insecticides. In addition, the antimalarial drug chloroquine, once very effective in protecting individuals against *Plasmodium,* has become ineffective, which has resulted in a resurgence of malaria. Scientists have identified a gene, called *cg2,* in *Plasmodium* that allows the *Plasmodium* to mount resistance to chloroquine. This research could be used by scientists to develop new versions of chloroquine that will sidestep the parasite's resistance and, therefore, effectively protect people against malaria.

– from Travis, 1997

36. Some investigators have suggested that some strains of *Plasmodium* have become chloroquine-resistant because these strains have an increased ability to pump chloroquine from their bodies. Other investigators suggest that the resistance stems from changes in some strains of *Plasmodium* that prevent chloroquine from entering the parasites in the first place. These two suggestions can **best** be described as

A. theories

B. hypotheses

C. conclusions

D. observations

Source: January 2002

37. A possible reason that the *Plasmodium* parasite may have resistance to chloroquine is that the *cg2* gene codes for a protein that seems to play a role in membrane transport of the drug. If this is true, researchers may want to develop compounds that specifically block this resistance mechanism by

A. preventing mutation of the *cg2* gene

B. stimulating translation of the *cg2* gene

C. preventing transcription of the *cg2* gene

D. stimulating DNA replication of the *cg2* gene

Source: January 2002

38. The increasing resistance of the *cg2* gene in *Plasmodium* to chloroquine is **most likely** a result of

A. the natural selection of the *cg2* gene

B. the non-random mating of resistant *Plasmodium*

C. the growing resistance the mosquito carrier has developed

D. an increase in mutation rate from the non-resistant to the resistant gene

Use the following information to answer the next three questions.

Komodo Island National Park is one of the last refuges of the Komodo dragon lizard. It is estimated that there are 3 500 Komodo dragons living in the 520 km² park. The Komodo dragon can grow to over three metres in length, weigh up to 70 kg, and run up to 20 km/h. These lizards grow slowly and can live up to 30 years. Female Komodo dragons mate once a year. Females may lay on the nest to protect the eggs. After the eggs hatch, young Komodo dragons live in trees until they are one year old to avoid being eaten by adult Komodo dragons and other predators.

– from Ciofi, 1999

7. What is the population density of Komodo dragons in Komodo Island National Park? _____ dragons/km²
(Round and record your answer to **three** significant digits.)

Source: January 2002

39. Because the retina of the Komodo dragon consists of only cones, Komodo dragons have a limited ability to see

A. colour

B. fine detail

C. prey at a distance

D. prey in low-intensity light

Source: January 2002

40. Komodo dragons have a poor range of hearing, partially because they have only one ossicle—the stapes. In humans, three ossicles work together to increase vibrations of the

A. cochlea

B. oval window

C. eustachian tube

D. tympanic membrane

Source: January 2002

Use the following information to answer the next question.

In heavily populated regions of Canada, the landscape is now dominated by what scientists call "invasive" non-native species. Horticultural expert Bill Granger has described the Norway maple as a "tree on steroids" because of its dense rooting system. This tree reaches sexual maturity quickly and spreads many seeds over a wide area. Another invasive species, pampas grass, is described by Dr. Spencer Barrett as an "excellent opportunist." Pampas grass relies on allies such as humans to cut out vegetative competition before it proceeds to dominate the landscape.

– from Cundiff, 1996

41. Two strategies that give the Norway maple a high biotic potential are identified in row

Row	Strategy 1	Strategy 2
A.	is on steroids	reaches sexual maturity early
B.	reaches sexual maturity early	has large number of seeds
C.	spreads seeds over a large area	is on steroids
D.	spreads seeds over a large area	has strong root system

Source: January 2002

Use the following information to answer the next two questions.

Because insects are probably our main ecological competitors, scientists search for ways to get rid of them. Scientists have discovered that the hormone ecdysone, produced by the prothoracic gland of all insects, stimulates moulting and development into adult insects. The corpora allata gland secretes another hormone, juvenile hormone (JH), which inhibits the effect of ecdysone and maintains the insect juvenile state (pupa). Typically, insects winter as pupae and emerge as adults in spring.

– from Wallace, Sanders, and Ferl, 1996

42. An effective insecticide would be one that

A. inhibits JH in the spring

B. stimulates ecdysone in the spring

C. maintains a high level of JH in the fall

D. inhibits the release of ecdysone in the spring

Source: January 2002

43. Which of the following statements gives a valid prediction about the effect of the increased light in the spring on the hormones that control the emergence of an adult insect from its pupa case?

A. The light stimulates the release of JH.

B. The light inhibits the release of ecdysone.

C. The light stimulates the release of ecdysone.

D. The light inhibits the release of both ecdysone and JH.

Source: January 2002

Use the following information to answer the next question.

The burrowing owl is an endangered species in Canada's western provinces. Research data collected in Saskatchewan's Burrowing Owl Recovery Project indicate that the population has declined by 20% per year over the past five years. In 1996, a population estimate showed that the number of burrowing owls had declined to 800 breeding pairs.

To obtain this population data, researchers reached into the burrows to collect and count baby owls. When they did this, the researchers heard a hiss like a rattlesnake coming from the baby owls in the burrow. The owls were attempting to scare off the intruders.

– from The Globe and Mail, 1997

44. The hissing behaviour of the baby owls is an example of

A. mimicry

B. mutualism

C. camouflage

D. commensalism

Source June 2001

Elephants communicate mainly by means of infrasonic sound. This means that the sound is below the frequency of sound that a human can hear. Elephants also emit a few higher-frequency trumpeting sounds that are audible to humans.

The infrasonic calls of elephants travel great distances. Researchers are now beginning to understand elephant behaviour based on this communication method. Certain calls are crucial in reproductive behaviour.
The females use a distinctive infrasonic call when they are sexually receptive, which occurs for only four days every four years.

– from The Edmonton Journal, 1997

45. In comparison with humans, elephants would be considered

   A. *r*-selected, and they have a lower biotic potential than humans

   B. *r*-selected, and they have a higher biotic potential than humans

   C. *K*-selected, and they have a lower biotic potential than humans

   D. *K*-selected, and they have a higher biotic potential than humans

Source: June 2001

The red-winged blackbird's adaptability has allowed it to become one of the most abundant birds in North America.

A Study of a Red-Winged Blackbird Nesting Site

The initial population of red-winged blackbirds was 208.

	End of Year 1	End of Year 2
Births	22	43
Deaths	4	7
Birds entering area	0	2
Birds leaving area	2	5

46. A conclusion about this nesting site study is that the red-winged blackbird population increased because

   A. natality plus immigration exceeded mortality plus emigration

   B. mortality plus emigration exceeded natality plus immigration

   C. natality plus emigration exceeded mortality plus immigration

   D. mortality plus immigration exceeded natality plus emigration

Source: January 2001

Use the following information to answer the next question.

Polycystic kidney disease (PKD) is a genetic disorder of the kidneys caused by an abnormal recessive allele. It is characterized by the presence of multiple cysts in the kidneys. Persian cats are known to have a very high rate of occurrence, with an estimated 37% of Persians being affected by PKD. This disease also affects humans, with 1 in 44 000 children being born with PKD.

47. What is the frequency of carriers in human populations?

   A. 0.3%

   B. 0.8%

   C. 16%

   D. 47%

Use the following information to answer the next question.

A high percentage of purebred dogs have genetic defects. Some examples of these defects follow.

1. Hip dysplasia, a defect in the hip joints that can cripple a dog, occurs in 60% of golden retrievers.

2. Hereditary deafness, due to a recessive autosomal disorder, occurs in 30% of Dalmatians.

3. Retinal disease, which may cause blindness, occurs in 70% of collies.

4. Hemophilia, an X-linked recessive disorder, is common in Labrador retrievers. Dwarfism is also common in this breed of dog.

– from Lemonick, 1994

CHALLENGER QUESTION   36.3

Numerical Response

8. What is the frequency of the abnormal allele that causes hearing defects in Dalmatians? ____
(Record your answer to **two** significant digits.)

Source: January 2001

Use the following information to answer the next question.

Many elk live in and around an 80 km^2 area that includes the Jasper town site.

48. If a disease were to kill 90% of these elk (an epidemic), what would be the likely consequence?

   A. The genetic variability in the population would decrease.

   B. The mutation rate in genes for disease resistance would increase.

   C. The population's resistance to all diseases would increase.

   D. The population's gene frequencies would return to pre-epidemic values through genetic drift.

Source: January 2000

ANSWERS AND SOLUTIONS—DIPLOMA EXAMINATION
SAMPLE 2

1. C	11. D	21. B	31. A	42. D
2. A	NR3. 4312	22. D	32. A	43. C
3. B	NR4. 1432	23. A	33. C	44. A
4. C	12. B	24. A	34. C	45. C
5. A	13. A	25. D	35. C	46. A
6. B	14. A	NR5. 1342	36. B	47. B
7. C	15. C	26. A	37. C	NR8. 0.55
NR1. 4231	16. D	NR6. 6432	38. A	48. A
NR2. 9040	17. B	27. C	NR7. 6.73	
8. B	18. B	28. C	39. D	
9. B	19. C	29. C	40. B	
10. D	20. B	30. A	41. B	

1. C

Calcium can either be found deposited in the bones and teeth, or dissolved in the bloodstream. When blood calcium levels fall, PTH is secreted. This results in increased absorption of calcium from the gut into the blood, and the dissolving of calcium and bones, increasing blood calcium levels. At the same time, the secretion of calcitonin, which acts antagonistically to PTH, will be decreased.

2. A

All of the alternatives list substances that have some effect on the release of thyroxine, but the question asks for the one that directly regulates the release of throxine. This is TSH, which stands for thyroid-stimulating hormone. TSH is produced by the anterior pituitary gland and stimulates the thyroid to release thyroxine. TRH, thyroid-releasing hormone, (sometimes referred to as TSHRF) is produced by the hypothalamus and causes the release of TSH. Iodine is needed for thyroxine production, so if there is a shortage of iodine, thyroxine production will be hampered. Thyroxine itself has an effect on thyroxine production because it exerts a negative feedback effect on the hypothalamus. Only TSH has a direct effect on thyroxine production.

3. B

Hyperthyroidism refers to an overactive thyroid producing excess thyroxine, resulting in a higher than normal metabolic rate. The high rates of cell respiration that result would deplete fuel stores and result in loss of weight. All the rest of the symptoms given would result if there were a shortage of thyroxine, which would cause a lower metabolic rate.

4. C

Aldosterone acts on kidney tubules to increase the active transport of salt (sodium) from urine into the blood. Because higher sodium levels in the blood make the blood hypertonic, water follows sodium by osmosis, increasing blood volume and thus blood pressure. Cortisol converts protein to blood glucose. Thyroxine increases metabolic rate and has no effect on salt. Epinephrine (sometimes referred to as adrenaline) initiates a "fight-or-flight" response. Epinephrine increases the conversion of liver glycogen to blood glucose, but has no effect on sodium.

5. A

Aldosterone release is controlled by blood volume and blood pressure. A decrease in blood volume (perhaps caused by blood loss due to hemorrhage) stimulates an increase in the secretion of aldosterone. Aldosterone increases the active transport of sodium ions from urine to bloodstream. This makes the blood hypertonic so water follows from the urine into the bloodstream by osmosis.

A reduction of the water content in the blood, as might occur as a result of dehydration, does not have the same effect. ADH responds to a drop in water content by increasing reabsorption of water directly.

6. B

In order to grow in height, children need to have calcium taken from the bloodstream and deposited in bones. They will therefore have relatively low parathyroid hormone levels. Pregnant women will have high PTH levels to produce high blood calcium concentrations. The fetus will need to absorb the calcium in the mother's blood to build bones and teeth. Elderly people who develop brittle bones (osteoporosis) are losing calcium from their bones into the bloodstream and would therefore likely have higher PTH levels. Babies who are not developing teeth normally are less able to take calcium from the blood and deposit it into teeth, so their PTH levels could theoretically be too high.

7. C

The occipital lobe, which is at the back of the cerebrum (the conscious part of the brain), is associated with the processing of visual stimulation. The frontal lobe (at the front of the cerebrum) is associated with personality traits and voluntary movement The parietal lobe is associated with processing of conscious sensation. The temporal lobe is associated with hearing, balance, and language

NR 1   4231

All reflex responses have this general pattern: sensory receptor → sensory neuron → interneuron → motor neuron → effector (muscle).

The size of the pupils is influenced by light intensity and is controlled by constriction and relaxation of the circular iris muscle in the eye. The reflex response will begin with the light receptors, which activate the sensory neurons of the optic nerve. These neurons synapse with interneurons where a response is coordinated. Finally, a response is sent through motor neurons that lead to the iris muscle which responds by constricting or relaxing in order to control the amount of light entering through the pupil.

NR 2   9040

When at rest, the membrane potential is –90 mV, which means that it is 90 mV more negative inside the neuron than outside. Stimulation of the neuron causes a flood of positive sodium (Na^+) ions into the neuron, making it more positive inside. This reversal of the membrane polarity is called depolarization. According to the graph, during depolarization the inside of the neuron reaches +40 mV. Note that different sources may state the resting membrane potential as being –70 or –90 mV. Similarly, the depolarization potential may be given as +30, +35, or +40 mV. Use the potentials as stated in the accompanying diagram.

8. B

A synapse or synaptic cleft is the space between the end of the axon of one neuron and the cell body or dendrite of the next neuron. Neurotransmitters such as dopamine and serotonin are released from the presynaptic membrane of the axon and diffuse across the synaptic cleft, binding to receptor sites on the postsynaptic membrane. Since MAO breaks down dopamine, it must function in the synaptic cleft.

9. B

The fight-or-flight response is an unconscious response in which the hormones epinephrine and norepinephrine prepare the body to deal with a perceived threat. The cerebrum sends sympathetic nervous signals to the adrenal medulla which in turn releases epinephrine and norepinephrine in response.

10. D

Use the mRNA Codon Translation Table to answer this question, matching the amino acids with possible mRNA codons. The sequence AUG UUU GGC GGC UAC is the only sequence to match the given amino acids.

11. D

The information explains that neural pathways involving dopamine cause pleasurable feelings. When the neurotransmitter dopamine is released from the presynaptic membrane, it diffuses across the synaptic cleft, binding to dopamine receptors on the postsynaptic dendrite. When enough dopamine receptors have been stimulated, the postsynaptic neuron's threshold is reached. At this point, sodium channels in the membrane open, depolarization occurs, and an impulse travels along the neuron.

NR 3   4312

High levels of androgens in the blood (**4**) will have a negative feedback effect on the hypothalamus/pituitary, causing them to stop releasing the gonadotropins FSH and LH (**3**). FSH stimulates sperm production in the seminiferous tubules of the testes, and LH causes the release of androgens from the interstitial cells of the testes. Without FSH and LH, sperm production will stop (**1**). This treatment is only effective for a few weeks because negative feedback from low sperm and high inhibin levels will cause FSH to rise again, increasing sperm production so the levels return to normal (**2**).

NR 4   1432

Production of sperm by the process of meiosis occurs in the seminiferous tubules (**1**). The epididymis, in which sperm mature (**4**), is a cap of coiled tubes at the edge of the testes. The vas deferens are two long smooth muscle tubes that transport sperm up from the testes, past the bladder, seminal vesicles, prostate gland, and Cowper's glands, to the urethra (**3**). FSH and LH are stimulated to be released from the anterior pituitary by releasing hormones produced by the hypothalamus (**2**).

12. B

Structure 2 is the prostate gland, where cancer occurs if the protein coded by the *p27* gene is absent. Structure 1 is the seminal vesicle, structure 3 is the Cowper's gland, and structure 4 is the testis.

13. A

Note that the molecule being read is DNA. This refers to the process of transcription where the base sequence on the active strand of DNA is copied in a complementary manner onto an mRNA molecule. This occurs in the nucleus. Later, in the cytoplasm, the base sequence on the mRNA molecules will be read in the process of translation resulting in the assembly of the desired protein.

14. A

Chordomas are believed to form from the cells of the notochord, which is derived from the mesoderm. The mesoderm gives rise to bones, muscles, and reproductive organs. Therefore, the likely site of chordoma development is within the bones. Both epidermis and nervous tissue arise from the ectoderm. The lining of the digestive tract arises from endoderm.

15. C

The corpus luteum produces progesterone and estrogen for the first trimester. The placenta takes over this endocrine function for the second and third trimesters. Low progesterone concentrations indicate a problem with the placenta. The amnion and amniotic fluid immediately surround the fetus, protecting it from impact. The chorion was involved with progesterone production in the first trimester. It produced the hCG that signalled the corpus luteum to continue to secrete estrogen and progesterone until the placenta could take over. The allantois is involved in blood vessel development in the umbilical cord and placenta.

16. D

Sperm production occurs in the seminiferous tubules of the testes. The sperm finally mature in the epididymis, but it is clear from the diagram that the mitotic proliferation stage is occurring long before the sperm are mature. The vas deferens is a tube that transports sperm from the epididymis towards the seminal vesicles. The seminal vesicles add fructose-rich fluid to the semen.

17. B

In the diagram, stage A cells are spermatogonial cells that are diploid, and are dividing by mitosis to maximize the number of primary spermatocytes that will go through meiosis. The diploid chromosome number in humans is 46. The two divisions of meiosis have been completed by stage B. Because meiosis cuts the chromosome number of cells by half, spermatids must be haploid and their chromosome number must be 23.

18. B

Because the diagram shows us that the Dionne Quintuplets formed from a single egg and a single sperm, they must be identical, not fraternal quintuplets. It is not likely that fertility drugs were involved because they cause multiple ovulation—the production of many eggs, and the diagram shows that only one egg produced all five babies.

19. C

The diagram shows that this individual has three chromosome 18s, which the information identifies as Edward syndrome. The sex is male because the last pair of chromosomes, the sex chromosomes, are different, an X and Y, not two Xs.

20. B

CVS stands for chorionic villus sampling. It involves taking a sample of cells from the chorion, the outer layer of the embryo. Because the chorion cells are derived from the zygote, they will be genetically identical to all cells of the embryo. Therefore, sampling the chorion cells will provide the same genetic information as sampling the actual embryo or fetus.

21. B

The diagram shows a well-developed fetus. At this stage the placenta (2) has long-since taken over the job of secreting hormones from the corpus luteum.

22. D

Insulin and glucagon are antagonistic hormones. When blood glucose is too high, insulin is released from the β cells of the islets of Langerhans in the pancreas. Insulin reduces blood glucose by increasing the permeability of cell membranes to glucose, allowing glucose to enter cells and be used as fuel in cell respiration. Insulin also causes the liver and muscles to store blood glucose as glycogen. The hormone glucagon is released when blood glucose gets too low. It increases blood glucose concentrations by decreasing the permeability of cell membranes to glucose, causing glucose to remain in the blood. It also causes liver and muscle cells to hydrolyze their stored glycogen, releasing it into the blood as glucose.

23. A

A zygote from which an individual is formed is composed of the nuclear material of a sperm and the entire cell of the mother's egg. Because mitochondria are part of the cytoplasm, mitochondrial DNA, including the mutation that causes KSS, comes from the mother. In the example given, the mother does not have the mutant DNA in her own somatic (body) cells. Therefore, the mutation must have occurred during the production of the egg (her oocyte).

24. A

The sperm is very tiny, and the egg very large. The sperm provides only nuclear material in the formation of the zygote. The egg contains a large amount of cytoplasm, along with its nucleus. This is the result of unequal cytokinesis in oogenesis. The first meiotic division forms one large secondary oocyte and a tiny polar body that dies. In the second division unequal cytokinesis occurs again, producing an enormous ootid with a lot of cytoplasm, and a second polar body which also dies. The egg contains abundant cytoplasm and organelles to power first the zygote then the embryo through its first week until it is implanted in the endometrium of the uterus and is able to obtain nutrients through the chorionic villli.

25. D

The distractors in this question refer to the series of events in translation, the part of protein synthesis where mRNA is read or translated into a string of amino acids that form the desired protein.

In translation a ribosome reads the mRNA strand in groups of three bases called codons. Each codon stands for a specific amino acid that is required to build the desired protein. The amino acids are present in the cytoplasm and will be delivered to the ribosome in the order in which mRNA requests them. When a specific mRNA codon is read, a tRNA molecule with an anticodon complementary to the mRNA codon will pick up the requested amino acid from the cytoplasm. The tRNA will deliver the amino acid to the ribosome where it is placed next to the amino acids that have already formed the beginning of the desired polypeptide chain.

NR 5   1342

Often people use the words gene and allele as if they mean the same thing, but they do not. A gene is a segment of DNA that codes for a specific trait, such as coat colour (**1**). The term allele refers to a specific version of a gene. For example one allele of the coat color gene with a certain base sequence codes for the tobiano protein. Another allele of the gene codes for a protein that results in non-tobiano coloring. Alleles are indicated as being dominant, by using an upper case letter, or recessive, by using a lower case letter (**3**). Phenotype refers to how an organism appears. These horses can appear as tobiano-colored or not tobiano-colored (**4**).

Each organism has two alleles for each gene; one that was given by the father in the sperm, and one that was given by the mother in the egg. The two alleles may be the same (*TT* or *tt*) or different (*Tt*). The alleles given by the parents make up the organism's genotype (**2**).

26. A

The following Punnett square shows that a cross of *Tt* × *tt* will yield a 1:1 genotypic ratio in the offspring. A cross of *Tt* × *Tt* will yield a 3:1 ratio. Tobiano and not tobiano are phenotypes, not genotypes.

$Tt \times tt$

	T	*t*
t	*Tt*	*tt*
t	*Tt*	*tt*

The genotypes of the offspring are 50% *Tt* and 50% *tt* (a 1:1 ratio).

NR 6   6432

A somatic cell is a normal body cell. It has two genes for each trait, one provided by the mother and one provided by the father. Because each cell has two genes for each trait, a normal cell is diploid or has the *2n* chromosome number.

A gamete is produced when a diploid cell in a gonad undergoes meiosis. During meiosis the chromosome number is halved, so gametes are haploid and have the *n* chromosome number.

If the diploid number is 64 then the chromosome number in a somatic cell is 64 and in a gamete it is 32.

27. C

The black allele is dominant over the chocolate and cinnamon alleles and the chocolate allele is dominant over the cinnamon allele. That means that when there is a heterozygous condition involving the black allele and a different allele (*Bb* or *Bb*^{l}), the individual appears black—the other colours do not appear. When there is a heterozygous condition involving the chocolate and cinnamon alleles (*bb*^{l}) the chocolate allele dominates, and the cinnamon allele does not appear.

28. C

Since the female is blue, she is *B_dd,* and the male, being cinnamon-coloured, is *b*^{l}*b*^{l}$\overline{D}$_. The unknown parts of the genotypes can be determined from the information provided about the offspring.

Since some of the offspring are *dd*, both parents had to be able to give a *d*. Therefore, the male is *b*^{l}*b*^{l}*Dd.* The female has one *B*—but is her other allele *b*^{l}, or *b*?

If the female is Bb^l, then her offspring will be black, cinnamon, blue, and fawn, and they are not. If she is Bb, then her offspring will be black, blue, chocolate, and lilac, which they are. Therefore, she must be $Bbdd$.

29. C

The following Punnett square shows the cross between a $BbDd$ (black-coloured female) and a fawn-coloured male (b^lb^ldd). Of the offspring, 25% will be chocolate coloured.

Parents bb^lDd		b^ld
male female	BD	Bb^lDd
	Bd	Bb^ldd
$BbDd \times b^lb^ldd$	bD	bb^lDd
	bd	bb^ldd

30. A

Female cats can be X^RX^R orange, X^rX^r black, or X^RX^r orange and black (tortoiseshell). Since this cat is X^rX^r, with no X^R, she will have no orange colour. Therefore, she will be black.

31. A

The following Punnett square shows that for this cross, there is only one phenotype of male offspring and one phenotype of female offspring. Only alternative **A** indicates two possible phenotypes of the offspring.

Parents		X^RB
$X^rYb^lb^l \times X^RX^RBB$	X^rb^l	$X^RX^rBb^l$
	Yb^l	X^RYBb^l

Offspring—50% tortoisshell female cats and 50% orange male cats.

32. A

Carriers are individuals who are heterozygous. Since sickle cell anemia is an autosomal (not sex-linked) recessive trait, the carriers will have the genotype Ss. If two individuals are Ss, the genotypes of the offspring are 25% SS (normal), 50% Ss (carriers), and 25% ss (with sickle cell anemia).

33. C

Currently, a person who is a carrier of sickle cell anemia has some ability to withstand malaria. If scientists were to eliminate malaria, the sickle cell allele will have lost its survival value. It is likely that the allele will reduce in frequency as it is removed by natural selection. In the short term it will not disappear since it can easily exist in heterozygous forms without resulting in the death of the individual.

34. C

Process 1 is gamete formation (from a diploid ($2n$) cell to a haploid (n) cell). Therefore, this process is meiosis. During process 2, there is an increase in numbers and it appears that the cells were $2n$ to begin with because they came from a zygote, so process 2 must be mitosis.

35. C

The first stage shows gametes, the plasmodium equivalent of human sperm and eggs. The gametes will fuse to form a zygote. The zygote would be $2n$ (chromosomes in pairs). The two gametes would be n. Each gamete provides one chromosome of each pair of homologous chromosomes to the zygote. From the zygote, a multicellular structure forms (labelled stage 2). The cells of stage 2 would be $2n$ like the zygote from which they formed.

36. B

A hypothesis is a possible answer to a question or problem. These two suggestions are possible answers to the problem, "How have some strains of *Plasmodium* become resistant to chloroquine?" A theory is an answer that has been well tested by experiments and has gained wide acceptance. Neither of these suggestions appear to have been based on direct observation and either of these suggestions could only be considered a conclusion if they were well supported by observation.

37. C

If the *cg2* gene codes for a protein that transports the drug out of the *Plasmodium*, then any organism that has that gene has some resistance to chloroquine. If researchers found a way to block transcription of the *cg2* gene, the transport protein could not be made. A mutation of the *cg2* gene would be a good thing in this case. Stimulating translation of the *cg2* gene would cause the transport protein to be made so researchers would not want to do that. As well, replicating the *cg2* gene may help make more of the transport protein, so researchers would not want to do that.

38. A

Plasmodium that bear the *cg2* gene are the most likely to survive exposure to chloroquine and continue reproducing. Therefore, they are naturally selected for when the drug chloroquine is employed. Resistant *Plasmodia* are no more likely to mate than non-resistant ones. There is no evidence that the mosquito that carries the *Plasmodium* is involved. The increasing resistance is not due to the fact that genes are mutating into the resistant form. The resistant gene (*cg2*) was always in the population, but because of the heavy use of chloroquine, more *Plasmodia* without c*g2* are dying, leaving more *Plasmodia* with c*g2* to reproduce.

NR 7   6.73

There are 3500 Komodo dragons and they live in an area of 520 km^2. To determine the population density, divide the population size by the area the dragons occupy.

3 500 ÷ 520 = 6.73 animals/km^2

This answer is given to two decimal places in the units dragons/km^2.

39. D

Humans have two types of light receptors in our retinas. Rods can detect low light levels but cannot perceive fine detail or colour. In contrast, the cones require bright light to work, but they are more sensitive to fine detail and can detect colour. If the Komodo dragons only have cones, then they have a limited ability to see in low-intensity light and thus have poor night vision.

40. B

In humans, sound waves in the air cause the tympanic membrane (eardrum) to vibrate. This vibration causes the three ossicles of the middle ear—the malleus, incus, and stapes—to vibrate. The last ossicle, the stapes, hits the oval window of the cochlea causing it to vibrate, setting up vibrations in the cochlear fluid. The eustachian tube equalizes air pressure between the pharynx at the back of the mouth and the middle ear. The eustachian tube does not directly affect hearing.

41. B

Having a high biotic potential means that it has a high reproductive capacity so that it can increase its population size quickly. Insects, whose populations can explode in a short time, have a high biotic potential. The Norway maple is not really "on steroids," that is just a figure of speech. Having a strong root system certainly helps the tree, but this is not directly related to reproductive rate. The tree reaches sexual maturity early, which means that it will start to reproduce at a young age, and it has a large number of seeds—two points that suggest that a tree will have a large number of offspring, increasing its biotic potential.

42. D

The hormone JH prevents the pupa from becoming an adult. The hormone ecdysone causes the pupa to become an adult in the spring. One way to keep the insect numbers down would be to keep them from becoming adults, so if the release of ecdysone could be blocked, then the pupae would not become adults and therefore could not reproduce.

43. C

It appears that during the spring, ecdysone is released, not JH. In the spring, there is a lot of light. Therefore, it makes sense that the presence of a lot of light stimulates the release of ecdysone.

44. A

Mimicry is an adaptation in which an organism appears to be another, perhaps more dangerous, organism. In this case, the defenseless baby owls sound like rattlesnakes. As a result, an approaching predator may back off, thinking that it has stumbled upon a rattlesnake den.

45. C

K-selected populations are ones that tend to maintain their population size near K, the carrying capacity. Typically, a K-selected population is made up of large, slow-growing organisms that have few offspring, provide good parental care, and have a good survival rate of the young. Elephants are a good example of a K-selected population. Biotic potential refers to the maximum reproductive rate. Since female elephants are sexually receptive only once every four years, their maximum biotic potential is lower than that of humans.

46. A

A population grows if the total of natality (births) plus immigration exceeds the total of mortality (deaths) and emigration.

In this case, natality for the two years was $22 + 43 = 65$ and immigration was $0 + 2 = 2$, for a total of 67. Mortality was $4 + 7 = 11$ and emigration was $2 + 5 = 7$, for a total of 18. As a result, the population increased by $67 - 18 = 49$ birds.

47. B

The frequency of the homozygous recessive genotype (kk) in humans is 1 in 44 000, or 0.000 02 or 0.002%. Use the Hardy–Weinberg genotype equation,

$p^2 + 2pq + q^2 = 1$; so, $kk = q^2 = 0.000\ 02$.

Therefore, the frequency of a single abnormal allele is $k = q$

$$= \sqrt{q^2}$$
$$= \sqrt{0.000\ 02}$$
$$= 0.004$$

To determine the frequency of the dominant allele (K), use the Hardy–Weinberg allele equation, $p + q = 1$; so, $K = p$

$$= 1 - q$$
$$= 1 - 0.004$$
$$= 0.996$$

Now, to determine the frequency of carriers who are heterozygous (Kk), again apply the Hardy–Weinberg genotype formula, where $Kk = 2pq$

$$= 2(0.004)(0.996)$$
$$= 0.008 \text{ or } 0.8\%$$

NR 8   0.55

This question requires the use of the Hardy–Weinberg equations.
$p + q = 1$

The information states that 30% of Dalmatians have this autosomal recessive disorder, $q^2 = 30\%$, which equals 0.3. Determine the frequency of the abnormal allele: q.

$$q^2 = 0.3$$
$$q = \sqrt{0.3}$$
$$q \doteq 0.55$$

48. A

With a large population becoming a very small population, the number of genes in the gene pool is bound to decrease. A logical conclusion that can be drawn is that the genetic variety of the population will decrease.

Appendices

BIOLOGY DATA

SYMBOLS

Symbol	Description	Symbol	Description
D_p	population density	♂	male
N	number of individuals in a population	♀	female
A	area occupied by a population	n	chromosome number
V	volume occupied by a population	B, b	alleles: uppercase is dominant, lowercase is recessive
t	time	I^A, I^B, i	alleles, human blood type (ABO)
Δ	change in	P	parent generation
K	carrying capacity	F_1	first filial generation
gr	growth rate	F_2	second filial generation
cgr	per capita growth rate	p	frequency of dominant allele
$>$	greater than, dominant over	q	frequency of recessive allele
$<$	less than, recessive to		

EQUATIONS

Subject	Equation
Hardy–Weinberg principle	$p^2 + 2pq + q^2 = 1$
Population density	$D_p = \dfrac{N}{A}$ or $D_p = \dfrac{N}{V}$
Change in population size	$\Delta N = \left(\text{factors that increase pop.}\right) - \left(\text{factors that decrease pop.}\right)$
Growth rate	$gr = \dfrac{\Delta N}{\Delta t}$
Per capita growth rate (time will be determined by the question)	$cgr = \dfrac{\Delta N}{N}$

ABBREVIATIONS FOR SOME HORMONES

Hormone	Abbreviation
Adrenocorticotropic hormone	ACTH
Antidiuretic hormone	ADH
Follicle-stimulating hormone	FSH
Gonadotropin-releasing hormone	GnRH
Human chorionic gonadotropin	hCG
Human growth hormone or growth hormone (somatotropin)	hGH or GH (STH)
Luteinizing hormone	LH
Parathyroid hormone	PTH
Prolactin	PRL
Thyroid-stimulating hormone	TSH

PEDIGREE SYMBOLS

Symbol	Meaning	Symbol	Meaning
□	Male	○—○ (joined)	Identical twins
○	Female	○ ○ (joined)	Non-identical twins
○—□	Mating	● ■	Affected individuals
○═□	Mating between close relatives	◐ ◧	Known heterozygous for autosomal recessive
I ○—□	Roman numerals symbolize generations	⊙	Known carrier of X-linked recessive
II □ ○ □ (1 2 3)	Arabic numbers symbolize individuals within a given generation	⊘ ⊘	Deceased individuals
	Birth order, within each group of offspring, is drawn left to right, oldest to youngest	◇	Sex unknown

Note: Pedigrees may or may not show individuals who are carriers for a particular trait.

MESSENGER RNA CODONS AND THEIR CORRESPONDING AMINO ACIDS

First Base	Second Base				Third Base
	U	C	A	G	
U	UUU phenylalanine UUC phenylalanine UUA leucine UUG leucine	UCU serine UCC serine UCA serine UCG serine	UAU tyrosine UAC tyrosine UAA stop** UAG stop**	UGU cysteine UGC cysteine UGA stop** UGG tryptophan	U C A G
C	CUU leucine CUC leucine CUA leucine CUG leucine	CCU proline CCC proline CCA proline CCG proline	CAU histidine CAC histidine CAA glutamine CAG glutamine	CGU arginine CGC arginine CGA arginine CGG arginine	U C A G
A	AUU isoleucine AUC isoleucine AUA isoleucine AUG methionine*	ACU threonine ACC threonine ACA threonine ACG threonine	AAU asparagine AAC asparagine AAA lysine AAG lysine	AGU serine AGC serine AGA arginine AGG arginine	U C A G
G	GUU valine GUC valine GUA valine GUG valine	GCU alanine GCC alanine GCA alanine GCG alanine	GAU aspartate GAC aspartate GAA glutamate GAG glutamate	GGU glycine GGC glycine GGA glycine GGG glycine	U C A G

* Note: AUG is an initiator codon and also codes for the amino acid methionine.

**Note: UAA, UAG, and UGA are terminator codons.

INFORMATION ABOUT NITROGEN BASES

Nitrogen Base	Classification	Abberviation
Adenine	Purine	A
Guanine	Purine	G
Cytosine	Pyrimidine	C
Thymine	Pyrimidine	T
Uracil	Pyrimidine	U

CREDITS

The publishers wish to thank all those who assisted in the creation of this publication. Some of the original graphics used in the Alberta Diploma Exams have been adapted, modified or replaced for this publication. Some images used in this publication are © Corel Corporation.

Examination questions, preambles and most graphics appearing in this booklet have been reproduced from the Biology 30 Grade 12 Diploma Examinations for January and June; 1999, 2000, 2001 and January 2002 with the permission of Alberta Education (http://education.alberta.ca/).

Every effort has been made to provide proper acknowledgement of the original source and to comply with copyright law. However, some attempts to establish original copyright ownership may have been unsuccessful. If copyright ownership can be identified, please notify Castle Rock Research Corp so that appropriate corrective action can be taken.

Some images in this document are from www.clipart.com, copyright (c) 2011 Jupiterimages Corporation.

NOTES

ORDERING INFORMATION

SCHOOL ORDERS

Please contact the Learning Resource Centre (LRC) for school discount and order information.

THE KEY **Study Guides** are specifically designed to assist students in preparing for unit tests, final exams, and provincial examinations.

THE KEY **Study Guides** – $29.95 each plus G.S.T.

SENIOR HIGH		JUNIOR HIGH	ELEMENTARY
Biology 30 Chemistry 30 English 30-1 English 30-2 Applied Math 30 Pure Math 30 Physics 30 Social Studies 30-1 Social Studies 30-2	Biology 20 Chemistry 20 English 20-1 Mathematics 20-1 Physics 20 Social Studies 20-1 English 10-1 Math 10 Combined Science 10 Social Studies 10-1	English Language Arts 9 Math 9 Science 9 Social Studies 9 Math 8 Math 7	English Language Arts 6 Math 6 Science 6 Social Studies 6 Math 4 English Language Arts 3 Math 3

Student Notes and Problems (SNAP) Workbooks contain complete explanations of curriculum concepts, examples, and exercise questions.

SNAP Workbooks – $29.95 each plus G.S.T.

SENIOR HIGH		JUNIOR HIGH	ELEMENTARY
Biology 30 Chemistry 30 Applied Math 30 Pure Math 30 Math 31 Physics 30	Biology 20 Chemistry 20 Mathematics 20-1 Physics 20 Math 10 Combined Science 10	Math 9 Science 9 Math 8 Science 8 Math 7 Science 7	Math 6 Math 5 Math 4 Math 3

Visit our website for a tour of resource content and features or order resources online at
www.castlerockresearch.com

#2340, 10180 – 101 Street
Edmonton, AB Canada T5J 3S4
e-mail: learn@castlerockresearch.com

Phone: 780.448.9619
Toll-free: 1.800.840.6224
Fax: 780.426.3917

CASTLE ROCK
RESEARCH CORP

ORDER FORM

THE KEY	QUANTITY	Student Notes and Problems Workbooks	QUANTITY	
			SNAP Workbooks	Solution Manuals
Biology 30		Math 31		
Chemistry 30		Biology 30		
English 30-1		Chemistry 30		
English 30-2		Applied Math 30		
Applied Math 30		Pure Math 30		
Pure Math 30		Physics 30		
Physics 30		Biology 20		
Social Studies 30-1		Chemistry 20		
Social Studies 30-2		Mathematics 20-1		
Biology 20		Physics 20		
Chemistry 20		Math 10 Combined		
English 20-1		Science 10		
Mathematics 20-1		Math 9		
Physics 20		Science 9		
Social Studies 20-1		Math 8		
English 10-1		Science 8		
Math 10 Combined		Math 7		
Science 10		Science 7		
Social Studies 10-1		Math 6		
English Language Arts 9		Math 5		
Math 9		Math 4		
Science 9		Math 3		
Social Studies 9				
Math 8			**TOTALS**	
Math 7			**KEYS**	
English Language Arts 6			**SNAP WORKBOOKS**	
Math 6			**SOLUTION MANUALS**	
Science 6			**SOLUTION MANUALS**	
Social Studies 6				
Math 4				
English Language Arts 3				
Math 3				

CASTLE ROCK
RESEARCH CORP

#2340, 10180 – 101 Street, Edmonton, AB T5J 3S4   **Phone:** 780.448.9619   **Fax:** 780.426.3917
Email: learn@castlerockresearch.com   **Toll-free:** 1.800.840.6224
www.castlerockresearch.com